MELANIE KLEIN

Melanie Klein is volume 2 of *Female Genius: Life, Madness, Words—Hannah Arendt, Melanie Klein, Colette*, a trilogy by Julia Kristeva.

EUROPEAN PERSPECTIVES

EUROPEAN PERSPECTIVES

A Series in Social Thought and Cultural Criticism
Lawrence D. Kritzman, Editor

European Perspectives presents outstanding books by leading
European thinkers. With both classic and contemporary works,
the series aims to shape the major intellectual controversies of
our day and to facilitate the tasks of historical understanding.

For a complete list of books in the series, see pages 297–98

Melanie Klein

by

Julia Kristeva

Translated by Ross Guberman

COLUMBIA UNIVERSITY PRESS   NEW YORK

Columbia University Press wishes to express its appreciation
for assistance given by the government of France through the
Ministère de la Culture in the preparation of this translation.

COLUMBIA UNIVERSITY PRESS

Publishers Since 1893

New York   Chichester, West Sussex

Copyright © 2001 Columbia University Press

Le Génie féminin, Melanie Klein © Librairie Arthème Fayard, 2000

Library of Congress Cataloging-in-Publication Data

Kristeva, Julia, 1941–

[Melanie Klein. English]

Melanie Klein / by Julia Kristeva ; translated by Ross Guberman.

p. cm. — (European perspectives)

Includes bibliographical references (pp. 277–84) and index.

ISBN 0–231–12284–5 (cloth : alk. paper)

1. Klein, Melanie. 2. Women psychoanalysts—Biography.

I. Title. II. Series.

BF109.K57 K75 2001

150.19'5'092—dc21   2001042226

Casebound editions of Columbia University Press books
are printed on permanent and durable acid-free paper.
Printed in the United States of America

c 10 9 8 7 6 5 4 3 2 1

CONTENTS

Madness

Melanie Klein
or matricide as pain and creativity

FIGURE I. Melanie Klein in 1912, aged about 30.
(With the permission of the Melanie Klein Trust, and
courtesy of the Wellcome Library, London.)

A woman of character & force some submerged—
how shall I say?—not craft,
but subtlety; something working underground.
A pull, a twist, like an undertow: menacing.
A bluff grey haired lady, with large bright imaginative eyes.

—The Diary of Virginia Woolf

Than soul, live thou upon your servant's loss [. . .]
So shalt thou feed on Death that feeds on men,
And, Death once dead, th's no more dying then."

—William Shakespeare, *Sonnets*, 146

FIGURE 2. The psychoanalyst.
(With the permission of Keystone, Paris.)

INTRODUCTION: THE
PSYCHOANALYTIC CENTURY

Men are so fundamentally mad that not to be mad
would amount to another form of madness.

—Blaise Pascal, *Thoughts*

1925: "She's a dotty woman. But there's no doubt whatever that her mind is stored with things of thrilling interest. And she's a nice character."[1] That was how Alix Strachey described Melanie Klein to her husband, James Strachey, who would become the celebrated editor and translator of the *Standard Edition* of Freud's writings and who was one of the leaders of the acclaimed Bloomsbury group in London. While Alix and Melanie were in Berlin together, they were analyzed by Karl Abraham and spent their evenings dancing in "leftist" bars of a more or less popular vein.

1957: Three decades later, Melanie Klein had achieved international renown as the founding mother of child analysis and, as a reformer in the wake of Freud, of the psychoanalysis of adults, particularly psychotics. As she wrote in *Envy and Gratitude*:

My work has taught me that the first object to be envied is the feeding breast, for the infant feels that it possesses everything he desires and that it has an unlimited flow of milk, and love which the breast keeps for its own gratification. This feeling adds to his sense of grievance and hate, and the result is a disturbed relation to the mother. If envy is excessive, this, in my view, indicates that paranoid and schizoid features are abnormally strong and that such an infant can be regarded as ill. . . . [In its later forms,] envy is no longer focused on the breast but on the mother receiving the father's penis, having babies inside her, giving birth to them, and being able to feed them.[2]

It is particularly creativeness which becomes the object of such attacks. Thus Spenser in "The Faerie Queene" describes envy as a ravenous wolf. . . . This theological idea seems to come down to us from St Augustine, who describes Life as a creative force opposed to Envy, a destructive force. In this connection, the First Letter to the Corinthians reads, "Love envieth not."[3]

Melanie Klein has since become a major figure of indisputable worth—just like the psychoanalysis that she practiced so ingeniously.

At the dawn of the third millennium, the discovery of the unconscious—whether it is considered to be a magnificent experience that has permeated our culture or an insignificant misperception under savage attack in certain quarters—remains an enigma. A century after the term "unconscious" first appeared,[4] we still have not fully absorbed the Copernican revolution launched by Sigmund Freud and his disciples. Psychoanalysis, which is a product of religion and philosophy as well as of late nineteenth-century medicine and psychiatry, has destroyed those disciplines only to rebuild them. In so doing, it has endorsed the idea that the human *soul*, which is bound up with the *body* and *language*, can not only be understood but, as a locus of pain that is vulnerable to destruction and even death, can become a privileged realm of rebirth as well.

With a passion typical of those who explore the unknown, the pioneers of this discovery made it the core of their very existence. In that spirit, they developed a new form of knowledge that reshaped classical rationality by expanding it to include the imaginary, which strengthens the bonds between two speaking beings. Although many people have been suspicious (and continue to be suspicious) of psychoanalysis—think of Heidegger and Nabokov, to name just the most outspoken critics—some of the most creative men and woman of the twentieth century—from Virginia Woolf to Georges Bataille, from André Breton to Jean-Paul Sartre, from Romain Rolland to Gustav Mahler, from André Gide to Emile Benveniste, and from Charlie Chaplin and Alfred Hitchcock to Woody Allen—either have read Freud or have lain themselves down on the psychoanalytic couch so they might better understand—or at least experience—this innovative path to self-knowledge, one that is both the precursor of a new form of freedom and a turning point in the history of civilization.

The fratricidal and institutional rifts that have accompanied and disrupted the psychoanalytic movement from its earliest days—and, in fact, throughout all its early history—result from more than just psychotherapists' close proximity to the very insanity that they endeavor to treat (which is what critics of psychoanalysis suggest). These rifts have not resulted solely from the truths that are often disclosed when powerful drives and words defy the conventions of civilized society. Rather, and more significantly, a more nuanced analysis reveals that the infighting within the analytic movement reflects the cruelty that is endemic to all of human culture precisely because innovations occur only at the outer bounds of possibility.

Mental illness, in fact, is what Freud and his "accomplices" considered to be the royal road toward understanding and liberating the human soul. Before Freud, many moralists and writers, particularly in France, took a first step down that path by describing the madness that lies at the heart of the human soul. Isn't it true that these precursors to Freud proposed a way of thinking about excess that flies in the face of the doctors and psychiatrists who relegate such excess to the realm of pathology alone? In fact, what do we make of "madness" when it is seen through the civilized lens of a La Rochefoucauld who wrote, "He who lives without madness is not as wise as one might imagine" or through the infernal knowledge of a Rimbaud who proclaimed, "Unhappiness has been my god. I have lain down in the mud, and dried myself in the crime-infested air. And I played the fool to the point of madness." Madness must not be ignored or brushed aside, but spoken, written, and thought: it is is a formidable transitory state, a tireless source of creativity.

An inherent paradox thus lies at the core of the incomprehension and resistance that psychoanalysis often inspires: How can pathology give voice to truth? By treating psychic malaise and by analyzing ill-being, psychoanalysis explores the logical processes underlying "normal" human experiences as well, and it thus learns to describe the conditions under which such processes degenerate into symptoms. From that perspective, the theory of the unconscious erases the boundary between the "normal" and the "pathological," and, without ceasing to engage in the analytic cure, it makes itself available to each of us in the form of an intimate journey to the end of the night. A psychiatric lexicon unhappily creeps in here: although psychoanalysis is based in some respects on madness, it is simply not true that analysts apply that label to everyone in an effort to prove all of us crazy. Instead, psychoanalysis approaches madness as if it were a set of models or structures that quietly lurk inside us and that encourage excesses and limitations—but also innovations.

The notion that the life of the mind is rooted in *sexuality* was the Archimedean point that permitted Freudian psychoanalysis to redefine the boundaries between normalcy and pathology and to bring about one of the most radical dismantlings of metaphysics that our century has ever seen. Freud's conception of sexuality, which he considered to be energy as well as meaning and biology and as a form of communication with the Other, does not transform the essence of man into something biological, which it has been accused of doing, but immediately incorporates animality into culture. To the extent that we are capable of symbolizing and sublimating, it is because we are endowed with a sexuality that inevitably fosters something that metaphysics considered to be a dualism: body and mind, drive and language. In truth, _desire_ always comprises both energy and intention, and it is by observing the vagaries of sexuality that psychoanalysis appreciates the failures of desire—which are what generate ill-being. Before we could rid ourselves of the guilt surrounding sexuality in a way that once enabled a Viennese Jew to turn sexuality into an object of study and then into the core of psychic life, we first had to wade through our biblical heritage as well as the entire libertarian development of European culture, from the time of the Renaissance and the Enlightenment until the Belle Époque at the end of the nineteenth century. Various libertarian minds have not failed to appreciate this subversive action, but the reach of Freud's discovery goes even further than that. Freud's version of sexuality, which deems sex to be neither licentiousness nor a source of provocation, is a focal point for solidifying the "essence of man" into a desire that is so indissolubly energetic and laden with meaning that it is inscribed with both the fate that holds us in check and the uniqueness that grants us our freedom. Freud's sexuality, indeed, is a desire that lies at the crossroads between the genetic and the subjective, between weightiness and grace.

In that sense, the _soul_, the descendant of what the ancients called a _psyche_, has become a "psychic apparatus" whose "topographies," though malleable (unconscious/preconscious/conscious, and then id/ego/and superego), never stop infiltrating the various economies and figures of desire, which themselves are always already psychosomatic. Freud staked his reputation on the notion that this double-sided desire could be detected in a _discourse_ addressed, through transference, toward the analyst-Other. Freud's was a wager that brimmed with optimism—a wager that was not spared the most brutal disillusionment, that made the _ear_ the most important organ, and that made _textual analysis_ the ultimate Judeo-Christian reference point in this prolonged adventure.

The heterogeneity between mind and body that Freud believed was woven by sexuality can be heard in discourse only if it opens up its surface, which is mastered by the conscience—and only if it carves out a space for the breach of a different logical process. The entire edifice of the *thinking subject*, who inherits the history of metaphysics and who is sealed shut by the Cartesian cogito, is disrupted as a result. The *Freudian unconscious*, for its part, becomes the "other area"—-accessible through the conscious but irreducible to it—that opens itself up to the analytic ear. The unconscious is able to avoid this irrationality: far from being an irreducible chaos, the unconscious possesses a structure all its own, however different that structure may be from the structure of the conscious. By overcoming the psychological secret that harbors familial shame and social mores, the unconscious shapes me to an unimaginable degree without my knowing as much. Once I am able to access my unconscious, moreover, my unconscious spares me my own inhibitions by restoring my freedom. I am not responsible for my unconscious, but if I do not respond *for* it, I respond *to* it—by rethinking it and re-creating it.

From that vantage point, unconscious sexuality offers a new perspective on the traditional difference between the two sexes. It is not the least of the revelations introduced by the psychoanalytic revolution to have participated in and stimulated the modern overhaul of the relationship between the sexes. It was by listening to *female hysteria* that Freud fine-tuned his ear to the logic of the unconscious. A host of female "characters" or "case studies" supported Freud's founding of psychoanalysis: think of Anna O., Emmy von N., Lucy R., Katharina, and Elisabeth von R., not to mention Dora, the most famous of all, as well as many other women, some of them better known than others. Freud, who in no way considered this symptomatology to be the sole domain of women, caused much controversy by acknowledging the existence of male hysteria as well, which was one of the ways he questioned the traditional split between men and women. Psychoanalysis begins by recognizing the psychic bisexuality endemic to each of the two biologically constituted sexes, and it concludes by revealing the sexual uniqueness of us all. Thus, although most analytical schools of thought assert that the heterosexuality that founds the family is the only form of sexuality to guarantee the subjective individuation of children, psychoanalysis explores and recognizes a sexual polymorphism beneath all types of sexual identity, and it relies on that recognition when it holds itself out as an ethics of subjective emancipation.

This intellectual context made it easier for women to participate in psychoanalytic practice, a domain that capitalized on women's talents more explicitly than did the other disciplines that reflected, to varying degrees, the social and political upheaval of the day. Despite the resistance and hostilities that such women faced in a male-dominated environment, and despite their exposure to the rigid and traditional hierarchies of the medical profession, many of them joined the psychoanalytic revolution, which later credited them for their contributions: think of Lou Andreas-Salomé, Sabina Spielrein, Karen Horney, Helene Deutsch, Anna Freud, Joan Riviere, Susan Isaacs, Paula Heimann, Jeanne Lampl-De Groot, Marie Bonaparte, and especially Melanie Klein, just to name a few of Freud's female contemporaries.

Worshiped to the point of dogmatic fanaticism by her disciples—and held in utter contempt by her detractors, some of whom did not hesitate to deny her the analyst title—Melanie Klein (1882–1960) wasted little time in becoming the most original innovator, male or female, in the psychoanalytic arena. Klein successfully introduced a new approach to the theory and practice of the unconscious without ever abandoning the fundamental principles of Freudianism (which distinguishes her from Jung and from the other "dissidents"). Klein's clinical and theoretical writings amount less to a canonical text than to the development of a potent practical intuition that, on the heels of many painful controversies, inspired the productive work so highly prized by modern psychoanalysis today, particularly in Great Britain.

Without Klein's innovation, the clinical practice that focuses on children as well on psychosis and autism, a practice dominated by such names as W. R. Bion, D. W. Winnicott, and Frances Tustin, would never have come to pass. We will see how this woman—an unhappy wife and a depressed mother who began an analysis with Ferenczi that she completed with Abraham and who was neither a physician nor a holder of any advanced degree—completed her first study on the psychoanalysis of young children in 1919 by relying on the analyses of her own children, and who then became a psychoanalyst herself in 1922 at the age of forty. In 1926 Klein moved to London and rose to meteoric fame with the 1932 publication of her collected essays *The Psychoanalysis of Children*. The differences of opinion she had with Freud and the disputes she had with Anna Freud, which culminated in the Great Controversial Discussions of the British Psycho-Analytical Society between 1941 and 1944, diminished neither her influence nor her resolve. In fact, Klein's direct and indirect influence has not stopped growing since her death, particularly in England and Latin American but also in France, and she has left her mark not only on clinical psychoanalysts but on sociologists and feminists as well.

Klein's major divergences with Freud have been well documented. Those differences were never styled as a true rejection of his thinking, however, but as a way to complete his theory of the unconscious. While the Freudian unconscious is structured by desire and repression, Melanie Klein focused on the newborn's psychic *pain*, on his *splitting processes*, and on his early capacity for a rather limited form of *sublimation*. The Freudian drive has a source and an aim, but no object, while in Klein's view, the newborn's drives are directed from the outset toward an *object* (the breast or the mother). In Klein's world the *Other* is always already there, and the dramas of the early bond between the object and an ego—with its just as early superego, which is generated by an extremely early Oedipus complex—unfold with the horror and the sublimity of a Hieronymus Bosch painting. Freud oriented the psychic life of the subject around the castration ordeal and the function of the father; Melanie Klein, who did not ignore these realities, buttressed them with a maternal function that was missing from the founding father of psychoanalysis's theories. As a result, Klein ran the risk of reducing the oedipal triangle into a dyad (although the couple was always present in her theory in the primary form of a "combined" parental object). At the same time, her efforts to privilege the mother in such a way hardly amount to raising the mother into some sort of cult, as Klein's adversaries have been so quick to accuse her of doing. In truth, *matricide*, which Klein was the first to have the courage to consider, is, along with envy and gratitude, at the origin of our capacity to think. Freud's invention of psychoanalysis was based on transference love, although he never completely theorized it; Klein, for her part, analyzed the maternal transference that her young patients directed toward the analyst-maternal substitute that she was, and she lent her ear to the fantasies that emerge when children play and that generate countertransference (as Klein's disciples pointed out) in the analyst herself. Dreams and language for Freud, the fantasy that permeates play for Klein: it was not only the young age of Klein's patients, who had not yet acquired language and who had not yet experienced roadblocks to speech, that demanded this new development in analytic technique. The Kleinian *fantasy* is at the heart of psychoanalysis for both the analyst and the patient; it is even more heterogeneous than is the Freudian fantasy, which itself is made up of both disparate conscious and unconscious elements and which the founder of psychoanalysis defined as being of "mixed blood." The Kleinian *phantasy* (as the Kleinians spell the word), which consists of drives, sensations, and acts as well as words, and that is manifested just as much in a child at play as in an adult who describes his drives and sensations from the analytic couch using a discourse bereft of any motor manifestations, is a veritable incarnation, a carnal metaphor, what Proust would call a transubstantiation.

This conceptual complexity is not unique to the Kleinian fantasy. As we will see, all of our author's notions prove to be ambiguous, ambivalent, and reflective of logical processes that are more circular than dialectical. Does this mean that our theorist was weak-minded? Or, on the other hand, does it vindicate the analytic insight that, by seizing upon regression, does not even require the notion of the "archaic" in order to make repression act as a repetition or a reduplication, or even as a subtle link between the substance and the meaning that dominate our thoughts and behavior in the same way as the major signs of the unconscious?

Once Klein's thought was consolidated into a veritable school of thought, it claimed to understand the unconscious, whose inner workings it often oversimplified. Klein's detractors, in fact, went so far as to accuse her of thinking that she herself was the unconscious! And yet, if we follow the development of Klein's theories and the alchemy of her "case studies" along with the evolution of her notions, we will be amazed to discover a permanent opening of the analyst's unconscious that emerged *alongside* the unconscious of her patients. The relationship that ensues is one of "at-one-ment," to use the term that W. R. Bion, one of Klein's most original followers, invented based on the notion of "to be at one with." Such a relationship is not too far removed from the pain that precedes the capacity to symbolize that same pain in order to get beyond it and to re-create that infinite fantasy known as life.

Because Klein understood anxiety, that conduit of pleasure, more deeply than did anyone else, she turned psychoanalysis into the art of caring for the capacity for thought. Attentive to the death drive that Freud had already incorporated into psychic life in his "Beyond the Pleasure Principle" (1920), Klein considered the death drive to be the primary agent for our distress, but also—and especially—for our capacity to become creatures of symbols. Freud essentially taught us that the repression of pleasure generates anxiety and the symptom. Under what conditions are the anxieties that tear us apart amenable to symbolization? That is the question that Klein uses as she reformulates the analytic problem, a question that places her work—unwittingly so since she was most notably a courageous clinician and in no way a "master of thought"—at the heart of humanity and the modern crisis of culture.

Yet beneath the apparent self-assurance of this woman, who became the leader of a school of thought, lay an exceptionally close relationship with anxiety, both in other people and in herself. Her cohabitation with anxiety, which was symbolized and thus made tolerable because it came to be superseded by thought, gave her the impetus and the strength she needed to avoid retreating from psychosis. On the contrary, in fact, Klein was more concerned with psychotic states than was Freud. Erasmus had already written his *In Praise of Folly* (1511) to communicate to Renaissance humanity that freedom is rooted in borderline experiences. When Freud, beginning with *The Interpretation of Dreams* (1900), taught us that our dreams represent our private madness, he was not denying illness as such but, rather, sketching out a fuller understanding of illness as being our own "uncanniness" and associating it with care as much as with benevolence. By detecting in the newborn a "paranoid-schizoid" ego or by pointing out that the "depressive position" is a precondition for language acquisition, Klein familiarized us with madness and exposed us to its inner workings.

Although Klein was moved by the dramatic history of the European continent, which culminated in the delirium of the Nazis, she did not focus on the political aspects of the madness that tainted the twentieth century. At the same time, even if she shielded herself from the horrors that surrounded her, Klein's analysis of private psychosis, whether in children or in adults, helps us identify the most deep-seated mechanisms that—along with economic and ideological influences—paved the way for the destruction of psychic space and the annihilation of the life of the mind that has threatened the modern era. Madness will prove to be the most pressing political characteristic of our day, and we would be well served to remember that psychoanalysis has been its contemporary—not because psychoanalysis has participated in a version of nihilism contemporaneous with secularization and that generated at once the death of God, totalitarian regimes, and "sexual liberation," but because, in the context of the deconstruction of metaphysics that we experience through varying degrees of pleasures and dangers, it has led us to the heart of the human psyche and has allowed us to see its madness, which is both its driving force and its most fundamental limitation. Melanie Klein ranks among those who have done the most to further our understanding of our being as an endemic state of ill-being in all its diverse manifestations: schizophrenia, psychosis, depression, mania, autism, delays and inhibitions, catastrophic anxiety, fragmentation of the ego, and so forth. Although Klein's work does not give us a ready-made fix to avoid such ill-being, she helps us adorn it with an optimal support system and an opportunity for change with a view toward a possible rebirth.

Even at this early stage, if we look past the particular destinies and differences between Hannah Arendt's and Melanie Klein's work, we can detect some similarities between their respective geniuses. Both women were interested in the object and the social bond, were drawn to the destruction of thought ("evil" for Arendt and "psychosis" for Klein), and resisted linear modes of reasoning. To those similarities were added some existential parallels: the two intellectuals, both of whom emerged from secular Jewish worlds, appropriated Christian philosophy, Enlightenment humanism, and contemporary science in a uniquely critical and highly personal way. In so doing, they endeavored to develop a certain freedom of behavior and thinking that is truly exceptional as compared with the existence of the other women and men of their day. Arendt and Klein, who were dissidents in their respective professional environments and who were subject to hostility from conformist factions even though they were also capable of fighting to the death to develop and defend their innovative ideas, were rebels whose very genius was rooted in the fact that they ventured to think.

I will attempt now to follow more methodically the evolution and the crystallization of the unique qualities that made Melanie Klein the boldest reformer in the history of modern psychoanalysis.

I

JEWISH FAMILIES, EUROPEAN STORIES: A DEPRESSION AND ITS AFTERMATH

LIBUSSA

Not surprisingly, the biography of Melanie Klein[1] reveals that the childhood experienced by this discoverer of the "object-mother" and of matricide was dominated by the imposing figure of her own mother, Libussa Deutsch.

Libussa, a black-haired beauty, intelligent and well educated, came from a family of learned and tolerant rabbis in Slovakia. She played the piano and learned French; her brother Hermann, who became a successful lawyer and who played an important role in the life of the Reizes family, attended a Jesuit school. At twenty-four years of age, Libussa met Moriz Reizes in Vienna and then married him. Moriz, a Polish Jew from a rigidly orthodox family in Galicia and a man twenty-four years her senior, was a general practitioner, a rather unimpressive one at that, who worked in

Deutsch-Kreutz, a small Hungarian border town about seventy miles from the couple's home in Vienna. Libussa and Moriz's union, a poor match because of their differences in age, status, and culture (Libussa's family, wealthier and better educated than Moriz's, was also dominated by a "pattern of matriarchy"[2]), does not appear to have been a marriage of love.

In Klein's brief *Autobiography*, which was written between 1953 and 1959 (and which remains the unpublished property of the Melanie Klein Trust), the psychoanalyst offers a vision of her life that is dramatically modified, if not idealized. She claims to have been fascinated by the scholarly atmosphere that pervaded the Deutsch family and to have admired her father's independent thinking that enabled him to defy the Hasidim and to embark on the study of medicine, and she also remained in awe of his command of ten languages! At the same time, Klein described her "revulsion" toward the ritual kaftan worn by her father's sister, and she did not hide her "scorn" for the Yiddish spoken by the Slovakian Jews on her mother's side of the family.

Libussa and Moriz had three children—Emilie, Emanuel, and Sidonie—before moving to Vienna and giving birth to Melanie. Emilie, Moriz's favorite, was envied by her youngest sister; Emanuel was the genius of the family and was close to Melanie; and Sidonie, the best-looking of the children and her mother's favorite, died of tuberculosis when she was eight years old and Melanie only four: "I remember that I felt that my mother needed me all the more now that Sidonie was gone, and it is probable that some of the spoiling was due to my having to replace that child."[3]

A "beautiful Jewish princess," Melanie appears to have been given much love during her childhood, and she became the favorite of her mother's brother and of Libussa herself after Sidonie's death.[4] On the other hand, Melanie admitted that she never understood her father because of his age, but also, most likely, because of his modest social status. Moriz served as a medical consultant in a music hall, a position that he loathed, as did his wife, who appears to have been unsatisfied with his predicament. The family's financial woes forced Libussa to open a shop, a rather odd pursuit for the wife of a doctor. She sold plants as well as reptiles, which resonates with what Klein later considered to be the fantasy of the mother's body, teeming with horrible "bad objects" that are anal or phallic. None of this inhibited our hero-ine, who said she was "absolutely never shy" and who claimed to have been "fired by ambition": she intended to study medicine (like her father) and, more curiously, to specialize in psychiatry— a most unusual goal for a girl, let alone a Jewish one! Propelled by a genuine intellectual fervor, Melanie made her brother into her "confidant," her "friend," and her "teacher," and she grew at his side, which filled the young man with pride.[5]

Although Melanie was an assimilated Jew and never subscribed to Zionism, she felt deeply Jewish, as did her family, and she acknowledged that she had been acutely aware of her marginality in a Catholic Vienna that did not refrain from persecuting the Jewish minority. Melanie's family maintained Jewish ritual cele-brations; she recalled that they celebrated Passover and the Day of Atonement, although she added that she could have never lived in Israel. Significantly, Klein remembered her mother's own rec-ollection of a student with whom she had apparently been in love and who declared, on his deathbed, "I shall die very soon and I repeat that I do not believe in any god."[6] In that sense, it is entirely inaccurate to assert, as some have done, that psycho-analysis took the place of this absent god to whom Melanie was "converted" as were so many other secular Jews before her. On the contrary, it was by accompanying the catastrophe of meaning as reflected in psychoanalytic experience that Melanie Klein, like some others, was able to articulate the fundamentals of nihilism and of religious belief and depression as well as reparation in an effort to deconstruct them all.

The "strong incestuous overtones"[7] that imbued the Reizes family were particularly pronounced in the relationship between Melanie and Emanuel. Emanuel, stricken with heart disease that stemmed from a childhood bout of scarlet fever, knew his days were numbered. Accordingly, he abandoned medical school for a life devoted to literature and travel. Ill and in debt, he explored Italy while keeping up a correspondence up with his mother and his sister, who responded with letters of her own that were replete with amorous sentiments and sexual connotations. It was this desperate relationship between twin souls, one in which brother and sister sought a passion that exceeded the bounds of friendship, that provided a backdrop for . . . Melanie's subsequent marriage.

Melanie was seventeen years old in 1899, when she met Arthur Stevan Klein, a second cousin on Libussa's side and a friend of Emanuel's. Arthur, for his part, was twenty-one years old and was a student of chemical engineering at the prestigious Swiss Federal Technical High School in Zurich. Libussa considered him to be a good match and perhaps even the most promising of Klein's suitors, and Emanuel was more impressed by him than was Melanie herself. Klein would later attribute her marriage less to love than to the pull of Arthur's "passionate temperament."

The following year, Melanie's father, Moriz Reizes, died of pneumonia. What the family considered "senility" was a form of degeneration that was likely due to a case of Alzheimer's disease that had been festering for years. Emanuel later died in Genoa, the victim of heart failure—unless, that is, he killed himself accidentally.[8]

Still overwhelmed by the mourning for her brother that shook her to her very foundations, Melanie got married on March 31, 1903, the day after her twenty-first birthday. According to a patently autobiographical story that she wrote later on (around 1913), she apparently felt nothing but disgust for sex. Her revulsion was probably linked to her feeling of having betrayed her brother, Emanuel. As her heroine, Anna, puts it, "And does it therefore have to be like this, that motherhood begins with disgust?"[9]

Arthur, who soon became unfaithful, went on frequent business trips and gradually began to distance himself from Melanie. At first the young woman occupied herself with publishing her brother's writings; in her *Autobiography* she expresses her thanks to Arthur for having helped her . . . retrieve Emanuel's manuscripts! Although Melanie believed that this marriage is what "made [her] unhappy" and that Emanuel himself may have realized that she was "doing the wrong thing"[10] by marrying her cousin, she remained close to her in-laws.

JEWS AND CATHOLICS

The Kleins were assimilated Jews: Arthur's father, Jakob Klein, who was merely a nominal member of the synagogue, managed the local bank and served as the mayor of Rosenberg (a small town with a population of about eight thousand in what was then the Hungarian province of Liptau) and as a senator for the town. Arthur attended a Jesuit school, as did Melanie's maternal uncle. The newlyweds settled in Rosenberg before Melanie gave birth— in 1904, and after feeling "miserably nauseated"—to her first child, Melitta, who unfortunately was not a boy as Libussa had wished (!)[11] Hans was born in 1907, and Erich in 1914.

The entire existence of the new Klein family was subject to the iron rule of Libussa. A possessive and abusive mother, Libussa sent letters offering advice before she eventually moved in with the young couple, asked for financial assistance, and even accompanied them in their travels to Italy. She deemed her daughter to be immature and neurasthenic and overwhelmed her with supervision to the point of taking the place of . . . "Frau Klein": "Libussa wanted to have a very special place in her daughter's life, and she proposed a curiously oblique way in which Melanie could communicate with her so that Arthur would not read the letter: simply by addressing it to Frau Melanie Klein." Under these conditions, Arthur became "difficult" and suffered from "nerves" and stomach complaints. Melanie's own illnesses were only aggravated in turn, as she suffered from "irritability," "depressive exhaustion," and a "paralyzing depression."[12] This atmosphere took its greatest toll on little Melitta: her grandmother favored Hans, and drummed into her the image of her mother as an "emotional cripple" who had to be separated from her husband as long as possible and then dispatched to treatments and various vacations and holidays: "Libussa wanted Melanie out of the way. She tried to create situations in which husband and wife saw each other as seldom as possible. . . . It infuriated her to think that Arthur was making private plans with his wife, and in subtle ways she discouraged him from writing to her."[13]

Melanie first tried to escape this hell by forming friendships with other women. She grew close to her husband's sister, Jolan Klein-Vágó, who impressed her with her stability and her warm sensitivity, and to Klara Vágó, the sister of Jolan's husband, Gyula. She was extremely jealous, on the other hand, of her sister Emilie's emotional depth and sexual freedom—or at least of what she considered to be such. We will encounter this same passion for the female in Klein's subsequent psychoanalytic theories, as well as in the professional skirmishes she had with her female disciples and adversaries.

As might be expected, Melanie's emotional difficulties were accompanied with spiritual doubts and religious crises. The much admired Jolan became a devout Roman Catholic, as did the other members of the Vágó family. At that point Melanie spent a good deal of time with Klara Vágó, with whom she apparently had a "relationship," as evidenced, in the opinion of Klein's biographer, by an affectionate poem Klein dedicated to her in 1920.[14] As a child, Melanie the Jew had been influenced by Catholicism, and she admitted feeling guilt over it. One could wonder, however, if that guilt did not emerge much later. Critics like to point out the similarities between certain features of Klein's theory and such Catholic notions as original sin, the Immaculate Conception, or expiation. In any event, through the impetus of Arthur Klein and with Melanie's consent, the Klein family converted to Christianity and joined the Unitarian Church, which they found easier to accept because it rejected the dogma of the Holy Trinity. And they had all of their children baptized.

As a result—and under the threat of Nazi persecution—Erich Klein moved to England, where he became Eric Clyne. None of these machinations kept Melanie Klein from remaining acutely aware of her Jewish origin and writing the following in her *Autobiography:*

I have always hated that some Jews, quite irrespective of their religious principles, were ashamed of their Jewish origin, and, whenever the question arose, I was glad to confirm my own Jewish origin, though I am afraid that I have no religious beliefs whatever. . . . Who knows! This might have given me the strength always to be *a minority about my scientific work* and not to mind, and to be quite willing to *stand up against a majority for which I had some contempt,* which at no time has been mitigated by tolerance.[15]

Arthur's work forced the family to move to Budapest in 1910. Although the year 1912 saw some happier times, the marriage between Arthur and Melanie continued to deteriorate during 1913 and 1914—around the time that Erich was born and Libussa died—as evidenced not only by Melanie's letters to her mother but also by the writings she composed between 1913 and 1920 as a way to hide from her depression. In these thirty poems, four stories, and an array of sketches and prose fragments,[16] it is easy to detect the desire for a life filled with sexual satisfaction. Melanie's style was influenced by erotic expressionist poetry, but also by the "stream-of-consciousness narrative" favored by Arthur Schnitzler and James Joyce,[17] as can be seen, for example, in her story of a woman who wakes up from a deep coma after a suicide attempt— and who is modeled after Emanuel's former lover! Melanie also exposed her hostile feelings toward Arthur, which are clearly fused with her unconscious hatred for her mother. At the same time, even in Melanie's *Autobiography,* she protected herself against any aggression toward her mother and persisted in idealizing her image of her: "My relation to my mother has been one of the great standbys of my life. I loved her deeply, admired her beauty, her intellect, her deep wish for knowledge, no doubt with some of the envy which exists in every daughter."[18]

Not surprisingly, Arthur received far less attention. While Melanie conserved nearly all of her letters from her mother and her brother, she retained only one letter from her husband.[19] Arthur Klein left for Sweden in 1917 and remained there until 1937, after getting remarried and then divorced. He died in Switzerland in 1939.[20] The Kleins themselves had divorced in 1923—though Melanie oddly reported the date as being 1922. Was it so she could draw a veil over her private life and divert attention instead to the other events that would enliven her existence?

SÁNDOR FERENCZI

Around 1913 Klein entered into analysis with Sándor Ferenczi in Budapest—her third analysis, this one the product of a concerted effort to be reborn! In 1920 she mustered up the courage to move away from Budapest and Rosenberg, leaving Melitta and Hans behind, and took up residence with Erich in Berlin, not far from the home of Karl Abraham, with whom she would continue her analysis.

Some letters written a few years later by Alix Strachey, another patient of Abraham's, portray a woman transformed. Melanie brought Alix one evening to a masked ball sponsored by a group of Socialists. The elegant British woman from the snobbish Bloomsbury group was disconcerted, to say the least: Melanie danced "like an elephant" and was "a kind of Cleopatra—terrifically 'décolleté,'" although she is "really a very good sort."[21] Another evening, during a performance of *Così fan Tutte* at the opera, Melanie subjected Alix to a nonstop "flood of conversation!" "A bit too simple & breezy for me," Alix declared, but she is "an engaging character all the same."[22] From the beginning of their friendship, Alix acknowledged being "immensely impressed"[23] by Melanie's competence and knowledge, and she admired her psychoanalytic creativity.

Released from her familial obligations, Melanie enrolled in a dancing class, where she met a journalist at the *Berliner Tageblatt* named Chezkel Zvi Kloetzel. Kloetzel was married; he bore a likeness to Emmanuel . . . and so she became romantically involved with him and bestowed on him the secret name of . . . Hans, the name of Melanie's older son. Her pocket diary, as well as her rambling, marked-up letters, reveal the depths of her passion—but also a deep-seated depression, the hidden force behind their relationship. Klein's lover took the affair less seriously than she did, and he informed her rather bluntly that he had decided to split with her.[24] As her biographer put it, Melanie was "an intelligent woman who was capable of losing her head."[25] Still, Melanie apparently exerted a strong sexual power over Kloetzel, as he continued to visit her periodically from the time she moved to London in 1926. Unable to find work in England, he emigrated in 1933 to Palestine, where he became a features editor at the Jerusalem *Post*.[26] Melanie never saw him again, and he died in 1952.[27]

The turning point in the first part of Melanie Klein's life, which we have just retraced in brief, began with her marital crisis between 1913 and 1914 and concluded with Libussa's death. From the moment the couple moved to Budapest, Arthur was engaged in a business relationship with Sándor Ferenczi's brother. Melanie, who suffered from an acute depression that would only get worse upon the death of her mother, entered into analysis with Ferenczi, most likely in 1912, and pursued it until 1919. She read Freud's "On Dreams"[28] in 1914, and familiarized herself with early psychoanalysis and with its free-thinking and impassioned pioneers. Sándor Ferenczi (1873–1933) was the most renowned analyst in Hungary, and Freud soon came to refer to him as "my dear son." Among "the early Christians in the catacombs,"[29] as Sándor Rádo, one of Freud's first disciples, called them, Ferenczi was an exceptionally talented and devoted practitioner. Along with Jung, Ferenczi joined the founder of psychoanalysis on his 1909 trip to America to introduce the Freudian discovery to the New Continent. Ernest Jones (1879–1958) and Géza Roheim (1891–1951) did their respective analyses with him.

Highly attuned to archaic and regressive stages and unusually innovative in his mode of listening and analytic technique, Ferenczi was a proponent of an "active"[30] technique that endorsed an intrusive and seductive closeness with the patient that Freud would subsequently criticize harshly. Ferenczi, for his part, criticized Freud for failing to analyze transference. In addition to imitating certain features of Ferenczi's style, Melanie Klein borrowed some of the concepts he set forth in 1913, such as the "introjection stage" (which Ferenczi believed was the stage of omnipotence) and the "projection stage" (or the reality stage). At the same time, she appropriated Ferenczi's ideas in her own original way and modified them substantially. After Freud published his case study of Little Hans, which analyzed a child ("Analysis of a Phobia in a

Five-Year-Old Boy"[31]), Ferenczi deepened our understanding of this new branch of psychoanalysis in his own 1913 case study entitled "A Little Chanticleer," which concluded that the young neurotic Arpád suffered from a phobia about cocks because he had been reprimanded for masturbating. Two of Ferenczi's analysands—the Polish Eugenia Sokolnicka, who worked in France, and Melanie Klein—devoted themselves to child analysis.[32] In a June 26, 1919, letter to Freud, Ferenczi informed him that "[a] woman, Frau Klein (not a medical doctor), who recently made some very good observations with children, after she had been taught by me for several years,"[33] was to become the assistant to Anton von Freund, the wealthy brewer who generously endowed both the Budapest Psychoanalytic Society and Freud's publisher, the Verlag.

In her *Autobiography*, Klein herself paints the clearest picture of her early experiences with psychoanalysis under the auspices of Ferenczi:

> During this analysis with Ferenczi, he drew my attention to my great gift for understanding children and my interest in them, and he very much encouraged my idea of devoting myself to analysis, particularly child-analysis. I had, of course, three children of my own at the time. . . . I had not found . . . that education . . . could cover the whole understanding of the personality and therefore have the influence one might wish it to have. I had always the feelings that behind was something with which I could not come to grips.[34]

The first time Klein presented a case of child analysis to the Budapest Psychoanalytic Society was in 1919, and her work was published the following year as "Der Familienroman in statu nascendi." The paper earned her a membership into the society—and without any supervision being required. Klein's study used the first name Fritz as it recounted the analysis of Klein's own son Erich, whom she had observed since he was three years old (which was not an unusual practice at the time), while her other two children were raised primarily by Libussa. I will return to the scandal that erupted over her decision to follow Erich as well as to its advantages and disadvantages—her observations of her son did not escape scrutiny, and she would eventually push the whole matter under the rug: "My first patient was a five-year-old boy. I referred to him under the name 'Fritz' in my earliest published papers."[35]

From that point on Klein's colleagues pointed out that her approach differed from that of Hermine von Hug-Hellmuth, the well-known child analyst from the early days of psychoanalysis, just as her approach was different from Anna Freud's because Klein distinguished the analytic experience from parental and educational influences. The previous year, Melanie Klein had met Freud during the Fifth Psychoanalytic Congress, which was held at the Hungarian Academy of Sciences on September 28 and 29, 1918. Relaxed, creative, and independent, the society was enjoying a short-lived period of exuberance. At fifteen years of age, Melitta herself was permitted to attend the meeting.

The First World War disrupted Europe and everyone's fate. Arthur was called to service and returned from the war with a wound to his leg. The couple went through the motions of being married, and little more. The defeat of the Austro-Hungarian Empire and the downfall of Count Michael Karolyi's government led to the rise of a dictatorship of the proletariat in Hungary under Béla Kun. Unlike the Stalinists, who declared psychoanalysis to be a deviant science, the Bolsheviks appointed Ferenczi to be a university professor of psychoanalysis! When the counterrevolution broke out and the Red Terror was followed by an anti-Semitic White Terror, however, Géza Róheim and Ferenczi were dismissed from their positions and subjected to death threats. Arthur Klein, who could longer continue in his profession, left to find work in Sweden. And Melanie met up with Karl Abraham in Berlin.

KARL ABRAHAM

Karl Abraham (1877–1925) is one of the great names from the early years of psychoanalysis. At the time it appeared as though he would be Freud's successor, although Freud was not fond of his detached personality. In 1910 Abraham founded the Berlin Psychoanalytic Society. He replaced Ferenczi as a mentor to Melanie, who at thirty-eight years of age had just begun to reveal a rich creativity that had previously remained inhibited. It is easy to see the extent to which Abraham—who developed more thoroughly than Freud the theory of the pregenital stages as well as the thesis of the death drive[36]—influenced Klein's work. In fact, just as Klein borrowed from Ferenczi the idea that nervous tics are a substitute for masturbation, explaining that it was essential to understand "the object relations on which it is based,"[37] so she discussed the anal-sadistic relations that Abraham had described in his study of the anal character. From that perspective, Klein's case study of the young Lisa (who, according to an unproved hypothesis, was really Klein's daughter, Melitta) concludes that it is the analyst who fulfills the function of primary object and who begins to analyze transference as well as the homosexual relationship.

Did Klein use her children as "guinea pigs?"[38] Erich disguised as Fritz, Hans as Felix, and Melitta as Lisa? Under the influence of Abraham, Melanie refined her ability to expose her "case studies" more clearly than before as much as she refined the subtleties of her play technique. She became an associate member of the Berlin Psychoanalytic Society in 1922, and won full membership in 1923.

In 1922 Klein delivered a paper to the Seventh Psychoanalytic Congress in Berlin, which was the last such congress that Freud would attend. Although Freud was most likely absent during Klein's presentation, he must have heard at least something of what she said—and he must have been displeased that Klein challenged his notion of the Oedipus conflict and offered her own notion of an early anal fixation in the baby that gives rise to inhibitions. At the same time, it was Freud's "Beyond the Pleasure Principle" (1920) that inspired Klein to modify his early theory: she was more receptive than were other analysts to the hypothesis of a death drive in the baby that responded to his fear of being destroyed—whereas Freud believed that the baby is wholly unfamiliar with death. And yet, by considering the drive to be more psychological than biological, Klein added that the death drive manifests itself only through its relation to an object. Abraham's work inspired Klein's own work on this subject,[39] and Melanie paid tribute to him in turn in her *Autobiography*:

> Abraham, who discovered the first anal phase . . . , came near to the conception of the internal objects. His work on the oral impulses and phantasies goes beyond F's work. It did not by any means go as far as my own. . . . I should say that A. represents the link between my own work and F.'s. . . . [My analysis] came to an end when Abraham fell very ill in the summer of 1925 and died at Christmas of that year; a great pain to me and a very painful situation to come through.[40]

It took little time for Klein's bold innovations to encounter opposition with the first incident occurring during Abraham's lifetime. At the International Congress at Salzburg in 1924, where Klein questioned when the Oedipus complex emerges, emphasized the role of the mother as opposed to the father in the organization of the neuroses, and described sexuality in terms of orality, her remarks drew strong objections. That did not keep her, however, from applying her views to a case study of Erna entitled "An Obsessional Neurosis in a Six-Year-Old Girl,"[41] in which she revealed the little girl's constitutionally strong oral and anal-sadistic predisposition, early Oedipus conflict, early and cruel superego, and homosexuality. Abraham had put Klein in contact with Nelly Wollfheim, a child therapist who ran a kindergarten in Berlin where Klein met little Erna. Wollfheim, who served as Klein's secretary for ten years before the two of them parted ways, was the first person to be at once impressed and intimidated by Klein's talent and confidence. Was Klein not projecting onto her own patients her devouring, even sadistic, character, which served as her best weapon for staking out a place and thriving in a hostile, suspicious environment?

After Abraham died, Klein's detractors made no bones about

their position: they derided the acclaim she had found in Berlin, they emphasized her lack of advanced training, and they drew attention to the inherent paradox of this woman who wanted to be a master, not to mention a child analyst! The assassination of Hermine von Hug-Hellmuth by her nephew, who had been a patient of hers, only encouraged the prevailing hostility to the psychoanalysis of children. Otto Rank's notion of the birth trauma—which posits that the separation from the uterus is a prototype of anxiety—resonates with Klein's view that guilt does not result solely from the late manifestation of the oedipal triangle but begins to take shape in the oral stage because of the child's ambivalent relationship to the breast. For the most loyal Freudians, such a notion proved Klein a dangerous dissenter.

LONDON

Ernest Jones (1879–1958), on the other hand, got wind of Klein's talents through James Strachey, who was himself intrigued by Alix's letters, and invited Melanie in July 1925 to deliver a series of six lectures—in English!—on child analysis. Alix Strachey, who translated the lectures, knew that Klein was considered in certain quarters to be "quite sound in practice, but feebleminded about theory."[42] To put it bluntly, Melanie Klein's cause was already widely misunderstood across the Channel by the time she left for England! Not to mention the problems brought on by Melanie's atrocious accent, Alix's English lessons notwithstanding, and her ugly hats: "By the way, Mélanie showed me a hat she's bought to lecture in London & knock her audience—& by God it *will!* It's a vastly, voluminous affair in bright yellow, with a huge brim & an enormous cluster, a whole garden, of mixed flowers somewhere up the back, side, or front—The total effect is that of an overblown tea-rose with a slightly rouge'd core (her phiz); & the ψ's will shudder."[43]

In the end, however, Melanie's presentation allayed all fears and exceeded all hopes. Frau Klein, soberly attired, described her analysis of *children*—that most English of themes!—by way of *play*—that most sensitive and empirical of techniques!—and made "an extraordinarily deep impression on all of us and won the highest praise both by her personality and her work,"[44] as Jones wrote Freud on July 17, 1925. At the time the British Psycho-Analytical Society had only twenty-seven members and twenty-seven associates, but the level of interest in Klein's lectures was such that their location had to be moved to the drawing room of Karin and Adrian Stephen (Virginia Woolf's older brother) at 50 Gordon Square. Melanie's triumphant entrée into London, then, occurred under the auspices of the Bloomsbury group. Immediately thereafter, Jones invited Klein to spend a year in England analyzing his own children. Say goodbye to Berlin, Budapest, and Vienna! Onward to London!

In London, Melanie lived the life of a luxurious nomad, moving from one temporary quarter to the next. The London Clinic for Psycho-Analysis had opened on Freud's birthday, May 6, 1926. The young British Psycho-Analytical Society was dynamic, unencumbered, almost brazen in its efforts to acquire knowledge in an attempt to innovate more effectively, and infused with an old-fashioned penchant for democracy and an avant-garde taste for eccentric people, perhaps even Jewish ones. Its founder (in 1913) and director was Ernest Jones, a Welshman from a middle-class background. Jones had enjoyed a brilliant career as a medical student and was fascinated by Freud's early work: he immediately set out to learn German so he could read Freud in the original. When Jones was later accused of using indecent language with some of his child patients, he sought refuge in Toronto and then quickly returned to London to devote himself to psychoanalysis in Great Britain and abroad. Appreciated by Freud because he was a "Gentile"—a trait rarely seen among Freud's disciples, particularly during the tumultuous time of his schism with Jung—this complex and highly diplomatic man later became Freud's biographer. Although Jones was rather faint at heart, he absorbed Melanie's innovative theories while remaining loyal to Freud and Anna Freud—and thus succeeded in attending to both the shepherd and his flock. The relationship between Freud and Jones was always "one of wary fencing,"[45] but Jones was nevertheless the one who sent Klein to London to dispense her analytic wisdom to Mrs. Jones as well as to their two children, Mervyn and Gwenith (the daughter died a tragic death in 1928).

Melanie's renown spread far and wide, so much so that Ferenczi, during his 1927 visit to London, wrote Freud about his consternation upon discovering the "domineering influence"[46] that Frau Melanie Klein exerted upon the British group. From that point on, Melanie Klein's life and the fate of her work became one: the conflict with Anna Freud, her rift with her daughter, Melitta, the loyalties and disloyalties of her female disciples, and the Great Controversial Discussions of the British Psycho-Analytical Society during the Second World War all affected the spirit of Klein's work as well as the varying degrees to which it was accepted. And so did the history of the century. In Klein's view, the emigration of Jewish psychoanalysts to England or the United States and the worldwide dissemination of psychoanalysis were no doubt related to her painstaking work in modifying the Freudian talking cure. Klein fought tooth and nail in the name of her *vurk*, as she called it in a strong German accent ("my other child—work").[47] For these reasons, her clinical practice and theoretical approach form the basis of my discussions of her, as I trace her journey until it reaches September 22, 1960, the day she passed away in London, conquered by illness, anemia, and old age at seventy-eight years of age.

Sensing that the end was near, Klein tried to rekindle her Jewish faith and sent for a rabbi. In the end, though, when faced with the complexity that such a plan would entail, she changed her mind and attributed her wish to a flight of sentimental whim. The elated grandmother who adored Diana, Hazel, and especially Michael,[48] the children of her son Eric and of Judy, had not taken on any young patients since the 1940s, but she continued to treat adults in training analyses and continued to supervise as well. She enjoyed spending her evenings attending concerts and plays. Her bursts of laughter during scientific conferences greatly amused her colleagues. Even though some of them always retained their doubts about her seriousness and her commitment, others idealized her and called her the "most impressive woman"[49] that had ever lived. During her cremation ceremony, Rosalind Tureck, a newfound, affectionate friend, soberly performed the andante from Bach's Sonata in D Minor.

For the moment, why don't we conjure up the image bequeathed to us by Melanie's faithful exegete, Hanna Segal, as she describes the way she walked: "Her shoulders were a bit forward, so was her head, and she walked with rather small steps, giving an impression of great attentiveness. Her head was a bit forward. Now I think this way of walking . . . belonged to the consulting room and waiting room. That's how she wanted to meet one. I don't think she was like that outside when she held herself much straighter and she didn't have the same sort of attentive posture."[50]

Melanie walks in our direction, but she has not yet reached us all the way.

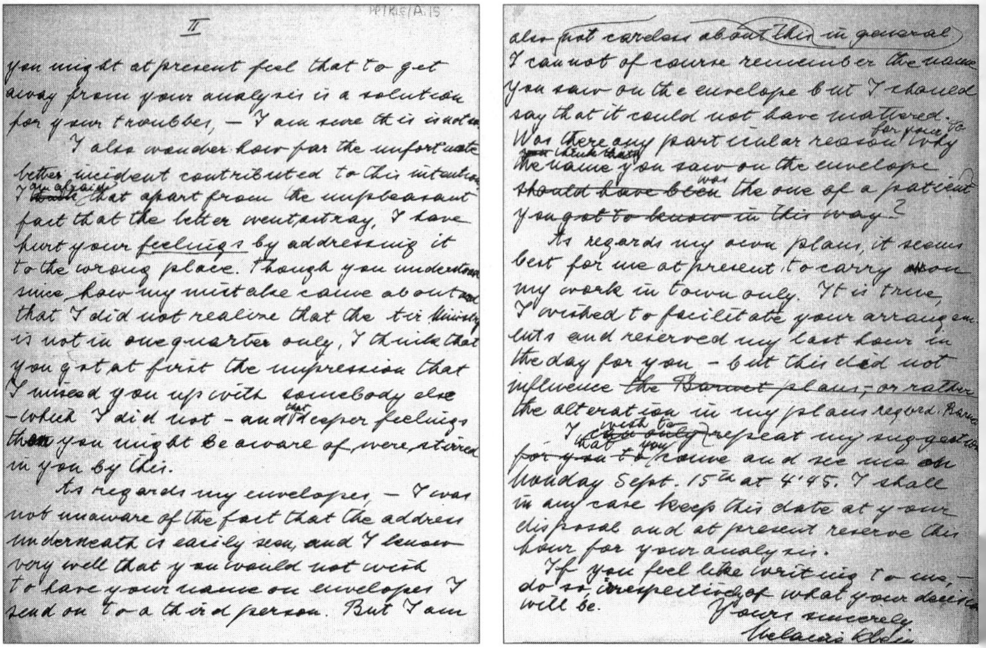

FIGURE 3. Letter written to a patient, August 11, 1941.
(From the Melanie Klein Personal Papers, with the permission of the
Melanie Klein Trust, and courtesy of the Wellcome Library, London.)

ANALYZING HER CHILDREN: FROM SCANDAL TO PLAY TECHNIQUE

Long before Freud, Wordsworth (1770–1850) wrote that "the child is father to the man." In the shadow of the signs of the baby Jesus and of Saint Augustine's *Confessions*, two models of childhood have competed for the English imagination[1]: first, the model set forth by John Locke in his *Thoughts Concerning Education* (1703) and Jean-Jacques Rousseau in *Emile* (1762), that is, the purified myth of childhood innocence; and second, the Calvinist belief[2] that the child is naturally perverse as a legacy of original sin, which justifies the often cruel severity of educational methods (whippings, deprivations, and intimidation).

Scholars as well as novelists have placed the child at the heart of the social bonds and of the magic of art. Even in the nineteenth century, for example, the writer Charles Kingsley, in his *Alton Locke*, proved to be an unexpected proponent of the puritanical thesis. His novel describes the educational efforts of a mother convinced that her child has a diabolical nature, and it recounts the child's "conversion" to Christian values as a result of the food deprivations and regular whipping sessions that taught him to curb his passions. This harsh approach reflects the ferocious efforts by nineteenth-century philanthropists to moralize working-class children. The cult novel of a triumphant bourgeoisie, Thomas Hughes's *Tom Brown's School Days* (1857), for example, recounts Thomas Arnold's transformation of a public school and depicts the metamorphosis of a shy, young boy into "the bad of school" who had abandoned the virtues of "muscular Christianity."

At the same time, other educational models advocated a version of communal living that was founded upon the equality of all human beings: think of Sir Thomas More's utopia, the Diggers' efforts during the revolution, Owen's experiences, and, during the twentieth century, A. S. Neill's work at Summerhill. The eighteenth century saw an onslaught of books on the education of boys, and of girls as well; among the most important pedagogues were Catherine Macaulay, Mary Wollstonecraft, Maria Edgeworth, and Hannah More.

In the nineteenth-century English social novel, childhood became the wall of tears that reflected the misery of the world, a vision that prefigured the Romantics' notion that reified the child and then made him, for better or worse, into the ancestor of man. Dickens, for his part, described his own miserable childhood. Lewis Carroll created in *Alice in Wonderland* a mythical childhood woven out of poetic daydreams and secret drives. Peter Pan, a fictional hero of whom a lifelike statue exists in London, has generated an incredibly popular myth that reflects a childhood that is at once forbidden and regretted. And this trend continued all the way until the modern William Golding, whose *Lord of the Flies* (1954) uses parody to contrast the fury of children's cruel perversity with their seductive inventiveness as they create a parallel society replete with intelligence and appealing fun. . . . The child appears to be the object of desire par excellence of the English imaginary, an imaginary we might refer to as *pedophilic* if that term still retained its innocently puritanical connotations.

From a more pragmatic perspective that examines the rise of child psychology and psychoanalysis in England following the Second World War (from Bowlby to Winnicott), Juliet Mitchell[3] has pointed out that, on the one hand, the independence that the overall mobilization for the war effort granted women paved the way for emancipating advances that continued until the 1960s, and that, on the other hand, this newfound peace localized the English family unit, at least for a time, within the confines of a moral artifice. In truth, both these competing developments helped shift attention toward the child.[4]

Was England an unwitting forerunner of Freud, and in particular of child analysis, which advocates that we rediscover the childhood within us so we might confront the pain of being? That is, while we wait for consumption and global marketing to put the child-client at the center of a humanity that is at the mercy of technology but that returns in actuality to its most primary needs for gratification . . .

Does this mean that it was real necessity, and not happenstance, that fated Klein to realize her talent in England rather than some place else? In any event, Klein declared England to be "her second motherland,"[5] and those who knew her remarked on how "alive" she became following her move there.[6] In fact, although the works I will discuss in this chapter all date from Klein's Continental period—from Budapest and Berlin—it was from the time of her move to London that she was able to give these texts their deepest meaning and to graft upon them a clinical and theoretical scope that could be shared with other people, thereby ensuring their fate. In 1932, as Melanie was taking on the task of developing the child analysis inaugurated by Freud in his study of Little Hans[7] and before she experienced her bitter debates with Anna Freud, she published a collection entitled *The Psychoanalysis of Children* that narrated twenty analytic treatments: four of them with children between the ages of two years nine months and four years three months (the oedipal period), five with children between the ages of five and six (the postoedipal period), five with children between the ages of seven and nine (the latency period), four with children between the ages of twelve and fourteen (puberty), and two with adults in classic analytic treatment.[8]

THE UNCONSCIOUS KNOWLEDGE (OF THE CHILD) VERSUS THE ENLIGHTENMENT (OF THE PARENTS)

Beginning with her first article, "The Development of a Child" (1921),[9] Klein engaged in a *reversal of position* that was no doubt rooted in Freudian thought but that she developed with much acumen on her own. Having begun by asserting that the repression brought on by education represses infantile sexuality and culminates in the inhibition of thought, Klein recommended that psychoanalysis play a part in the education of all children, even for those who appear free from cognitive or behavioral difficulties. This educational premise was based, it would appear, on Enlightenment principles, a connection the author does not fail to address as she recalls that parental authority tends to draw support from the authority of God, whose existence is difficult to prove, and that the logical imbroglios spawned by the inevitable religious disagreements between the child's two parents generate confusion, even mental slowness, in the child. Happily, the astute psychoanalyst that Klein was (an analyst who had the good fortune to live very close to the parents of Fritz and who could thus follow the boy as if . . . she were his own mother—and an atheist mother at that!) had the wherewithal to associate the *metaphysical* curiosity about the existence of God with the *sexual* curiosity that the child both experiences and represses. In this way Klein exposed the child's troubles, and, by sparing the parents their ideological disagreements, relaxed their authority and allowed their offspring's thought to develop. Up to that point, all of this is straight Freudian orthodoxy!

Little Fritz (keep in mind that he was Klein's own son Erich in reality) learned to speak late, had trouble expressing himself, and secluded himself in a world of repetitious sounds. In sum, Fritz appeared "slow" and "behind" for a boy four years of age.[10] It was at that point that his mother, with the help of the analyst (or was it the other way around?), had said a few words to him about the nonexistence of Santa Claus and about the origin of babies. Fritz began to ask questions, grew curious about the world, became interested in feces and urine, and developed a sense of reality. At times he remained stagnant, and even regressed when his overwhelmed mother or analyst ceased making interpretations. In the end, though, Fritz was able to abandon his belief in the omnipotence of his infantile thought, express his desires more clearly, and, eventually, attain a wholly satisfying level of intelligence.

And yet, without the benefit of the second part of Klein's work, which would modify this optimistic, "eighteenth-century" vision of children's psychic life,[11] Klein, as early as the fourth page of her study, had already begun asserting that interpretation, which has the desirable effect of undermining both God's authority and the authority of the parents themselves, is in no way a simple result of education—that is, of sexual enlightenment or *Aufklärung*. In fact, the repression that plagued Fritz went deeper than did the secondary repression brought on by his moralizing education: "a certain 'pain' [on the part of Fritz], an unwillingness to accept (against which his desire for truth was struggling) was the determining factor in his frequent repetition of the question."[12] That was enough to relax religious or moral authority—and in Fritz's family, as we have seen, such authority was not very strong in the first place because of the discord between his parents. In truth, Fritz's inhibition was not the product of external educational pressure but of a mental universe that was already present. His inhibition expressed an *unconscious knowledge* that was structured through the weight of desires, on the one hand, and by the power of repression and the incest taboo, on the other. To summarize, although we have an "innate tendency to repression," Melanie Klein was already describing a sort of *split* between Fritz's "strong sexual curiosity" and his formidable "repression."[13] Accordingly, Fritz saw sexuality through the lens of an indomitable repulsion. The young boy, whose enlightened parents never repressed or threatened his sexual antics, nevertheless resisted enlightenment; he "simply [did] not accept it." "Repudiation and denial of the sexual and primitive . . . set repression in operation by dissociation."[14]

At that point Klein makes a hypothesis, one that she would later present as a truism. The child's unconscious forces us to confront *another form of knowledge*, an enigmatic knowledge that character- izes the *fantasy* and that remains resistant to "enlightenment," a knowledge that does not wish to be *familiar* with the real world through learning and adaptation to reality. Such *knowledge* staves off *awareness*. This unconscious knowledge is phylogenetically con- stituted and innate: it is tantamount to a castration complex "that had certainly developed on the basis of the Oedipus complex."[15] It adheres to the enigma of the incest taboo and is thus laden with desire *and* prohibition.

The analyst was convinced that when she peered into Fritz's unconscious, she could witness *original repression* itself! From that point on, her goal was not only to respect this unconscious knowledge (which contravenes our enlightened principles) but also to share in it and help it adhere, for only then are we able to work through it. In that sense, such knowledge can afford itself an opportunity—despite all odds—to become familiar with exis- tence on the heels of a lengthy process that is no longer a means of adaptation (which is what the parents want) but a negotiation between fantasy and reality. Therein lies the goal of Kleinian psy- choanalysis—and its parameters began to take shape in her earli- est works: the excess of the drive, the power of unconscious pro- hibition, splitting, the gradual deterioration of the fantasy (which is replaced by a never-fully-realized awareness of reality), and the imaginary nature of an ego confronted from the start with inter- nalized objects that are wholly desired and wholly forbidden. . . . It is said that genius can be detected from its earliest manifesta- tions, and that certainly applies to Melanie.

INVENTING STORIES WITH ERICH/FRITZ

This maternal-analytical insight (which was encouraged, as Melanie acknowledged, by Anton von Freund, who advised the young analyst to interpret not only the underlying conscious material but the deep unconscious material as well) encouraged Klein to take her interpretations one step further. She went beyond the conscious and educational level, and even beyond the level of the Freudian unconscious to which Anna Freud would try to limit herself a few years later, and dared to directly interpret fantasies that, as luck would have it, profoundly affected the child. To what can we attribute this sudden emergence of truth? To the fact that the child has fewer defenses and is less repressed than is the adult, and to the fact that the child can absorb interpretive speech when it has the courage to listen carefully to the rift between desire and repression—that is, to "pain":

> He listened with enjoyment to the story about the woman upon whose nose a sausage grew at her husband's wish. Then quite spontaneously he began to talk, and from then on he told longer or shorter phantastic stories. . . . I give a few excerpts from some of these phantasies:
>
> Two cows are walking together, then one jumps on to the back of the other and rides on her, and then the other one jumps on the other's horns and holds on tight. The calf jumps on to the cow's head too and holds tight on to the reins. . . . On bidding good-morning to his mother he said after she had caressed him, "I shall climb up on you; you are a mountain and I climb up you." . . . After a further period he again began to ask a few questions with great ardor. . . . Hand in hand with this he began to play.[16]

And what did the mother-analyst do? She made up stories, she played, and she told tales. She shared in the sexual curiosity and the castration anxiety or fear of death that fed the child's fantasies, and she did not hesitate to offer up a few stories of her own when Fritz remained silent. She projected herself onto Fritz's splitting; she lived in it, in its place, in the tension between desire and repression—endowing it with words, with stories that she was convinced were her own.

"It's just suggestion!," some will cry. "I'm just playing a game," Klein responds in turn. Although her words did not communicate an "enlightening" meaning, they allowed the child's fantasies to be translated into playlets, into tales reconstructed for the adult through a playful exchange that was at once complicit and distant. Fritz, in turn, was drawn to his mother's and/or his analyst's discourse about the little seeds that grow in women's bellies, and he then began to take an extraordinary interest in . . . the stomach. But which was it: the belly or the stomach? Fetus/child or food/excrement? The mother/analyst has listened, reaped, and sowed; she associated, and Erich/Fritz joined her. In fact, it would require a child's stomach to digest all that Melanie has revealed! A long, involved story awaited them:

> He had spoken of his "kakis" as naughty children who did not want to come. . . . I ask him, "These are the children then that grow in the stomach?" As I notice this interests him I continue, "For the kakis are made from the food; real children are not made from food." He, "I know that, they are made of milk." "Oh no, they are made of something that papa makes and the egg that is inside mamma." (He is very attentive now and asks me to explain.) . . . From this time on too his extraordinary interest in the stomach decreased greatly.[17]

The Kleinian child is not, as we see here, innocent in Rousseau's sense, nor is he "simply," if we could call it that, what Freud would call a perverse polymorph. To the extent the child is phobic, he fears a powerful stimulant as much as a strict taboo. Or, on the other hand, to the extent the child's admittedly polymorphously perverse stimulation and sexual curiosity underlie neurosis in Freud's view, for Klein they tread a dangerous path toward a much deeper unconscious, a primary unconscious that allows for the very possibility of original repression and, concomitantly, for the capacity—or lack of capacity—for language and thought. To declare that "Freud acquainted us with the child in the adult, and Klein with the infant in the child and the adult," as Hanna Segal so eloquently put it,[18] does not reveal the whole story. From the outset Klein lent her ear to original repression as it manifests itself in the child, fails in the psychotic, and reveals itself in borderline states. At the same time, Klein's breakthrough did not simply question the pedagogical and normalizing goals of a certain style of child analysis, as was believed to be the case in the 1930s and 1940s, nor was it a subversive call for the liberation of a sexuality that was uninhibited in families relieved of their authority, particularly paternal authority, as was claimed in the wake of the 1968 uprisings and the feminist movement. Rather, from the time of Klein's earliest clinical efforts, her innovation emerged as a *psychoanalysis of the capacity to think*, which is how it was understood and developed by Bion and Winnicott and by all of their followers who have sought to treat child psychosis and autism.

The renowned analysts who have breathed new life into psychoanalysis by introducing new domains of psychic investigation did so by transforming their secret and their passion into an epistemological goal. From her earliest writings, Melanie's own secret, passion, and goal were on full display: she sought to listen to— and to solicit—a *desire that thinks*. Are we witnessing here a mother concerned about the proper development of her child? Or is it Libussa's daughter grappling with her mother's grip on her as a young girl while functioning at the outer limits of incestuous stimulation and depressive suffocation?

> The *conflict* that the developing reality-sense has to wage with the innate tendency to repression, the process by which (as with the acquisitions of science and culture in the history of mankind) knowledge in individuals too must be *painfully* acquired. . . . In the case described, the foundations for his inhibitions and neurotic traits seem to me to reach back before the time even when he began to speak.[19]

Under certain conditions, the human family—as well as psychoanalysis, which may be able to help that family along—learns to transform the "conflict" and "pain" endemic to the realm of our thinking into a successful outgrowth of thought and culture. To do so, it must account for social bonds, that is, for the sundry "object relations," as Klein will later call them, that allow desire to generate meaning—through pain and despite pain—rather than remaining trapped by inhibition. The primary linchpins of Klein's thought are already present in her analysis of Fritz: desire, sublimation, and symbolization.

Eric Clyne recalled that his mother, in Rosenberg in 1919 and then in Berlin in 1920, spent an hour each day analyzing him before putting him to bed. Did the maternal bond make it easier for Klein to listen to him, or did it make it more difficult? The answer to that question, one that has been debated incessantly by Klein's disciples as well as her detractors, can only be ambiguous: the process was made both easier *and* more difficult. As a mother, Melanie was her son's object of unconscious desire, just as he was hers. This closeness—was it denied or was it overinvested?—helped Klein pick up on the subtle signs of Erich's sexual curiosity about his two parents. At the same time, in Klein's role as the analyst that she sought to be and that she for the most part successfully became, she was also an agent—if not of an optimal inhibition, at least of a sublimating negation of this desire: through interpretation, she encouraged Erich/Fritz to symbolize. From the beginning, she proved herself attentive to this dual function without ever being aware of the difficulties and obstacles that confronted the two protagonists:

> Owing to bringing into consciousness his incest-wishes, his passionate attachment to his mother is markedly shown in daily life. . . . His relationship with his father is, in spite (or because) of his consciousness of his aggressive wishes, an excellent one. . . . The process of liberation from the mother is already partly begun, or at least . . . an attempt at it will be made.[20]

Is it not through this mother/analyst coupling that we can understand why "the part played by the father was not referred to?" Almost as if Klein suspected that the answer to that question

would be troubling, she explained—perhaps a bit too simplisti-
cally—that "[Erich] had not at that time asked directly about
it."[21] She later added that, "The father's part in the birth and the
sexual act in general were not directly asked about. But even at
that time I thought these questions were unconsciously affecting
the boy."[22]

It is clearly impossible for a mother to play the role of an object
of desire while playing the role of a subject-presumed-to-know the
unconscious. We should also remember that Klein never advocated
that a mother play these dual roles, and she even tried to forget that
she had attempted to do so herself. Similarly, we should remember
that Klein was aware that the familial realm must be separated from
the analytic one: "I came to the conclusion that psycho-analysis
should not be carried out in the child's home."[23]

At the same time, Klein's strong tendency to "mother" the
unconscious[24] endured and even insinuated itself into her most
coherent and objective practices later in her career. This tendency
is apparent in the effort—more characteristic of the Kleinians, it
would seem, than of Klein herself—to emphasize original repression and the unconscious to the point of objectifying them and
molding them into dogmatic "positions," if not into preset interpretations that are both stereotypical and suggestive. A different
sort of capacity for a more playful and serene motherhood—the
sort of mother described by Winnicott—is what has enabled the
"seeds" (to use Melanie and Fritz/Erich's term) that Klein dissem-
inated through the psychoanalytic terrain to avoid the dogmatism
of maternal control and to develop instead into the recognition
that a "good enough mother" resides in the analyst himself (or
herself), in the form of an invitation to create a "transitional
space"[25] between the mother and baby as well as between the analyst and the patient.[26]

HANS AND (PERHAPS) MELITTA

Melanie's first son, Hans, did not escape his mother-analyst's
attentions either. Granted the name "Felix" in "A Contribution to

the Psychogenesis of Tics,"[27] Hans/Felix is said to have been subject to a stretching of the foreskin at three years of age and, at eleven years of age, to a nasal exam that reactivated this trauma and that encouraged his tendency to masturbate.

Masturbation was singled out for repression by his father, who, upon his return from the war, was very strict with his son. Felix developed tics that the analysis saw as a displacement of genital stimulation and masturbation. By decomposing Hans's three irrepressible movements—the sensation of pressure on his neck, the compulsive flipping back of his head accompanied by a sharp turn to the side, and finally his pressing of the chin down hard on his chest—Melanie Klein associated them with his recollection of the child's mother (who of course was in reality Klein herself). Before Felix's sixth birthday, he shared his parents' bedroom and wanted to participate in their lovemaking: his movements or tics mimicked his mother's presumed passivity and his father's active penetration of her. The analyst detected "his anal fixation to [his mother]" as well as "his repressed homosexuality."[28] As simplistic as these interpretations may appear, they do not merely regurgitate the Freudian notion that the hysterical symptom symbolizes a part of the body (in Freud and Breuer's *Studies on Hysteria,* for example, the paralyzed arm is considered to be the equivalent of an erect penis that the patient, in Freud's view, desires or seeks to possess). Klein is beginning here to form her theory of *object relations* by situating the symptom in the particular realm of the child, in the objects of his desires—his mother and father: "Experience has convinced me that the tic is not accessible to therapeutic influence as long as the analysis has not succeeded in uncovering the object relations on which it is based. I found that underlying the tic there were genital, anal- and oral-sadistic impulses toward the *object.*"[29]

And as for Melitta, it has been assumed that she was presented in a less flattering light, first as an anonymous case study and then under the first name of Lisa.[30] As a parallel to the story of Felix, Melanie reported the case of another child who had a sister "in a family with which I am well acquainted"[31] and that she described idealistically (which comes as no surprise, as it is her own!): "The children concerned are very well disposed and very sensibly and lovingly brought up."[32] Unhappily, although the fifteen-year-old adolescent (who shared the same age as Melitta did in 1919, when the first part of this essay was written) was at first gifted with solid intellectual abilities, she languished as she got older. The child was superficial and exhibited no curiosity about the world. As Klein put it, "The child never asked for sexual enlightenment at all,"[33] which could very well be taken to mean that poor Melitta was neither a shining light nor possessed of an "enlightened mind!" In summary, Klein notes, "she has, so far at least . . . shown only an average intellect."[34]

It is possible that, from the 1920s on, the war between mother and daughter, which did not truly begin until 1933, already consumed her. Can we not detect maternal envy or vengeance—in a woman who nevertheless projected a calm visage during this drama—in Klein's decision to portray her daughter so negatively long before the conflict was effectively unleashed? Lisa/Melitta personalized letters and numbers bizarrely rather than using them in the conventional way: she glorified the letter *a*, for example, by associating it with an image of her father, whose first name (Arthur) began with the same letter: "Then, however, she thought that 'a' was, perhaps, after all a little too serious and dignified and should have at least something of the skipping 'i.' The 'a' was the castrated but, even so, unyielding father, the 'i' the penis."[35]

Melanie diagnosed this underachiever as having a "sadistic idea of coitus"[36] and a castration complex that hindered her mathematical abilities. . . . Lisa/Melitta's paternal complex would achieve full force only when she was analyzed by Edward Glover,[37] as if it were an attempt to rehabilitate a father who had been "castrated but, even so, unyielding" in the face of an overwhelming, domineering mother.

And yet, through these rigid templates that the analyst-mother appears to have forced on her own children and that betray her own defenses against guilt, if not her maternal hatred toward her offspring, the pertinence of Klein's insight never ceases to amaze us, particularly because it so readily reveals a watershed event that lends itself to corroboration even as it relaxes the ever-threatening tension inherent in orthodoxy: an event that was none other than Klein's *invention of play technique.*

Klein traveled down that path by paying attention to Erich/Fritz's play and by participating, in her maternal capacity, in her children's fantasies as if she were "playing the game" while revealing its unconscious meaning. But it was with other children, those of her colleagues, particularly in Berlin, that Melanie, under the direction of Karl Abraham, refined her play technique.

PLAYING? INTERPRETING

At seven years of age, Rita disliked school and showed no interest in drawing. One day, however, she colored a piece of paper black, ripped it into pieces, and threw the shreds aside while murmuring, "dead woman."[38] Therein lay the source of the nocturnal terrors that caused the little girl to be brought in. Melanie understood that the "dead woman," a woman who threatened her and who had to be killed, was both the analyst and Rita's mother: transference became an essential object of interpretation. Klein also realized right away that paper, drawing, and water were indispensable to the "language without words" that appeared to characterize Rita's fantasies: for Klein, play was the royal road to the unconscious, the same function that the dream served for Freud. Melanie wasted no time before entering the room next door to look for her children's toys, and Rita began to enact various catastrophes with the miniature cars, trains, and dolls that the analyst brought back for her. Through Rita's play, Melanie saw a dramatization of her sexual adventures with a classmate. This irritated Rita at first, but she was soon appeased: play technique had begun to take shape.

I should like to explain briefly why these toys afford such valuable assistance in the technique of play analysis. Their smallness, their number and their great variety give the child a very wide range of representational play, while their very simplicity enables them to be put to the most varied uses. Thus toys like these are well suited for the expression of phantasies and experiences in all kinds of ways and in great detail. The child's various "play thoughts," and the affects associated with them (which can partly be guessed at from the subject-matter of its games, and which are partly plainly expressed), are presented side by side and within a small space, so that we get a good survey of the general connections and dynamics of the mental processes that are being put before us, and also, since spatial contiguity often stands for temporal contiguity, of the time-order of the child's various phantasies and experience.[39]

Klein would return later to the ideas expressed here, emphasizing that these toys should be "non-mechanical," as simple as the facilities in the playroom itself, and that the "the human figures, varying only in colour and size, should not indicate any particular occupation," so the child will use them for whatever purposes emerge during play.[40]

Although Klein was also cognizant of the aggression expressed during play, and although she paid assiduous attention to the destroyed object, she still forbade any act of physical aggression toward the analyst.[41]

Play, however, is not the abstract dramatization of "objects" of desire or of hatred symbolized by toys. Klein's conception of play is rooted in the body and in the world: play *exists* to the extent that it moves forward, burns, breaks, wipes, dirties, cleans, destroys, constructs, and so forth. . . . Accordingly, Klein needed surroundings that were altogether different from the somber analytic couch: "There has to be a quantity of illustrative material in the room. The most important of these is a wash-basin with running water."[42]

At three years and nine months, Peter was a very difficult child, inhibited in his play, strongly fixated on his mother, and "unboyish." During his very first session, he took a horse and carriage and bumped it into another one: "I asked him what the carriages were doing. He answered: 'That's not nice,' and stopped bumping them together at once, but started again quite soon." And during another session, " 'That's how they bumped their thingummies together.' . . . So I continued my interpretation and said: 'You thought to yourself that Daddy and Mummy bumped their thingummies together and that is how your little brother Fritz came.' "[43]

Trude, at three years and three months, was very neurotic and unusually fixated on her mother. During her first session, she insisted that Klein remove a flower from a vase. "My immediate interpretation of these utterances [was] in the sense that she desired to do away with her father's penis."[44]

Klein observed children destroying objects: did that not represent in the unconscious the destruction of the father's genitals?[45] She was careful to interpret *negative transference*[46] at the first signs of anxiety and resistance. The interpretation of negative transference was thus another of Melanie's contributions to psychoanalysis: in no way ignoring it, she was so sensitive to it that some have even accused her of soliciting it. What she was really seeking, however, was her patients' aggressiveness—their restrained death drive—because it was by freeing up the death drive that she believed she could free up thought. Klein applied here the lesson Freud taught us in his writings contemporaneous with his discovery of what lies beyond the pleasure principle, in particular in his "Negation" (1925)[47]–or, more precisely, she subjected them to her own original development.[48]

As Klein continued to expand her analytic practice with children, it became clear to her that play affords the same ability to access the unconscious as does an adult's free association or an analysis of a dream, perhaps even more so because play is more amenable to the expression of a pre- or transverbal unconscious. As a result, Klein incorporated into her account of Richard's treatment the following phrase from Montaigne's *Essays*: "As indeed it must be noted that children's games are not games, and must be judged in children like their more serious actions."[49]

PLAIN WORDS, NEGATIVE TRANSFERENCE, AND
DECONDENSATION OF THE PHANTASY

To carry out an analysis, however, it is not enough to project one-self onto the space of child at play and to reach the child's unconscious through a maternal-analytic osmosis: "The *form* in which an interpretation is given is also of great importance." Peter, as we remember, pointed to the swing and said: 'Look how it dangles and bumps.' And so when I answered: 'That's how Daddy's and Mummy's thingummies bumped together', he took it in without the slightest difficulty."[50]

We see that the highly empirical Melanie Klein had a keen sense of the linguistic "signifier," and that she made her interpretations, which often appear quite simplistic, with scrupulous respect for the child's particular use of language: "One of the necessary conditions of a successfully terminated treatment is that the child, however young, should make use of language in analysis to the full extent of its capacity."[51]

She offers a revealing example of this process: a five-year-old boy who completely repressed his fantasies nevertheless expressed them when he played, though he "show[ed] the tendency not to realize" the significance of his words. One day, while the two of them were playing a game of buyer and seller, the analyst asked him to choose a name for her. "I was to be 'Mr Cookey-Caker' . . . [and] to sell engines, which represented for him the new penis." Melanie understood that "Cookey-Caker" referred to "making cakes" and expressed the fantasy of making children orally and anally. The boy gave himself the name of "Mr Kicker," who had "gone away somewhere." "He soon realized that Mr Cookey-Caker had been killed by his kicking him . . . [and] realized after this interpretation his aggression against his father."[52]

This is all worlds apart, of course, from the technique that Freud used with Little Hans in relation to the boy's father: Freud's cautious approach—as compared with Melanie's outbursts—led him to claim that Hans was jealous because he wanted to share the same mustache as his father! There was no question of Freud's claiming that Hans wanted the same penis as his father. Klein's approach was nothing of the sort. With the help of Mr. Cookey-Caker, she forged ahead. Lacan and others would later observe that the signifier alone traced the path of her interpretive audacity. Still, she already found herself hearing the signifier ("cookey-caker, kicker"—but she curiously declined to note the importance of the "k" sound in Mrs. Klein, nor did she comment upon her being identified with a man), shifting from words to things, and recounting the fantasy. She limited herself to pointing out the following: "The word 'Cookey-Caker' is the bridge to reality which the child avoids as long as he brings forth his phantasies only by playing. It always means progress when the child has to acknowledge the reality of the objects through his own words."[53]

Klein's play technique proves to be inseparable from her style of interpretation, one in which a fantasy *enacted into play*, turned into a fantasy *narrated by two people*, leads to an awareness of reality. To the extent that little Rita[54] invented *play technique* with the help of Fritz, Peter, Felix, Trude, and others (just as Freud's patient Anna O. invented the "talking cure"), Kleinian *interpretation* is an integral part of this technique, and in fact the essence of her work.

Let us return to Fritz/Erich so we can better appreciate Klein's methodology.

Before introducing play itself, Melanie Klein used a two-step process to follow the child into his fantasies—which he communicated through repetitive utterance or through inhibited or compulsive behaviors. On the one hand, she named his fantasies by using plain words to "call a cat a cat," as Freud put it[55]: "If we want to gain access to the child's unconscious in analysis (which, of course, we have to do via the ego and through speech), we shall only succeed if we avoid circumlocution and use plain words."[56] On the other hand, she applied the logic of interpretation to the condensed interpretation intrinsic to the fantasy. Her goal was to draw out and then to free this web of identifications in order to determine the locus of the specific identification that informs the child's fantasy. Fritz's fixation on the stomach, for example, diminished only when—in the course of one of his sessions, as he was repeating the expression "cold in the stomach"[57]—he described the organ in question as a room that someone had entered in order to destroy. The mother-analyst responded by asking him the following:

> "Who is the someone and how did he get inside?" He answers, "A little stick came through the wiwi into the belly and into the stomach that way." In this instance he offered little resistance to my interpretation. I told him that he had imagined himself in his mamma's place and wished his papa might do with him what he does with her. But he is afraid (as he imagines his mamma to be too) that if this stick—papa's wiwi—gets into his wiwi he will be hurt and then inside his belly, in his stomach, everything will be destroyed, too.[58]

Interpretations of this sort presume that the child is capable of understanding the *semantic* value of the direct words used by the analyst as well as their *symbolic* value, which is derived from translating the interlocking gestures of identification (in this case, Fritz's identification with a "destroyed" mother and a "dirty mamma"[59]— as reflected by his anal-sadistic interpretation of intercourse—but also his fear of being that mother, which represented the homosexual component of his psyche). Klein's interpretation also assumes that, because children have an easier time communicating between the conscious and the unconscious, analytic speech, which reveals a deep and unpleasant reality, will inevitably grant relief. But Klein also ran the risk of underestimating the child's defenses and preconscious:

> He enquires quite cheerfully whether what he finds "horrid" will, after I have explained it to him, become pleasant again for him just as with the other things so far. He also says that he is not afraid any more of the things that have been explained to him even when he thinks of them.[60]

This interpretive style, which was rooted in Klein's analysis of her own children, developed and solidified with the play technique that was gradually taking shape. An example of this may be found in Rita: the young girl, who suffered from "night terrors" and animal phobias, and who was ambivalent toward her mother even though she clung to her, displayed all of the symptoms of an obsessional neurosis alternating with depression. During Rita's first session with Klein, she was afraid to be alone with the analyst in her office and wanted to go out into the garden. The child's mother and aunt accompanied the child, as they were already fearing failure, but Melanie agreed to play the game and knew that changing venues was a necessary part of it:

> While we were outside I had been interpreting her negative transference (this again being against the usual practice). From a few things she said, and the fact that she was less frightened when we were in the open, I concluded that she was particularly afraid of something which I might do to her when she was alone with me in the room. I interpreted this and, referring to her night terrors, I linked her suspicion of me as a hostile stranger with her fear that a bad woman would attack her when she was by herself at night. When, a few minutes after this interpretation, I suggested that we should return to the nursery, she readily agreed. . . . This case strengthened my growing conviction that a precondition for the psycho-analysis of a child is to understand and to interpret the phantasies, feelings, anxieties, and experiences expressed by play or, if play activities are inhibited, the causes of the inhibition.[61]

Melanie Klein examined the *realm of play* as a dreamlike scene subjected to the primary processes (condensation and displacement) and, of course, to the child's *language*, but she also took into account the *diverse semiology* of his affects, which she intuited from his corporeal and emotional behavior or from his nonverbal gestures. A vast array of signs were at her disposal as she sought to interpret negative transference, which is itself formulated in a sequence that is typically supported through causal links and that provides the path to the heart of the unconscious: Frau Klein = bad mother = Mummy who prevents me from sleeping and who threatens me like a witch = because I desire Mummy and/or because I am jealous that she sleeps with Papa and/or because I want to destroy her or them. . . . Melanie Klein's pronouncements, as well as the relationship she establishes between them, clearly are not wanting for semantic and logical coarseness. But it would be unfair to accuse her of making interpretations that are merely . . . "symbolic" in the sense of being based on an instinctual sexual symbolism that is stripped of preconscious bonds, unaware of the linguistic signifier, and dismissive of the child's receptivity.

Just like her brisk, overtly sexualized discourse, Klein's interpretation of negative transference from the outset of treatment—a focus that radically differentiates her technique from that of Anna Freud or of Freud himself—has the advantage, she believed, of establishing from an early stage a candid rapport with the patient, whether a child or an adult. While Anna Freud and her father committed themselves to establishing a bond of trust between the patient's ego and the analyst's ego before beginning any deep interpretive work, Klein believed that directly targeting the unconscious is what set this transference relationship into motion and paved the way for the analytic work to follow.

Such an approach, which can work quite well with young children, encounters more resistance with other age groups and psychic structures. The latency period, for example, poses particular problems that threaten to invalidate Klein's proposed technique: with that age group, the young child's play is no longer accessible, and the free association of the adult is not yet a possibility. In that case, isn't there a risk that a deep interpretation and an interpretation of negative transference could incite or exacerbate feelings of anxiety? And yet even here, the examples that Klein gives show that the child's indifference during the latency period, his withdrawal from transference, and his defensive isolation into psychic and discursive monotony can be approached through analytical interpretations about the sexual relations between the parents, masturbation, or oedipal rivalry. The apparent savageness of such interpretations reflects a disclosed unconscious truth that the analyst believes the patient is capable of absorbing, a secret with which the analyst entrusts the patient. At the same time, the analysand readily affirms the importance of this method by establishing or reinforcing his transference.

Does such a technique risk subordinating the patient or seducing him or intruding on his life? Aren't such suggestions rather manipulative? Are such interpretations sensitive to the original unconscious, or do they risk dominating it altogether? Is it not the case that the archaic analyst-mother allows herself to be carried away by a fantasy of being able to grasp what lies at the very origins of it all? Such questions about Kleinianism are legitimate, and the work of her followers on the secondary effects of transference as well as countertransference helps us avoid such problems today. That said, Klein's interpretive technique, which is explicitly anchored in play and which takes into account the many facets of play—semiotic codes that embellish verbal language, condensed multifaceted identifications that lie within acted-out or reified fantasies, and the negative or positive transference onto the analyst—offers an extraordinarily fertile ground for investigating the depths of the unconscious.[62]

Karl Abraham was correct when he proclaimed the following to the First Conference of German Psychoanalysts in Würzburg in 1924: "The future of psycho-analysis lies in play technique."[63] By relying on the interplay of the child's diverse semiotic codes, the creativity of psychodrama, and the interplay among the signifiers of free association, Melanie unwittingly foresaw the path that analytic treatment would take in the wake of Freud. And yet she left unanswered a question that is the fundamental question of all psychoanalytic interpretation—one that Klein was brave enough to even consider: Can I reveal everything that I know is taking place in my patient's unconscious? The "instinct," which senses everything, and perhaps even truth itself, *is not all there is*: nothing can be everything in the game of sensory fantasies. One sometimes has the impression that, for Klein, the psychic realm that she has enabled us to see concretely becomes, paradoxically, transparent, and that it loses its three-dimensionality when she disrupts it with ill-timed interpretations. The flair for the imaginary requires a good deal of tact in order to discover the unconscious and then to revive it indefinitely.

THE PRIORITY AND INTERIORITY
OF THE OTHER AND THE BOND:
THE BABY IS BORN WITH
HIS OBJECTS

NARCISSISM AND THE OBJECT

The hypothesis that a stage extending over several months precedes object-relations implies that—except for the libido attached to the infant's own body—impulses, phantasies[,] anxieties, and defenses either are not present in him, or are not related to an object, that is to say, they would operate *in vacuo*. The analysis of very young children has taught me that there is no instinctual urge, no anxiety situation, no mental process which *does not involve objects, external or internal; in other words, object-relations are at the centre of emotional life.* Furthermore, love and hatred, phantasies, anxieties, and defences are also operative from the beginning and are *ab initio* indivisibly linked with object-relations. This insight showed me many phenomena in a new light.[1]

Belated yet definitive, Klein's declaration sets forth the parameters of her fundamental debate with Freudian theory. In fact, what Freud (whose views on this subject were ever changing) describes as the young child's first (objectless) state of narcissism, Klein describes as an object relation that operates from the time of birth.[2] Although the divergence between these two theoretical stances is undisputed, these differences are more complex than they first appear.

When Freud began to develop his concept of narcissism in "On Narcissism: An Introduction" (1914),[3] he described an "auto-erotism"[4] that emerges early in life, an instinctual and, even more important, archaic, self-gratification for the baby that precedes a "new psychical action" known as "narcissism" in which the ego as a totality is deemed an object of love. In the years leading up to this discovery, Freud discussed narcissism in the context of homosexuality and psychosis: his studies on Leonardo Da Vinci (1910),[5] President Schreber (1911),[6] and the Wolf Man (which he worked on between 1910 and 1914 and published in 1918)[7] developed the notion of a narcissistic act that emerges on the heels of an identification. Da Vinci repressed his love for his mother by putting himself in her place: he identified with her and was thus drawn to objects of love that reminded him of her; if he chose to love young boys, it was because he loved them in the same way his own mother had loved him. In a different though somewhat similar way, the Wolf Man identified alternatively with his father and his mother in the context of a primal scene rife with anal sadism. What is more, the Wolf Man's identification with his Nanya only reinforced his adoption of a passive feminine position with respect to his father, with the result that his repressed homosexuality culminated in a narcissistic identification. President Schreber, who, like Da Vinci and the Wolf Man, invested heavily in anality and displayed a feminine passivity and a rather exalted interest in religion, withdrew his libido from objects and localized it in his own ego instead. Freud noted the following in response: just as the transference neuroses enabled him to illustrate the dynamic drives endemic to the psychic apparatus, *dementia praecox* and paranoia guided him toward the psychoanalysis of the ego. Until that point, narcissism was integrated with the demands of the ego—and it protected that ego.

Beginning with "Mourning and Melancholia" (1917),[8] Freud emphasized the identification with the lost object and its ambivalent internalization (at once love and hatred) within the mourning or depressed ego. "Beyond the Pleasure Principle" (1920),[9] on the other hand, replaced the "ego drives"—which were contrasted with the "sexual drives"—with a new duality of drives: the "life drive" and the "death drive."[10] Finally, with "The Ego and the Id" (1923)[11] Freud outlined a new structure for the psychic apparatus that would later form the basis of Melanie Klein's own conception of narcissism.[12]

With Freud's "second topography" (the id, the ego, and the superego), narcissism, which had been previously defined as a function of ego investment[13] through a surge of identifications withdrawing from objects, became "secondary narcissism." The term "primary narcissism," on the other hand, was now used to describe an objectless state characterized by the total absence of any relationship with other people and by a lack of any differentiation between the *ego* and the *id*. Intrauterine life and sleep are the closest approximations we have of this objectless narcissistic state.

Several critics[14] have found Freud's notion of narcissism to be imprecise and inadequate. Indeed, if narcissism is already an internalization of an object relation, can we really speak of a truly objectless state? And even if an objectless state exists, which still remains to be seen, the phrase "primary narcissism" would be inapposite because it represents the beginnings of an object relation. Finally, it is difficult to understand "just how [we are] supposed to picture the transition from a monad shut in upon itself to a progressive discovery of the object."[15] Recent studies that are sensitive to the work of Melanie Klein, particularly the work of André Green, have refined this notion by distinguishing "life narcissism" from "death narcissism" and by deeming narcissism to be not a state but a structure.[16]

This brief discussion helps us better understand the role that Klein accords to the object relation, and more specifically to the "internal object." Klein broadly outlines her notion of the object, which in her view takes on the true meaning of "object"—as opposed to the "ego"—only through the "depressive position." What is more, narcissism does not truly disappear in Kleinian theory and practice; instead, it takes the form of a "narcissistic state" in which libido withdraws from external objects and directs itself exclusively toward internalized objects.

Finally, it is worth noting that other theories of child psychology offer competing views on the subject of narcissism. At the same time, however, the hypothesis that a baby is capable of establishing a certain type of object relation has become widely accepted in recent years, which tends to confirm Klein's insights.

In Piaget's view, for example, "the universe of the young baby [which Piaget calls stage 3: the stage between the ages of five and seven months] is a world without objects, consisting only of shifting and unsubstantial 'tableaux' which appear and are then totally reabsorbed, either without returning, or reappearing in a modified or analogous form."[17] Although the baby establishes contact with an identical being that nevertheless changes its position and its state, there is no permanent scheme in the cognitive sense that would suggest the existence of an initial "object" (which will not be acquired until stage 4, that is, between the ages of nine and ten months). Henri Wallon, on the other hand, has posited the existence of a radical subjectivism that operates from the time of birth based on the baby's jubilation upon seeing his own image and on his imitation of his mother's facial gestures.[18] More recently, C. G. Carpenter has asserted that a two-week-old infant is capable of synthesizing the parts of his mother's body into a unified and complete visual image that he associates with her auditory traits.[19] Various cognitive science studies have wholeheartedly endorsed such views,[20] and among psychoanalysts, Michael Balint has acknowledged the existence of a primary object relation.[21]

Using her own unique psychoanalytic perspective—and while reworking her notions as the years went by—Klein theorized the early existence of an extremely early "object," an object that she would later term, very cautiously at that, a "bodily presence." Her writings on the subject, which she began in 1919–1921 and which were published in a 1932 anthology, started going down this path, but it was more precisely her 1934 discovery of the "depressive position" that reinforced her notion of the child's relationship with the object. At the same time, although Klein described the paranoid position in her later works—her 1946 formulation of a "paranoid-schizoid position" was associated with the notion of "projective identification"—her study of the universe that *precedes* the depressive position would cause her to modify her theory considerably. The two-volume study of Klein by Jean-Michel Petot[22] painstakingly retraces this evolution, which I am unable to discuss in detail here. I will limit myself to presenting the most essential features of Klein's notions to the extent they reflect the totality of her journey and in the context of its final destination, particularly in the seminal texts she wrote in 1952 that illustrate the ultimate coherence of her doctrine.[23]

INSIDE/OUTSIDE

Klein believed that the child, from the very beginnings of life, is consumed with anxiety and racked by destructive drives that put him in danger of being disintegrated. We see here a return, and an intensified one at that, to Freud's notion of the "death drive."

For Freud, however, neither the unconscious nor the baby knows death. At first Melanie adopted Abraham's view that aggressiveness in children appears only during the oral-sadistic stage, which led her to theorize a "pre-ambivalent oral stage." In her later work, however, she asserted that the death drive exists from the moment of birth:

From the beginning *the destructive impulse is turned against the object* and is first expressed in *phantasied oral-sadistic attacks on the mother's breast,* which soon develop into onslaughts on her body by all sadistic means. The persecutory fears arising from the infant's oral-sadistic impulses to rob the mother's body of its good contents, and from the anal-sadistic impulses to put his excrements into her (including the desire to enter her body in order to control her from within) are of great importance for the development of paranoia and schizophrenia.[24]

And as she also stated:

> I have often expressed my view that *object-relations exist from the beginning of life*, the first object being the mother's breast which to the child *becomes split into a good* (gratifying) *and bad* (frustrating) *breast*; this splitting results in a severance of love and hate. I have further suggested that the relation to the first object implies its introjection and projection, and thus from the beginning object-relations are moulded by an interaction between introjection and projection, between internal and external objects and situations. These processes participate in the building up of the ego and super-ego and prepare the ground for the onset of the Oedipus complex in the second half of the first year.[25]

A close reading of these passages shows that, even though Klein uses such terms as "object" and "ego," she also establishes, with respect to this early stage at the beginning of life, a distinction between *inside* and *outside*, between *inner* and *outer*. The early ego, in summary, is deemed to be exceptionally fragile, so much such that, under the weight of both the anxiety-death drive that lies at its origins and the intolerable feeling of being abandoned by the object (the mother), the ego gives way to an incessant back-and-forth motion and to projection-introjection. To defend itself against being the sole target of this primary destructiveness and to stave off separation, the ego jettisons that destructiveness in part and redirects it toward the outside world. At that point, the ego is drawn into what might be called a quasi-object—the breast—in the sense that the fragile ego is not truly separated in the sense of a "subject" separated from an "object," but it incessantly consumes the breast from within and ejects the breast into the outside world by constructing-vacating itself while constructing-vacating the Other. This dynamic is dominated by the fantasy-like omnipotence that the child exerts over his mother.

As if Klein were suggesting that this "primary" object—the breast—is unstable, she modifies her theory substantially: at a very early stage, the child perceives the breast as being the "part object" of nursing, but also as other parts of the mother's body (her voice, her face, her hands, and her bosom) that constitute a bodily "presence."[26] The mother's holding and handling of the baby impress him with a "physical closeness" with the no less "unstable" wholeness of an *Other*—or, more accurately, a *container*.[27] It is a container that is merely part of the process of differentiating with the ego. Isn't it true that the ego is founded upon "some indefinite connection between the breast and other parts and aspects of the mother"?[28]

Furthermore, although this quasi-object that is the primary breast exists completely in an outside world in which the infantile ego deems it to be an externality from the very beginnings of life, it is just as much a *construction from within*, that is, an internal image, to the extent that the fragile ego, as it constructs and deconstructs the boundary between the inside and the outside, is where this quasi-object (or this object-being-constituted) is formed. From the outset, then, the *primal object* of the paranoid-schizoid position emerges, in Klein's view, if and only if it is an *internal object* constructed through a fantasy of omnipotence.

At the same time, this internal focus has no purely drive-based or spectral quality. It is not only the drive that is projected and introjected (as love or hatred, desire or destruction), but bits of the baby as well (his organs—the mouth, the anus, and so forth—as well as his bodily products). Klein's view on this subject differs from Freud's. In addition, however much the internal object reflects the imaginary and attests to the presence of the fantasy in the early ego, it is also made up of substantive and sensorial elements: good or bad "bits" of the breast are situated within the ego or expelled from it into the mother's breast. Nourishing substances such as the mother's milk or excremental substances such as urine and feces are projected and introjected. Klein's internal object is an *amalgam* of representations, sensations, and substances—in a word, it is a diverse array of heterogeneous internal objects. Her notion of the internal object is entirely distinct from Lacan's *imaginary*, for Lacan believed that narcissism takes hold through the intermediary of the object as a function of the subject's absorption into his mirror image—into the very place where he realizes he is an Other who is sustained by the alterity of a mother already placed under the rubric of a third-party phallus. And yet this spectral distortion—which, for Lacan, has the advantage of highlighting the role that the scopic function plays in structuring the ego and the object, but especially of situating the binary relationship *inside* the triangulation dominated by the symbolic function of the father—is bereft of the *heterogeneity*[29] that characterizes Klein's notions of the internal object and of fantasy. Klein's thinking here evokes a cornucopia of images, sensations, and substances whose theoretical "impurity" is superseded by the clinical advances she proposes: the complexity of the internal object, in Klein's view, is indispensable for tracking the specifics of the fantasy in childhood as well as in borderline states or psychosis.

Finally, this early world is founded upon a process of "discriminating" between inside and outside, between good and bad, and so forth, that shares in the construction of the ego and the superego, unless that very construction is what leads to the discrimination.[30] In connection with the fragility of the early ego as it responds to the death drive, and before we examine the details of how the early ego functions, we should consider the importance of the capacity for making binary distinctions: in Klein's view, such a capacity ushers in an early form of *semiosis* that functions as an innate precondition to the child's subsequent acquisition of the symbol.[31]

We see below that, when Klein analyzed Rita, she situated the construction of the *internal object* within the dynamics of anxiety, of the destructive drive, and of guilt, all the while elucidating the mechanisms of projection and introjection:

Before she was two years old, Rita became conspicuous for the remorse she used to feel at every small wrongdoing,

and for her over-sensitiveness to reproach. . . . What determined her identification with the bear was her fear of her
real father's displeasure. Here inhibition in play originated
from her sense of guilt. When she was only two years and
three months old she used to play with her doll—a game
which gave her little pleasure—and would repeatedly
declare that she was not the doll's mother. Analysis showed
that she was not permitted to play at being its mother,
because, among other things, the doll-child stood for her
little brother whom she had wanted to steal from her
mother during the latter's pregnancy. The prohibition,
however, did not proceed from her real mother, but from
an introjected one who treated her with far more severity
and cruelty than the real one had ever done. Another
symptom—an obsession—which Rita developed at the age
of two was a bed-time ritual which took up a lot of time.
The main point of it was that she had to be tightly tucked
up in the bedclothes, otherwise a "mouse or a Bűtzen"
would get in through the window and bite off her own
"Bűtzen." . . . On one occasion during her analytic session
she put a toy elephant to her doll's bed so as to prevent it
from getting up and going into her parents' bedroom and
"doing something to them or taking something away from
them." The elephant was taking over the role of her internalized parents whose prohibiting influence she felt ever
since, between the ages of one year and three months and
two years, she had wished to take her mother's place with
her father, rob her of the child inside her, and injure and
castrate both parents. . . .

These games also proved that this anxiety referred not
only to the child's real parents, but also, and more especially,
to its excessively stern *introjected parents*. What we meet
with here corresponds to what we call the super-ego in
adults. . . . Early analysis shows that the Oedipus conflict
sets in as early as the second half of the first year of life and
that at the same time the child begins to build up its superego.[32]

THE "PARANOID-SCHIZOID POSITION": SPLITTING
AND PROJECTIVE IDENTIFICATION

Beginning with this clinical essay and before her subsequent formalization of the "paranoid-schizoid position," Klein described an ego "dealing with anxiety." For Klein, unlike Freud, it is not the *organism*, but the *ego*, however immature it may be, that projects and introjects the drive. Rita's ego had a fear of annihilation that she experienced as a sort of persecution by an object to which her anxiety was drawn, an object that was powerful and uncontrollable. An initial mechanism emerged that helped her defend herself against this object: *splitting*. The object is split into a "good" object and a "bad" object, with the prototype of this division being the gratifying "good breast" and the frustrating "bad breast." Splitting is accompanied by other movements and mechanisms that the ego can capitalize upon at a very early stage: *projection, introjection, idealization*, and *denial*. The way one experiences this threat from this external object led Klein to speak of a "paranoid position" that she based on the work of Fairbairn,[33] whose originality she admired although she diverged from his path. While Fairbairn emphasizes the ego's relationship with objects, Klein, for her part, focuses on anxiety. Although Klein recognized that aggression and hatred exist from the beginning of life, she did not forget that the "good" breast—which, in the context of this position, she termed the "idealized breast"—already exists for the ego as a "paranoid-schizoid position," which means that the "bad" breast is by no means the only breast that is internalized.

Klein's concept of the "position," then, invokes neither a "stage" as the term was understood by the psychoanalysts who preceded her, nor a "structure" in the modern postlinguistic sense of the word. Klein found herself speaking of masculine, feminine, libidinal, oral, and other "positions," thereby describing a shifting psychic vantage point and challenging the strict chronology claimed by the proponents of psychoanalytic stages. Once Klein's concepts were solidified into a "paranoid-schizoid position" and a "depressive position," they began to connote a certain structure of emotional life—one that appears at a particular moment of history and that is susceptible to reappearing in the unconscious: "the regular association of a series of anxiogenic situations with a series of determinate defense mechanisms."[34]

Attendant to the "paranoid-schizoid position" that Klein came to discover late (in 1946) but that she placed at the forefront of her developments, the *splitting* of qualities in the object also emerges inside the ego itself. The violence of the fissure that splitting creates between the "good" and the "bad" protects the object, at least a part of which turns out to be accepted, and thus protects the ego. At the same time, sadism directed toward the Other, as reflected in this fracture, does not protect the ego entirely: the ego, through incorporation, "is in danger of being split in relation to the internalized object fragments."[35] Furthermore, although this internal and external splitting is fantasy-like, the child still experiences it as being "very real," with the result that his feelings, his objects, and, later, his thoughts, are "cut off from one another."[36]

And yet nothing is so simple in this Dantean world. The "good breast," which becomes the core of the ego and that guarantees its strength, is also laden with traps. The *idealization* of the breast, which is a counterpart to the splitting of the ego, encourages the exaggeration of its good qualities in order to counteract the fear of the persecutory "bad breast." Although idealization is concomitant with the fear of being persecuted, it is just as much a function of the drive-based desires that seek an unchecked degree of idealization.

And there we encounter the childhood hallucination that Klein conceptualized so differently from Freud. In Freud's view, once the baby has sufficiently experienced gratification, he is capable of hallucinating gratification—that is, of experiencing gratification as if it were truly lacking—in a process Freud would later describe as being a "hallucinatory wish-fulfillment." In Klein's view, in contrast, as long as the infant is dominated by the paranoid-schizoid position, he is incapable of experiencing absence, with the result that he will experience the absence of the good object as an attack by the bad object. The infant will then proceed to split the object into a good part and a bad part while denying both frustration and persecution. He therefore denies the existence of the bad, but he vitiates psychic reality all the same because it is nothing but pain and thus bad. This omnipotent and maniacal omnipotence, which is what leads to hallucinatory wish-fulfillment in young children, is tantamount, for the unconscious, to an annihilation of painful circumstances, of the relationships that led to such circumstances, and of the ego forced to confront them. Denial and omnipotence thus play a role that is comparable to the role repression plays in optimal development, although in the schizophrenic these forces lead to delusions of grandeur and persecution.

All drives—oral drives as well as anal and urethral—participate in this logical process as part of their effort to wound, control, and possess the object. As a result, the various attacks and disturbances inflicted on the internal object "result in the feeling that the ego is in bits"[37] and can also result, in the schizophrenic, in intellectual deficiencies. Or instead, under the weight of the projective process, such attacks can appear to arise from a violent eruption of the external in the internal, of a control of the psyche by other people, and of the sort of fantasies that culminate in paranoia.

As is often the case when Klein initiates radical innovations, she reassures us—and reassures herself—as she rediscovers Freud's authority. In her view, Freud's case study of President Schreber, which she reread in the wake of the master, appears to have analyzed Schreber in a way that recalls her own notion of the paranoid-schizoid position. Didn't Schreber describe how his Doctor Fleschig's soul was first split into a live image, then into a persecuting image, and finally into forty or sixty bits, with God eventually reducing the life of the soul to only one or two forms? Freud concluded that the division was between God and Fleschig, who respectively represented the patient's father and brother. Klein elaborated upon this conclusion, adding that Fleschig's many souls reflected not just a splitting of the object but "a projection of Schreber's feeling that his ego was split" as well. "The anxieties and phantasies about inner destruction and ego-disinte-gration bound up with this mechanism are projected on to the external world and underlie the delusions of its destruction."[38]

Didn't Freud reach the same conclusions when he pointed out that Schreber rationalized his feeling of internal fragmentation by likening himself to "miracled up, cursory contraptions"[39] and by emphasizing that the paranoid person's "world catastrophe" is the "projection of this internal catastrophe"?[40] Melanie Klein hailed—and highlighted with italics—Freud's revolutionary insight that, in addition to the libido's effect on the ego, "*a secondary or induced disturbance of the libidinal processes may result from abnormal changes in the ego. Indeed, it is probable that processes of this kind constitute the distinctive characteristic of psychoses.*"[41] Even more similar to Melanie, Freud noted that these problems arise "somewhere at the beginning of the course of development from auto-erotism to object-love."[42] These remarks by Freud validate, in sum, the paranoid-schizoid position that Melanie invented as well as the projective identification that later became, for our theorist, an integral part of Freudianism.

Klein's novel theories illuminate, among other things, the problematic forms of schizoid and paranoid defenses that she had previously observed, even in patients who were not psychotic: defenses that take the form of detached hostility or of an apparent lack of anxiety manifested as indifference. When a patient claims that he understands his analyst's speech but that it "does not mean anything to him," Klein interprets his words to mean that aspects of his personality and emotions are split and removed. She thus interprets his aggressiveness toward the analyst (in the context of a comparable aggressiveness toward his mother); the patient lowers his voice in response and claims to be "detached" from the totality of the situation. Klein saw all of this as a sign of his fear of losing her, a fear that he did not express through guilt or pain but, rather, counteracted with splitting. At the same time, her interpretations altered the patient's mood: he found himself "hungry" and told her as much during his session. The emergence of the affect of appetite shows that introjection emerged as a result of libido: the patient began to experience more fully the ambiguity of his drives, both positive and negative. A synthesis of splitting was underway, which palliated the schizophrenic phenomena even though at first it exacerbated depression and anxiety.

Another one of Klein's case studies, the case of Mr. A., reveals the essential mechanism of the paranoid-schizoid position that she theorized late in her career, one that is worth reiterating and that is at issue here.[43] During his analysis, this thirty-five-year old homosexual, who suffered from "disturbed potency" and obsessional neurosis with paranoid and hypochondriacal features, came to associate his fear of women with fantasies in which he saw his mother engaged in uninterrupted intercourse with his father. The patient's energy dwindled as he spied on his parents; his masturbation was linked to fantasy scenes in which his parents destroyed each other. He was afraid of the father's penis, which interfered with both his heterosexual and his homosexual position. Identifying with his mother, he experienced her as being essentially bad, and he expressed this fear by likening his analyst's words to poisonous excrements—or by imagining that his father was speaking through his own mouth. Mr. A. had been "led . . . very early to introject a poisoning and dangerous mother-imago who impeded the development of a 'good' mother-imago,"[44] so much so that the imago could not defend against the threat posed by the father's penis. The themes of poisoning and persecution grew accordingly and culminated in a hypochondriacal syndrome:

> The fear of damaging the woman with his "bad" penis (or rather, of not being able to restore her in intercourse) was, apart from his fear of his mother's dangerous body, the basis for Mr. A's disturbed potency.[45]

Projective identification, which is central to this aspect of Klein's theory, is thus manifested as the projection of the parts of the self onto an object in order to possess that very object: the mother's breast and the father's penis contain the violence of the attack and the split that project them outside the world as bad objects: "It may result in the object being perceived as having acquired the characteristics of the projected part of the self but it can also result in the self becoming identified with the object of its projection."[46]

Mr. A conducted himself as a "bad" person, that is, as feminine and ill, homosexual, and hypochondriacal. Pathological projective identification is "a result of minute disintegration of the self or parts of the self which are then projected into the object and disintegrated; it results in the creation of 'bizarre objects.' "[47]

It follows, then, that if the goal of projective identification is the freedom from the unwanted part of the self that is threatening because it has been disintegrated by the death drive with a concomitant reversal of identities, such identification culminates in destroying the object—in vitiating it in order to possess it. But if projective identification projects onto the Other the good parts of the fragile ego in order to protect them from the outside world, it can result in an idealization of the object that, though excessive, devalues the ego. In either case, projective identification dominates a narcissistic structure because the object is internalized from within and is deprived of its own qualities from without, as identity is assured only at the expense of support from the Other. From that perspective, Klein's notion of the "narcissistic structure" is based on this *surging of the object onto itself*, which weakens the ego, renders it incapable of love and transference, and reduces it to "a mere shell for such internal objects."[48] The narcissistic structure is thus distinguishable from "narcissistic states," which are states of identification with an internal ideal object, and thus recalls Freud's auto-erotism. If primal splitting is the first step in differentiation, projective identification is the first step in bonding with the outside world.[49] This stage can be painful and unsatisfying if it fails as a defense, but if it projects a fragile ego, it can endure as a psychotic structure.

These various features of projective identification lend themselves to two applications. On the one hand, projective identification describes pathological states, particularly states of manic-depressive psychosis or psychosomatic illness. On the other hand, however, the endless game of projection and introjection constitutes what Florence Guignard calls a veritable "psychic exhalation" because its underpinnings reveal a sort of normalcy, even universality.[50] As Guignard points out, mourning and successful oedipal identifications are the only ways to avoid the effects of projective identification.[51] In fact, we cannot prove Klein's hypothesis that the infant engages in projective identification without conceding, as does Bion, that all forms of psychic life depend on the help of another form of psychic life that uses projective identification to "dream" of a newborn child with a psyche. Taking this notion to its logical extreme, one could say that it is the mother's—and the analyst's—projective identification that corroborates the normalcy—or the abnormality—of projective identification as a universal function that stimulates the psyche— even though psychotic symptoms, among other things, rigidify its underlying logic and cause it to generate symptoms.

Is the mother a quiet paranoid-schizophrenic who flirts with projective identification? In truth, the totality of fantasy functioning, the birth of secondary symbolization, particularly that of language, and psychoanalytic interpretation are all concerned with projective identification—which, incidentally, is at the heart of the interpretive process itself. In any event, this is a hypothesis, a painful one if there ever was, that should be reflected upon by mothers . . . and by psychoanalysts.

But to return to what Klein considered to be the primary appearance made by projective identification in the paranoid-schizoid position, such identification convinces us—if we need any convincing—that relationships and identifications are unstable during that stage, or mode, of the psyche. The very notion of the object becomes increasingly irrelevant in the light of the fluid exchange of fragments expelled without and integrated within.

Accordingly, because we cannot be certain of the identities that describe the archaic link between the ego and the Other, it may be more helpful to speak of an *abject* rather than of an ego or an object already there. The future subject is founded upon a dynamic of abjection whose optimal quality is fascination. And if this future subject readily grants himself a "presence" of other people that he internalizes as much it expels, he is not facing an object but, in fact, an *ab-ject*, with this *a* understood in the privative sense of the prefix, that is, as vitiating the object as well as the emerging subject. It is a subject and an object that, as such, are crystallized only through what Klein calls the "depressive position" or, strictly speaking, through the castration ordeal, the resolution of the Oedipus conflict, and the creative acquisition of language and thought.

Before the formation of the oedipal *triangle*, which divides the protagonists of the family, a *trio*, also oedipal but founded provisionally upon the uncertain identities of the protagonists (in reality, on their narcissistic and objectless unconscious), plays a role of its own, in Klein's view, in the paranoid-schizoid position. Like a band in a Möbius strip that is characterized by its limitlessness, the future subject is forever transported toward the "ab-ject" (on the side of the mother) and toward "primary identification" with the "father of personal prehistory" (on the side of the loved and loving pre-oedipal father, who displays the traits of both parents). As a figure of fascination as well as abjection, this narcissistic state of the early object relation, which I have described as *abject* and an *abjection*, challenges not only pathology but limit states of sublimation as well: it challenges the sacred and the mystic as well as the difficulties posed by modern art.[52] Melanie Klein exposes us to this sort of understanding of the archaic object, but only if we are willing to merge its genius into a consideration of the symbolic function of the father as set forth in Freud's conception of the Oedipus conflict and Lacan's notion of the Name-of-the-Father—a function that is lacking in the matriarch.

THE DEPRESSIVE POSITION: THE WHOLE OBJECT, THE PSYCHIC REALM, AND REPARATION

In Kleinian theory, it is only through the "depressive position" that we can maintain a sufficiently stable and satisfying relationship with the object: the depressive position generates symbolization and language, which in turn designate an object for the ego. Melanie Klein introduced the concept of the "depressive position" in 1934 and expanded upon it in articles published in 1940, 1948, and 1952[53] as she localized the evolution of the child *after* the "paranoid-schizoid position," a position she did not theorize until 1946.

Much closer to an organizing principle that is Freud's notion of the Oedipus conflict, the "depressive position" is a theoretical construct that Melanie developed on the heels of a grief-ridden period that tore her apart. In April 1934, Hans Klein, Melanie's eldest son, died in a mountain accident. While working in a paper factory founded by his paternal grandfather, he often sojourned in the Tatra mountains in Hungary. On one excursion the path crumbled away beneath him and led him to a fatal fall. His mother was so distraught that she was unable to attend his funeral in Budapest, remaining in London instead. At first Hans's death was considered a suicide, but Eric Clyne has categorically denied that possibility, and Hans's wife herself agreed that he had overcome his homosexual tendencies and anxieties. Still, "everything about Hans remains disturbingly shadowy."[54] The Thirteenth International Psychoanalytic Congress took place on August 26–31 that same year; the grieving mother, although unable to attend her son's funeral, traveled to the conference to read a paper entitled "A Contribution to the Psychogenesis of Manic-Depressive States," which she also delivered to the British Psycho-Analytic Society in 1935. These two events—the mourning of her son and the invention of the "depressive position"—are no doubt linked: her paper described the psychic work of mourning while contributing to the development of the concept.

We are now quite familiar with the primary features of Klein's "depressive position." In her view, where she departed from previous psychoanalytic theory was in her belief that the child, beginning at six months of age, is capable of experiencing the loss of a *whole object* (the mother herself, and no longer simply the *part* object that was the breast) as a result of his diminished degree of splitting, and that this *experience of loss* is concomitant with the *introjection* of that object: "Not until the object is *loved as a whole* can its loss be felt *as a whole.*"[55]

This psychological development is made possible thanks to neurobiological maturation, which ushers in a better synthesis of perceptions and a more sophisticated memory. Once the baby

THE PRIORITY AND INTERIORITY OF THE OTHER / 75

sees his mother as a unified or whole object, he can recall the gratification she has given him in the past, even if he finds himself
frustrated in the present. At the same time, the child's psychomo-
tor maturation, cognitive development, and ability to walk hasten his awareness that the mother exists outside his field of
vision—in a neighboring room for example—and that she will
return to him (this development occurs during the beginning of
the second year of life). The child is thus able to apprehend his
mother as a whole, "both good and bad, but at once one and different" from him as well as from other members of the family—
from the father, to begin with, and then from his brothers and sisters. This recognition of the mother as a complete person is
accompanied by an integration of the ego, which is itself experienced as a total ego. From the inside as well as the outside, good
and bad objects are linked with one another to the extent that
they are distinguished from one another; these objects become
less malformed; projection diminishes; integration increases; and
the separation from the ego and the Other becomes more tolerable.

It is true, of course, that Klein came to this realization in part
through the views of Karl Abraham, who, in addition to having
already distinguished between the "part object" and the "whole
object," hypothesized beginning in 1923 an *Ur-Verstimmung* in
childhood, which served as a model for the subsequent onset of
melancholia and that linked this infantile *Ur-Melancholie* with
oral eroticism.[56] Yet as attentive a student as Melanie was, she still
sustained ideas of her own. In Abraham's view, for example, the
oral and anal stages are narcissistic, while for Klein, object relations originate with the oral-sadistic stage and are rooted in the
emergence of the whole object in depressive ambivalence and
anxiety. In that sense, Klein elevated what Abraham called the
"stage" or symptom he termed "primal depression" into a "central
position" around which psychic life is organized.

And yet, as is always the case with our analyst, psychic gain
comes at a cost. A new form of distress enters the picture: the
child discovers his dependence on his mother as a person as well
as his own jealousy of other people; the *paranoid anxieties* brought

on by this position are followed by new *depressive anxieties*. When the child finds himself in the paranoid-schizoid position, he is afraid that he will be destroyed by the very bad objects that he has projected outside him; when in the depressive position, on the other hand, he feels more ambivalent:

> And it is not only the vehemence of the subject's uncontrollable hatred but that of his love too which imperils the object. For at this stage of his development loving an object and devouring it are very closely connected. A little child which believes, when its mother disappears, that it has eaten her up and destroyed her (whether from motives of love or of hate) is tormented by anxiety both for her and for the good mother which it has absorbed into itself.[57]

By retaining the memory of a good object, the child acquires a nostalgia for it that is comparable to mourning. But because this love, during the oral phase, is a love of devouring that is heavily laden with sadistic drives, the feeling of losing the good object is buttressed by a feeling of guilt over having destroyed it by assimilating it: "a characteristic depressive experience" originates from the "the sense that he has lost the good object through his own destructiveness."[58] Fears of retribution, which were specific to the paranoid-schizoid position, endure, but now they are combined with the new feeling of *guilt*. Both this encroachment of the two positions and this prevalence of orality explain why infants have eating difficulties during this period and why both children and adults experience hypochondriacal anxieties. The paranoid person is afraid of being poisoned by external objects (food) onto which he has projected his aggressiveness, while the depressed hypochondriac is afraid for his organs, which represent internal objects and which must be constantly watched over, protected, and cared for.

In the new psychic dynamic introduced by the depressive position, the child discovers his own *psychic reality*: he begins to distinguish external reality from his own fantasies and desires. He modifies his belief in the omnipotence of thought, which he had previously subscribed to (and which, in the end, is *magical* rather than true *thinking*): he learns to distinguish between real things and their symbols, which signals the beginning of language acquisition. The depressive position is thus a precursor to our attainment of ideas, and the readers of *In Search of Lost Time* already know that Klein's hypothesis finds unexpected support in none other than Marcel Proust, who wrote, "ideas come to us as the substitutes for griefs."[59]

Simultaneously, as the regime of the infantile superego moors a good object in the deepest recesses of the self, it adopts a new form. The severity of the melancholic superego is threatening, but it is different from the severity of the paranoid-schizoid position. At that point, to the attacks from the bad objects during the prior position is added "the urgent necessity to fulfill the very strict demands of the 'good objects,' "[60] which nevertheless remain uncertain and which are capable of being easily transformed into "bad" ones. Racked by "contradictory and impossible claims from within"—a situation experienced as a sort of "gnawing of conscience"[61]—the ego is assailed by the "remorse of conscience":

These strict demands serve the purpose of supporting the ego in its fight against its uncontrollable hatred and its bad attacking objects, with which the ego is partly identified. The stronger the anxiety is of losing the loved objects, the more the ego strives to save them, and the harder the task of restoration becomes, the stricter will grow the demands which are associated with the super-ego.[62]

The child nevertheless abandons some of the parents' tyrannical or monstrous features that constituted the persecuting archaic superego in the name of a whole object that he loves, however ambivalently. Because the superego therefore ceases to be a mere source of guilt, it becomes a source of love as well as a potential ally of the ego.

So which defenses remain at the disposal of the young ego so it can protect itself against the ambivalence (both the love and the hatred) that characterizes this depressive position? In place of the splitting, idealization, ejection, and destruction that we saw in the paranoid-schizoid position, the depressive position generates *manic defenses*. Though similar to their predecessors, these defenses offer something novel: they seek to exert omnipotence over the object-to-be-lost, and they do so triumphantly and contemptuously. Initially, these manic defenses are not pathological, and they play a positive role in development by protecting the ego from unbrided despair, particularly because *reparation*—the other mechanism that facilitates the resolution of mourning in the depressive position—is put into place only gradually.

Mania employs the same logical processes that appeared in the previous position—splitting, idealization, projective identification, and denial—but in mania these processes are better organized, the ego is more integrated, and the defenses are directed less toward the persecuting object than toward depressive anxiety and guilt itself. Focusing on the sensations themselves, they are drawn to the feeling of dependence. Thus, in order for the ego to defend itself from ambivalence, it splits off the internal world and the external world, to the point of denying the internal world itself along with all potential relationships (we should note that the mechanism of denying the internal world and its link to the external world allows us to diagnose the psychic source of social "anarchy" and the cult of the "solitary ego"). At that point a feeling of omnipotence emerges, one that is comparable to the paranoid-schizoid position and that relies on the mechanism of *negation* (in Klein's reinterpretation of Helene Deutsch's understanding of the term), with the initial negation centered on anxiety itself, as well as on the psychic reality that generates that anxiety.[63] The manic person appears indifferent because his defenses are directed, from the outset, toward the psychic reality that he pretends to undo, and if the subject finds himself in analysis, those defenses attack the very goal of the analysis while attempting to paralyze the analyst. At the same time, the maniacal ego subjects the internal or external object to a threefold treatment made of control, triumph, and scorn. The maniacal ego thus denies the importance of good objects; the manic person undervalues and absorbs them, with his detachment being the measure of his feeling of omnipotence over an eviscerated Other.

Klein's depressive position offers yet another innovation, one that will eventually encourage creativity: the feeling of depression mobilizes the desire to *make reparation to* objects. The baby, by believing that he is responsible for the loss of his mother, also imagines that he can undo the nefarious effects of his aggression through her love and care for him. "The depressive conflict is a constant struggle between the infant's destructiveness and his love and reparative impulses."[64] To deal with the depressive suffering that results from his feeling of having damaged the external and internal object, the baby tries to make reparation and restoration to the good object. His love only grows in the process: "The reappearance of his mother and her care for him are essential to this process. . . . The non-appearance of his mother or the lack of her love can leave him at the mercy of his depressive and persecutory fears."[65]

This amounts to reparation, no doubt, but it is hardly idyllic as it is tainted with despair:

It is a "perfect" object which is in pieces; thus the effort to undo the state of disintegration to which it is has been reduced presupposes the necessity to make it beautiful and "perfect." The idea of perfection is, moreover, so compelling because it disproves the idea of disintegration.[66]

In truth, sublimation has the distasteful task of preserving "the bits to which the loved object has been reduced" through a supreme "effort to put them together. . . . It appears that the desire for perfection is rooted in the depressive anxiety of disintegration."[67]

We can now better appreciate the difficulty of the baby's psychic work during the depressive position—as well as the difficulty of mourning that so struck Freud in his "Mourning and Melancholia" (1916).[68] Why, in fact, is it so difficult to accept that the loved one no longer exists in reality? Klein's response is that the work of mourning is directed not toward the actual person but toward the internal object, and that it reflects the need to overcome any tendency toward a regression to paranoid sentiments or to manic defenses. Only then can the mourning work restore a lively and livable internal world: its goal is to tolerate the absence of the external object without falling prey to projective identification.

As we have seen, this painful ordeal offers substantial benefits as well: the pain of loss, the suffering of mourning, and the reparative drives that overcome manic defenses result in the reconstruction—that is, in the symbolization—of the internal and external lost object. It is thus that pain, suffering, and reparation are at the foundation of creativity and sublimation. If it is true, as Freud believed, that sublimation results from a successful abandonment of both the aim of the drive and the residual effects of the death drive, Klein adds that such abandonment occurs through the work of mourning, with the residual effects of the life drive. She highlights the creative side of the depressive position: if the ego is capable of making reparation to the lost object, rather than responding with manic defenses it can take root in a creative work that contains both pain and the work of mourning in the name of generating the symbol. "I suggest that such an assimilated object becomes a symbol within the ego. Every aspect of the object, every situation that has to be given up in the process of growing, gives rise to symbol formation."[69]

The "central position"[70] accorded to the depressive position significantly modifies Klein's notion of the Oedipus conflict. In her early work the Oedipus conflict is front and center; Oedipus comes to the fore when hatred is at its peak, with the result in both boys and girls that the primordial bond with the breast also focuses on the father's penis, which is fantasized as living inside the mother's body. Later, upon discovering the depressive position, she changed her mind. From that point on Klein believed that the Oedipus conflict begins with the emergence of the depressive position—and that the Oedipus conflict is in fact endemic to that position. Parents, then, are perceived as separate beings—that is, they are no longer perceived as being combined parents—and the couple forms good whole objects: the child directs his ambivalent fantasies toward his parents, particularly when his parents are united through intercourse. Accordingly, it is not the fear of castration, aphanisis, and death that causes the child to abandon his oedipal desires (which is what Freud believed), but—long before the onset of the genital stage—the ambivalence that characterizes the depressive position itself (the love for one's parents *combined with* the fear of hurting them through an ever-present destructive aggression). If the child avoids relying on manic defenses, reparation can enable him to dominate his oedipal desires and to transform them into creativity. Hence, it is through reparation that the mourning process can finally be completed. And when that fails to occur, a pathological manic-depressive state can come about:

> The manic-depressive and the person who fails in the work of mourning, though their defenses may differ widely from each other, have this in common, that they have been unable in early childhood to establish their internal "good" objects and to feel secure in their inner world.[71]

From the perspective of the depressive position, the task of resolving the Oedipus conflict requires that a good breast (a good mother), a good father, and a good creative couple are established inside the ego. That entails introjecting the two sexes—the *two Others*—as manifested in the suffering common to depressive working-through. The *difference between the sexes* emerges against the backdrop of the depressive position. What's more, although Klein does not dwell on this point, the distinction the child makes between the two protagonists of the couple reveals that the path to heterosexuality is an optimal way of resolving the depressive position.[72]

This process entails considerable psychic difficulty, which helps explain certain failures—particularly the sort of failures generated by the formation of "clusters of defenses" that protect the child from depressive suffering, though at the price of a paranoid-schizoid regression that impedes intellectual development.

It is clear that in this Kleinian purgatory, every point turns into its counterpoint, but in a way that nevertheless portrays the paradise of sublimation—a sort of sublimation that can always be more effective, particularly through the help of analysis. And perhaps through the mother's gratifying care as well . . .

ANXIETY OR DESIRE:
IN THE BEGINNING WAS
THE DEATH DRIVE

Whereas for Freud the unconscious foundation of psychic life is centered on desire and on the repression of desire, all of Melanie Klein's work is dominated by an interest in anxiety. Still, could she be said to have eviscerated libido for the sake of the death drive or to have discarded Eros to take comfort in Thanatos, as some have accused her of doing?

The archaic ego, as fragile as it is, desires the breast, but because it strives for an immediate, infinite, and impossible gratification, it does so excessively, so much so[1] that it encounters *frustration*. In Klein's view, frustration is not a "lack" that is limited to renewing desire until it can become the "hallucinatory wish-fulfillment" that makes us lose touch with the boundary between what Freud termed representation (fantasy-like) and perception (realist), or that makes us explore the always open and metonymic trajectory of what Lacan calls "the object petit a."[2] For Klein, the intensity of frustrated desire is described, rather, as *anxiety*, which is "automatic"[3] before it is separated into paranoid-schizoid anxiety and depressive anxiety. Before frustrated desire begins the long process of integrating the ego, its violence is such that it does not tolerate the lack but attaches instead onto an object-target, a pseudo-object, or an *abject*. There is nothing missing, then, to be desired, but everything wounds, gets wounded, and allows itself to be attacked according to the principles of retributive justice.

Because of Melanie's focus on the death drive, her critics have often erroneously concluded that she was complacent about death and ignored the erotic forces of life. Klein's explicit debate on the subject, which took place rather late in her life, in 1948, provides us a more accurate perspective that merits some discussion before we continue to explore Klein's thought.

After reminding us that Freud, in his "Inhibition, Symptoms, and Anxiety" (1926), argued that "the unconscious seems to contain nothing that would lend substance to the concept of the annihilation of life,"[4] Melanie boldly states as follows: "I do not share this view because my analytic observations show that there is in the unconscious a fear of annihilation of life."[5]

Klein's belief could not be clearer: with the death drive, she presumes that "in the deepest layers of the mind there is a response to this instinct in the form of *fear of annihilation of life*."[6]

Under the effects of the death drive, the psyche expresses a fear *for life*. For the sake of life, it affords itself a way to respond to the fear of the annihilation of life, and its most fundamental mechanisms are nothing more than defenses against any such annihilation. The death drive is immediately and dialectically restored to its positive version, which is the very preservation of life.

This passage is interesting not only because it takes issue with Freud, who, as Melanie wrote, avoided "regarding the fear of death"[7]—in contrast to her, who, as we have seen, "regards" this fear, reinforced as she was by her clinical experience with psychosis, as a particularly early infantile psychosis. What is particularly interesting is that the psychoanalyst adopts—and then expands—Freud's efforts to attribute to the psyche the actions favorable to life: "the fear of death (or *fear for life*),"[8] she writes. And it is this very "fear for life," "arising from the inner working of the death instinct," that is the "first cause of anxiety." Even more specifically, the fear in question here is a fear for the life of the object (the mother), and even more so for the life of the ego. Accordingly, because the struggle between the two drives endures throughout our life, "this source of anxiety is never eliminated." It becomes clear, then, that Melanie considered the "inner working"[9] of the death drive to be directly linked to the life drive, and not dissociated from it. Dissociation emerges instead in psychosis, and it poses equally interesting questions of its own. But here, in this debate with Freud, we are operating at a level of universality that considers all manifestations of the drive, even the most normal ones, to be contingent on the *death drive that itself subsists on a fear for life*. In a word, it is for Eros's sake that our anxiety about the annihilation of life penetrates the deepest layers of the psyche.

Without being vitalist in any way, and while even suggesting that a fear for life neglects the erotic and/or life drives, Klein's theory of anxiety is dominated, quite explicitly, by such a fear. Is it a female subject who is emerging here, a confederate of a psychoanalyst who paid close attention to the various psychoses? Is it a woman who has no fear of regarding death because she fears for the life that it affords, and who faces head-on the dangers of annihilation that weigh on this life from its very beginnings? Is it to better defend herself from these dangers, especially because her familiarity with the "fear of death" showed her how much this initial negativity—this phobia of being, this nonbeing—can become (under certain biological and environmental conditions) a veritable work of the negative, even a renaissance?[10]

Though on the opposite side of the spectrum from Hannah Arendt, Melanie nevertheless appears to have shared Arendt's concern for the sort of life that emerges through the revelation and accompaniment of that which threatens it.[11] "Full of birth," as Arendt would put it, which Melanie showed herself to be through the therapeutic relentlessness that pervaded her incisive interpretations—and also through the privileged mode she assigns to the death drive, which is first described as a sadistic desire, as a type of envy, as she would later put it. In sum, the death drive is a condensation of love and hatred, otherwise known as paroxysmal desire.

Eros is hardly extinct, then, in this primary capturing of the object that operates through desire transformed into anxiety— either orally, anally, or genitally. Eros, in fact, has a "fear for life" and is in no rush to reappear in the privileged form of pleasure— which in Klein's view is essentially the pleasure of intelligence. Although the anxiety that is interpreted through transference develops in clearly delineated phases, it is able to confront split- ting and repression, and, by lifting repression, it is transformed into a symbolization of sorts: an uninhibited libido is a libido that thinks, and a desire separated from anxiety is a capacity for sym- bolization.[12]

We are familiar with Freud's resistance to the notion of an unconscious affect: "Thus the possibility of the attribute of unconsciousness would be completely excluded as far as emo- tions, feelings and affects are concerned."[13] As for anxiety, the founder of psychoanalysis believed that it was either a sign of increasing stimulation in the psychic apparatus (which is the case of current neuroses, an "innocuous" example of which being the anxiety of virgins) or the effect of repressed libido (which is the case with the psychoneuroses).

Melanie Klein, in contrast, was immediately drawn to uncon- scious anxiety, particularly when she listened to her son, whom she referred to as Fritz and Felix.[14] Although Klein did not, strictly speaking, develop a theory of affects, her explicit study of anxiety became the foundation for a post-Freudian conception of affects that is still being developed today.[15] Melanie Klein thus specifically related anxiety to the inhibitions, which are spared the symptom, though at the cost of a distortion of thought, or tics. Because desire is fundamentally a type of anxiety, the ego erects psychic barriers designed to curb its growth—precautions, inhi- bitions, and taboos that resemble certain forms of phobic defenses. Castration anxiety, which was manifested in Felix, joins this tableau and buttresses Klein's idea of a commonality between desire and anxiety.

But it is the sadism of the archaic ego, more than anything else, that prolongs original anxiety. A strong oral desire to devour, which is manifested at the very beginning of life, returns to the subject with the same content but with a different target: it is not I who wishes to devour, for I am afraid of being poisoned by the bad breast in which I projected my bad teeth—such is the logic of the sadistic fantasy that corresponds to primary paranoid-schizoid anxiety. Although Klein associated such anxiety with oedipal aggression (Rita, she pointed out, wished to steal children on the verge of being born out of their mothers' stomachs and also became competitive with her father), genital drives are inextricably linked with oral, urethral, and anal sadistic drives. It turns out that oral sadism, which is often identified with Kleinian theory,[16] emerged rather late in her development, while aggressive anality caught Klein's attention as early as 1924, during her analysis of Trude, a girl aged three years and three months:

> Early on in her analysis she asked me to pretend that I was in bed and asleep. She would then say that she was going to attack me and look into my buttocks for faeces (which I found also represented children) and that she was going to take them out. Such attacks were followed by her crouching in a corner, playing that she was in bed, covering herself with cushions (which were to protect her body and which also stood for children); at the same time she actually wetted herself and showed clearly that she was very much afraid of being attacked by me.[17]

And it was not until Klein's analyses of Ruth and Peter, which took place between 1924 and 1925, that she became aware of the "fundamental rôle"[18] played by oral-sadistic drives in sadistic fantasies and in their corresponding anxieties:

> [I found] in the analysis of young children full confirmation of Abraham's discoveries. These analyses, which gave me fur-

ther scope for observation, since they lasted longer than Rita's and Trude's, led me towards a fuller insight into the fundamental rôle of oral desires and anxieties in mental development, normal and abnormal.[19]

From that perspective, Klein associated her own observations, the story of Peter, and the story of two criminals as reported by the press: one of a man who engaged in homosexual relations with young men whom he would then kill by decapitating them and then cutting them into pieces, and the other of a man who killed his victims and made them into sausages.[20] Peter had a fantasy in which he was masturbating with his father and his young brother, and he represented that scene through the help of dolls that he decapitated, selling the body to a butcher and retaining the head, which he believed was the most appetizing body part. During his analysis, moreover, he succumbed to countless dismemberings and devourings of icons and dolls. Immediately imprinting this sadism in the Oedipus conflict and in the desire to be punished that generates the early guilt of the superego, Klein wrote the following:

> One may regard it as a rule that in every so-called "naughty" child the desire to be punished is at work too. I should like to quote Nietzsche and what he called his "pale criminal"; he knew much about the criminal driven by his sense of guilt.[21]

This unconscious sadism defends itself, as we have seen, by splitting the internal object as well as the external object into a good breast and a bad breast. This helps us appreciate the difference between this sort of fantasy, which Klein attributed to the earliest stages of the ego, and what Freud called hallucinatory wish-fulfillment.[22] In both cases, the perceptions of reality are replaced by a representation that deforms them in response to unconscious drives. For Freud, however, desire prevails, and libido, unlike frustration, builds up an idyllic vision that replaces gratification with an idealized representation of gratification.

Klein, for her part, recognizes the destructive violence of desire even more radically than does the Freud of "Beyond the Pleasure Principle" (1920).

On the one hand, this early violence reins in anxiety—imperfectly at that—only by *splitting the fantasy* itself and by leaving its negative mark on the fantasy by *splitting the object* of anxiety: a split between good and bad. On the other hand, although Klein always acknowledged the fantasy of the good breast and even made it into the focal point of the ego (as if she were defending herself in anticipation of those who would glean nothing more from her theory than the mere presence of the bad breast), the negative of the death drive constantly reappears in order to generate new defenses that are partly beneficial and partly destructive. Accordingly, Klein replaces the plenitude of bliss implicit in Freud's concept of "hallucinatory wish-fulfillment" with a constant work of the negative and an interminable sublimation of mourning, with the death drive sustaining psychic development—and yet hindering that development all the while even though it never truly subsides.

The intensity of this destructive drive is innate, Klein believed, a conviction that only grew in her later writings. Although Klein believed that "states of frustration or increased anxiety" resulting from an insufficient reality *reinforce* "the oral-sadistic and cannibalistic desires," she still insisted on their importance: "Accordingly, the strength of the destructive impulses in their interaction with libidinal impulses would *provide the constitutional basis for the intensity of greed.*"[23]

Such remarks might lead us to believe that the analyst's mind succumbed to therapeutic pessimism. Indeed, how can analytic treatment interact with this "constitutional basis" that Klein evokes so regularly and so passionately? Is it only by encouraging the optimal realization of what is innate, without changing the fundamental and genetically determined balance between love and hate? Or is it by transforming this very equilibrium through transference, interpretation, and a new environment?[24] This question remains unanswered, so much so that Klein's work bears witness to a generalized pessimism about the relevance of analytic treatment, even as she concedes its limitations. Klein appears to believe, paradoxically, that a good environment does not modify the constitutional basis, which she believes manifests itself even in the face of superior mothering.[25] A deficient environment or extensive deprivation, on the other hand, will aggravate any innate aggressive qualities. It is the psychoanalyst, then, who must perform a task that is not entirely unfeasible: to reduce splitting and to assist the ego in integrating the split-off parts.

THE GRIEF THAT AFFORDS US A SOUL

At the heart of this destructive universe, the analyst posits that the evolution of the ego in the normal course of development—and analytic treatment when it is successful—allow for the working through of destructive anxieties and sadistic fantasies. *The ego takes shape by way of a depressive working through.* Our ability to mourn the lost object completely replaces primal sadism with *psychic discomfort*: nostalgia and guilt, then, form the quieter side of Thanatos. Anxiety has not disappeared, as it is always present with Klein, but it chooses another domain: rather than splitting or fragmenting and rather than destroying and tearing into pieces, anxiety is tolerated as a source of pain relating to the Other and a source of guilt about having taken pleasure in hurting him. The sadism and persecutory anxiety of the first three months of life are followed by the capacity of a strengthened ego—the ego of the "depressive position" that emerges at six months of age—to introject the good object. The ego can do so more easily if it possesses an innate capacity for love:

> One major derivative of the capacity for love is the feeling of gratitude. . . . Gratitude is rooted in the emotions and attitudes that arise in the earliest stage of infancy, when for the baby the mother is the one and only object. . . . But the internal factors underlying it—above all the capacity for love—appear to be innate.[26]

Naturally, the depressive position offers considerable benefits: sadism becomes grief, nostalgia abates destructiveness, and the black sun of melancholia develops the ego, which, rather than splitting and denying, works through/represses/makes reparation to/and creates.

In tracing the metamorphosis of the death drive into what Klein refers to as "psychization," one cannot help but find the mother of psychoanalysis to be eminently Shakespearean. Is it not the case that the playwright's sonnet 146 already implies that the sublimating excess of "Death once dead," or "putting Death to death," is realized only through the internal life of the "poor soul," and only then if the soul is capable of consuming within itself the death that originates from the outside?[27]

Klein's Shakespearean vision of psychic functioning—a vision of a soul that sustains itself through (and that subsists on) the death that devours men—is directly reflected in her analytic technique. The analyst's task is to listen to—beyond and through desire—psychic *suffering* as well as to its companion, *aggressive anxiety*. As a separate but related matter, the analyst also "intervenes at the locus of maximal latent anxiety"[28] in order to listen more attentively to the anxious and aggressive material that presents itself in analytic sessions so she can interpret it directly and frequently. Although this perspective may invite fears of an excessively rapid acceleration of anxiety through the analyst's psychic encroachment upon the child, one could also counter, as does Florence Bégoin-Guignard, that the opposite approach, one that spaces out children's analytic sessions in order to "respect" them more and to practice "nonintervention," is an "invitation to intensify the child's tendencies toward massive projective identification with the omnipotent internal objects that he uses to intrude into the analyst's psyche and to exert total control over his thought."[29] At that point, we discover reinforced splitting and the formation of "false selves." And what is the cure? The analyst must consider his own pregenital conflicts, his cannibalistic or other forms of aggressiveness, and his own potential for overcoming the "depressive position"—all of these being traps that the analyst's countertransference directs toward his own sadism and pain. These traps grow in size and strength as the analyst listens to children, and then to adults, because infantile defenses are at once more powerful and less fixed than they are in adults, and thus openly appeal to the child inside the analyst.

The very least we can say is that Melanie Klein did not succumb to such appeal. She began her work as an analyst when she was around fourteen years old, and her disciples devoted a special issue of *International Journal of Psycho-Analysis* to her for her seventieth birthday in 1952. In 1955 the issue's contents, along with a few other commentaries and two articles by Klein herself, were included in a volume entitled *New Directions in Psychoanalysis*. One could easily have surmised at that point that Klein's work had come to an end, but then all of a sudden, in 1957, the "mother of psychoanalysis" published *Envy and Gratitude*. Klein's emphasis on a primordial aggressive drive, a theme already present in her earlier works—especially those that touch upon the paranoid-schizoid position—reappears in that volume in the form of an *envy* of the breast. Is this a return of Christian sin? St. Paul, St. Augustine, and Shakespeare are mentioned, and Othello joins Milton, Chaucer, and Spenser to provide a basis, *within the bounds of tradition*, for Melanie's prior clinical observations about aggressiveness and its elaboration, which are synthesized into a new binary vision: envy *along with* gratitude.

THE POWER OF ENVY AND A
WAGER ON GRATITUDE

Whereas jealousy is associated with a love of an object, envy precedes it and is more archaic. Jealousy is alleviated by a regained love while envy is never alleviated; jealousy is triangular and envy is binary.

The working through of envy by means of jealousy is at the same time an important defence against envy. Jealousy is felt to be much more acceptable and gives rise much less to guilt than the primary envy which destroys the first good object.[30]

Supported by primal greed, envy seeks to possess its object completely without concerning itself with its possible destruction: envy wishes to appropriate all that is good in the object and, if that proves impossible, does not hesitate to destroy the object in order to avoid the origin of the envious feeling. Although envy is rooted in primitive love and admiration, it is distinguishable from greed: as submerged as it is by the death drive, it reflects a lesser degree of Eros.

Readers of Freud are already familiar with his notion of envy, whose most fundamental manifestation is "penis envy" in women—the counterpart to the castration complex, which is itself a source of inhibition, frigidity, and negative therapeutic reaction. In Klein's view, oral envy—the envy of the mother's breast—dominates the psyche long before penis envy does:

> In this context I wish to consider the woman's penis-envy mainly in so far as it is of oral origin. As we know, under the dominance of oral desires, the penis is strongly equated with the breast (Abraham) and in my experience the woman's penis-envy can be traced back to envy of the mother's breast. I have found that if the penis-envy of women is analysed on these lines, we can see that its root lies in the earliest relation to the mother, in the fundamental envy of the mother's breast, and in the destructive feelings allied with it.[31]

Envy encourages everything, even as it impedes the development of the psyche: it grants the psyche a beneficial object, but it is an object that must be appropriated until it is vitiated or destroyed. As Melanie embarks on this final journey, she revisits her beloved theme of the loved-and-hated primary object. The breast, which is an aftereffect of nostalgia for the womb—itself a remnant of the birth trauma—is fantasized as being an inexhaustible breast, one that is idealized and thus intensifies hatred—because the real object never corresponds to the psychic object. To this fundamental situation is added deprivation: the breast is withdrawn, it is missed, the mother's care is not always adequate, and so forth. Excessive frustration, but also excessive indulgence (isn't Winnicott's "good enough mother" also a "bad enough" one?), serve only to aggravate this innate envy:

> I have often referred to the infant's desire for the inexhaustible, ever-present breast. But as has been suggested . . . it is not only food he desires; he also wants to be freed from destructive impulses and persecutory anxiety. This feeling that the mother is omnipotent and that it is up to her to prevent all pain and evils from internal and external sources is also found in the analysis of adults.[32]

At the same time (and here, the *good* breast returns with a vengeance), if the child feels satisfied after having first experienced a certain degree of frustration, he becomes better able to deal with his anxieties. The mother thus *contains* destructive anxieties, and, like a *containing* object, she encourages the integration of the ego. The bliss and gratitude brought on by the *container*, then, counterbalance the destructive drives as they diminish envy and greed. What Melanie Klein is describing here is a *jubilant bond* with the mother, on which she had never previously focused in quite the same way, and one that is rooted in the preverbal stage as a basis for the gratitude that will subsequently generate the capacity for reparation, sublimation, and generosity. And yet, because nothing is so simple in the world of the death drive, the analyst does not forget that gratitude itself can be "enacted" by guilt, in which case it would be distinct from "true" gratitude:

> All of this is felt by the infant in much more primitive ways than language can express. When these pre-verbal emotions and phantasies are revived in the transference situation, they appear as "memories in feelings," . . . and are reconstructed and put into words with the help of the analyst. In the same way, words have to be used when we are restructuring and describing other phenomena belonging to the early stages of development.[33]

Petits Fours, kleine Frou, Frau Klein . . .

One of author's clinical examples makes clear the extent to which
primordial envy is unconsciously transmitted to adults and curtails
their capacity for gratitude, love, and fulfillment as well as the analytic work that they nevertheless choose to undertake. A patient
describes the following dream: she was seated in a restaurant but,
when nobody came to serve her, she decided to join a queue. In
front of her was a woman who took several "*petits fours*" (the
woman said in French "*petits fru*" rather than "*petits fours*") and
walked away with them. The analysand, who was behind her, did
the same thing. Klein and her patient trace the associations: the
cake woman looks like the analyst, and "*petits frou*" (*kleine Frou*)
makes her think of *Frau Klein.* The analyst interprets the dream as
follows: the patient had missed some sessions, allegedly because of
a sore shoulder and her childish need to receive affection and be
taken care of, but no one came. The dream recaptured the grief
that appeared during the missed sessions and that was associated
with an unhappy childhood and with unsatisfying breast-feeding.
The "two or three *petits fours*" (*kleine Frou*), like the two breasts,
linked *Frau Klein,* through identification and projection, to the
patient's greed. The cakes represent the mother and the analyst's
frustrating breast as well as the breast of the patient, who agreed to
feed herself in the end by taking her place in the queue.

> To frustration had thus been added envy of the breast. This
> envy had given rise to bitter resentment, for the mother had
> been felt to be selfish and mean, feeding and loving herself
> rather than her baby. In the analytic situation I was sus-
> pected of having enjoyed myself during the time when she
> was absent, or of having given the time to other patients
> whom I preferred. The queue which the patient had decided
> to join referred to other more favoured rivals.
>   The response to the analysis of the dream produced a
> striking change in the emotional situation. The patient now
> experienced a feeling of happiness and gratitude more

vividly than in previous analytic sessions. . . . She was aware
that she was envious and jealous of various people but had
not been able to recognize it sufficiently in the relation to
the analyst because it was too painful to experience that she
was envying and spoiling the analyst as well as the success of
the analysis.[34]

It was thus in Klein's later writings, after she interpreted the
violent nature of envy as being the definitive version of the death
drive, that she expounded upon the capacity for love. Although
Klein reminds us that Freud, in his "Inhibition, Symptoms, and
Anxiety" (1926), proclaimed that the unconscious ego has no
capacity for representing death ("the unconscious seems to contain nothing that could give any content to the concept of the
annihilation of life"),[35] she indicates where she diverges from the
master:

The threat of annihilation by the death instinct within is, in
my view—which differs from Freud's on this point—the primordial anxiety, and it is the ego which, in the service of the
life instinct—possibly even called into operation by the life
instinct—deflects to some extent that threat outwards. This
fundamental defence against the death instinct Freud attributed to the organism, whereas I regard this process as the
prime activity of the ego.[36]

It is thus the ego, and not the organism, that is the agent of
hatred, but also of love, envy, and gratitude. Through splitting,
the ego defends itself from destructiveness and thus envy *until it
becomes capable of experiencing love*: a capacity that reinforces the
"depressive position" in particular inasmuch as that position
begins the process of resolving the Oedipus conflict. It is on that
basis that the struggle between the two forces continues throughout psychic life, with varying degrees of success for the two protagonists. Klein, for her part, lauds the many thinkers before who
have reproached envy as being the worst sort of sin because it
opposes life itself. "Love envieth not" (First Letter to the

Corinthians); Saint Augustine describes Life as a creative force that stands in opposition to a destructive force; in Milton's *Paradise Lost*, envy connotes a destruction of creativity; Chaucer condemns envy as being "the worst sin that is; for all other sins are sins only against one virtue, whereas envy is against all virtue and against all goodness." Klein's exploration of the duality between envy and gratitude concludes provisionally with the following heartfelt tribute to the forces of enjoyment and sublimation:

> I suggest that the happiness experienced in infancy and the love for the good object which enriches the personality underlie the capacity for enjoyment and sublimation, and still make themselves felt in old age. When Goethe said, "He is the happiest of men who can make the end of his life agree closely with the beginning," I would interpret "the beginning" as the early happy relation to the mother which throughout life mitigates hate and anxiety and still gives the old person support and contentment. An infant who has securely established the good object can also find compensations for loss and deprivation in adult life. All this is felt by the envious person as something he can never attain because he can never be satisfied, and therefore his envy is reinforced.[37]

We should not be deceived by what we read here, for this brief interlude does not introduce some sort of idyllic state, and Klein continued to be drawn to anxiety and destructiveness. Was it because those symptoms are more prominent in those sufferers who look to psychoanalysis for assistance? Or was it because the death drive is the more persistent of the two drives? It may well be that in the beginning is the good object along with the love that it inspires, as we have just seen is the view shared by Goethe and Klein. And yet, if we begin by analyzing this beginning, as Klein never stopped doing even though she remained skeptical of all beginnings, we may very well discover a large display of envy, ingratitude, sadism, and suffering. As she put it:

Excessive envy interferes with adequate oral gratification and so acts as a stimulus towards the intensification of genital desires and trends. This implies that the infant turns too early towards genital gratification, with the consequence that the oral relation becomes genitalized and the genital trends become too much coloured by oral grievances and anxieties. . . . With some infants, the flight into genitality is also a defence against hating and injuring the first object towards which ambivalent feelings operate.[38]

It is clear that we can never be too suspicious of the many faces of envy! By analyzing them and theorizing them, Melanie Klein no doubt continued her own analysis and worked through her countertransference toward the negative therapeutic reaction. Did she not write the following in her unfinished *Autobiography*?:

When I abruptly finished my analysis with Abraham, there was a great deal which had not been analyzed and I have continually proceeded along the lines of knowing more about my deepest anxieties and defences. In spite of the scepticism which I said was quite characteristic of a large part of my analytic life, I have never been hopeless, nor am I now.[39]

This tends to validate the view of Didier Anzieu, who cites the passage above, that all theories have an unrealized fate, particularly those that examine, as Klein's does, the prematurity of the human newborn. It also vindicates his view that the freshness of Klein's work is like a "promise of a youth forever rejuvenated through psychoanalysis."[40]

A MOST EARLY AND
TYRANNICAL SUPEREGO

FROM THE EARLIEST STAGES OF
THE OEDIPUS CONFLICT

In Klein's theory of the psyche, oral sadism goes hand in hand with a tyrannical superego. Toward the beginning of her clinical experience, the psychoanalyst set forth the early genesis of the superego in "Early Stages of the Oedipus Conflict and of Super-Ego Formation," an article that contains hints of an earlier 1928 study and that was published in *The Psychoanalysis of Children*.[1] Klein returned to the subject—with a new perspective and a new sense of purpose—in "The Oedipus Complex in the Light of Early Anxieties," which she published in *Love, Guilt, and Reparation*.[2]

The sadism phase, which intensifies from birth on and which Klein designated in 1946 to be the "paranoid-schizoid position," focuses, along with the breast, on *the inside of the mother's body* that contains the father's penis. There we shall find, as does Jean Bégoin, the prototype of *the psychic realm*.[3]

Klein describes two psychic events that will form the basis of the superego: first, the internalization of the incorporated object (the mother's breast + the father's penis) that defends the ego from the attacks of the id and that creates the core of the superego, and second, the ejection of this core into the anal-sadistic stage. The following are what Klein considers to be the three stages of this process:

1. The early stages of the Oedipus conflict and of the formation of the super-ego extend, roughly, from the middle of the first year to the third year of the child's life.[4]

2. According to my observations, . . . the Oedipus conflict and the super-ego set in under the supremacy of the pre-genital impulses, and the objects which have been introjected in the oral-sadistic phase—the first object cathexes and identifications—form the beginnings of the early super-ego. . . . It would follow logically that the ego would regard the internalized object as so cruel an enemy of the id from the fact that the destructive instinct which the ego has turned outward has become directed against that object, and consequently nothing but hostility against the id can be expected. . . . The father of the primal horde was the external power which enforced an inhibition of instinct. . . . And cruel as this super-ego formed under the supremacy of sadism may be, it nevertheless even becomes at this early stage, the agency from which instinctual inhibitions proceed, as it takes over the ego's defence against the destructive instinct.[5]

3. In the early anal-sadistic stage what [the child] is ejecting is his object, which he perceives as something hostile to him and which he equates with excrement. But as I see it, what is already being ejected in the early anal-sadistic stage is the terrifying super-ego which he has introjected in the oral-sadistic phase. Thus his act of ejection is a means of defence employed by his fear-ridden ego against his super-ego; it expels his internalized objects and at the same time projects them into the outerworld.[6]

Thus, as soon as sadism grows more intense, the extensive use of projective identification leads to persecutory anxieties associated with splitting, and these initial introjects construct a devouring superego that evokes a pitiless Saturn. The gradual discovery of the two positions, "depressive" and "paranoid-schizoid," as well as the discovery of their fluctuation and their reciprocal recovery (which has been termed, after Bion, "Ps-D"), modifies the superego just as the Oedipus conflict is getting underway. Oral frustration is projected from the outset onto the two parents, who, according to the child's fantasies, afford each other "mutual sexual pleasures"[7] that they withhold from him. Beginning in the sixth month of life, along with the depressive position comes a true Oedipus conflict and a shift from the part object to the whole object: with weaning, the fantasy of the lost (or dead) mother generates guilt, and the persecuting superego is transformed into a "remorse of the conscience" that mourns the fact that it was never able to protect the "good object" from internalized persecutors. Object relations will then fight among themselves, mirroring the ego's relationship with the superego and the id, or perhaps the superego's relationship with the ego.

Klein's divergence from Freudian theory is apparent and acknowledged. The Freudian superego, which appears in the second topography (id/ego/superego), is not truly dissociated from the ideal of the ego and the ego ideal, and it is often considered in the context of idealization[8] rather than in the Kleinian context of the terror that characterizes its function in the paranoid-schizoid position (even though it evolves after that position). It is as if Freud did not fully realize the consequences of his own theory of the death drive—consequences that Klein, on the other hand, understood quite deeply. The Freudian superego intervenes quite late, moreover, because it is a contemporary of the Oedipus conflict, and more specifically of the phallic stage (which Klein prefers to call a genital stage) where the superego evaporates, a stage brought on by the abandonment of incestuous desires. For Klein, the superego is thus both younger and crueler: it is always oedipal, as we have seen, but in the sense of a Kleinian Oedipus conflict, an early one at that, and one that makes its debut with oral sadism.

NEITHER BOYS NOR GIRLS CAN AVOID IT

The dual projective identification with the mother and the father is propelled by early genital desires that impregnate oral, urethral, and anal desires: libidinal stages emerge, in Klein's view, during the first months of life. Klein's 1945 article on the Oedipus complex[9] clarifies the way the two sexes form the superego as she follows the fluctuation of the Oedipus complex throughout what will be termed the "paranoid-schizoid-depressive position":

> In my view, infants of both sexes experience genital desires directed toward their mother and father, and they have an unconscious knowledge of the vagina as well as of the penis. For these reasons Freud's earlier term "genital phase" seems to me more adequate than his later concept of the "phallic phase." . . .
>
> The first introjected object, the mother's breast, forms the basis of the super-ego. Just as the relation to the mother's breast precedes and strongly influences the relation to the father's penis, so the relation to the introjected mother affects in many ways the whole course of super-ego development. Some of the most important features of the super-ego, whether loving and protective or destructive and devouring, are derived from the early maternal components of the super-ego.[10]

Freud, who associated the emergence of the superego with the castration complex, believed that women were much less equipped for it than men.[11] Melanie, on the other hand, simply because she linked the superego with the internalization of the bad persecuting breast, was far more generous toward little girls: she believed that the superego is no less developed in girls than in boys, though theirs is of a different sort. In the end, a veritable sexual duality structures the earliest manifestation of the superego and generates the different Oedipus conflicts experienced by boys and by girls.

More precisely, a boy's phallic stage succumbs to the threat of castration on the part of a father with whom he identified during his "primary identification with the father of personal prehistory." A girl's anxiety, on the other hand, is rooted in her fear of losing her mother's love, which is associated with her fear of the mother's death.[12] Klein will return to these ideas in *Envy and Gratitude*.[13]

PERSECUTING IDEALIZATIONS AND "CONCRETIZATIONS"

In this context, idealization takes on persecuting tones. As distinguished from the "good" object, the "idealized" object emerges as a defense against the fragile young ego's inability to fully internalize the good object:

> Some people deal with their incapacity (derived from excessive envy) to possess a good object by idealizing it. This first idealization is precarious, for the envy experienced towards the good object is bound to extend to its idealized aspect. . . . Greed is an important factor in these indiscriminate identifications, for the need to get the best from everywhere interferes with the capacity for selection and discrimination.[14]

Because idealization is a function of persecuting anxiety more than of the capacity to love, and because idealization stems from the "innate feeling"[15] that an "extremely good"[16] maternal breast exists, this idealized object is invariably ambivalent.[17] On the one hand, it counterbalances persecutory anxieties to some degree, but on the other hand, it persecutes itself because it contains powerful tyrannical elements that are not split. "The ideal breast is the counterpart of the devouring breast,"[18] but "infants whose capacity for love is strong"[19] feel less of a need for excessive idealization, which "denotes that persecution is the main driving force."[20]

Only an effective working through of the depressive position—a working through that is always underway and that is never fully realized—can successfully integrate the split-off parts while reconciling the persecutor and the ideal to form the "good" object and to abate the tyranny of the superego. Once the sexual identity of the "self" (a term that Klein increasingly used instead of "ego" to designate the totality of the psyche as opposed to the external object) takes shape, the child introjects the sexual functions at the genital level and detaches himself finally from his parents. This optimal evolution is followed by the formation of what Donald Meltzer calls the "Super-ego-Ideal."[21]

Psychotic structures, in contrast, forever carry the burden of this persecuting Kleinian superego because they need it to counterbalance the despair that results from primary destructiveness and from the failure of all early object relations. In fact, the idealized tyrant—protective in turn—that consists of the ferocious superego of psychosis (when it proves itself to be a last-ditch defense against the total annihilation of psychic life and of life) continues to impede the development of the psychic realm: the *biological* survival of the psychotic personality comes at the cost of a maddening inhibition or distortion of *psychic* life.

The realm of the mind thus finds itself to be quashed at least in part by "concretizations," in the sense that internal objects as well as the superego function as external objects, which leads to a denial of internal reality as well as of the link between the two. The psychic realm, which is a *representation*, is therefore experienced as an *incarnation*, as a container of objects that are perceived very concretely, that center on a container, and that inhibit symbolization as a result.[22] The passage that Klein often quotes from Milton's *Samson Agonistes* rings true here: "Thou art become (O worst imprisonment!) / The dungeon of thyself." Alongside symbolization, which the psychotic subject is somewhat capable of, we find another reality, a "concrete" reality in which the word is the thing and the thing is the word. This process, already recognized by such close Kleinian disciples as Joan Riviere and Susan Isaacs, has been fully developed by the post-Kleinians.[23] But Klein had already touched on it herself, particularly in her case studies of Dick and of Richard, where she relied on the healthy parts of the personality—those that were capable of joining the split-off parts—to interpret persecutory anxieties through transference in an effort to transform them into depressive anxieties and to extend symbolization to the entire psychic realm. From that perspective, Klein's case study of Richard reflects the degree to which abating the severity of the superego—as well as making interpretations that are susceptible of revealing that severity and of counteracting it with a verbalization shared with the patient through transference—are essential to the treatment of psychosis.

THE CASE OF RICHARD:
GOODNESS VERSUS HITLER-UBU

Klein completed her clinical work with Richard (who was ten years old at the time) in 1941. The Controversial Discussions with Anna Freud were in full force, as was the Second World War, which insinuates itself into the story of Richard.[24] The title of the case study, *Narrative of a Child Analysis*, suggests that it is a *narrative* of an analysis. Narration, the ultimate imaginary act, proves here to be a breeding ground for Klein's work. Whether the text is recounting Richard's words, relaying Klein's interpretations, or clarifying those interpretations through her commentary, the entire analysis is structured as a narration, and not at all as a system of knowledge. Klein in fact subscribed to a certain cult of the narrative: she was drawn to Colette's libretto for Ravel's *L'Enfant et les sortilèges*, to Julian Green's novel *If I Were You*, and, a bit further afield, to the myth that she wove around Aeschylus's *Oresteia*.[25] Her imaginary version of truth links her, unexpectedly, to a tribute to the *narrated life* that we have already observed in Hannah Arendt.[26]

During Richard's latency period, he suffered from characterological difficulties: insincerity, hypocrisy, and dissimulating charm. He also presented with inhibitions: he could no longer attend school because he suffered so from agoraphobic and claustrophobic anxieties. Richard was afraid of other children, although his fears, which were manifested at the beginning of treatment, were not excessive. Klein's interpretations brought his anxieties to the fore, which in turn unleashed his tyrannical superego. As was the case with Richard's sessions, what emerged from her study was a truly sadistic persecution that greatly surpassed the rigidity of the child's stern and puritanical parents. This "paranoid object," which inhabited Richard *concretely*, took the form of the family maid Bessie, seen as a Germanophobe and a poisoner, but also of Hitler, the most celebrated of the contemporary persecutors, who fascinated Richard as much as he terrified him, and with whom the young patient occasionally identified.

During the ninth week of Richard's treatment, which lasted sixteen weeks in all, he fell into a manic state that was subsequently abated. When Richard expressed his fear of his father's impending arrival, Klein's interpretation revealed to him that he desired his father's penis, an interpretation that immediately incited some violent material centered on a "monster" whose "meat was delicious"[27] and that was followed by Richard's handling a yellow pencil that he constantly shoved in his orifices—his mouth, his ears, and his nose—and his nibbling as he told the story of a mouse that had scurried about his parent's bedroom. During the following session, he described a dream about a trial that was very Kafkaesque (as Meltzer has wisely pointed out). In the dream, he was brought before a court without knowing exactly what he had been charged with:

> Richard was at a law court. He did not know what he was accused of. He saw the judge, who looked quite nice and did not say anything. Richard went to a cinema, which seemed also to belong to the court. Then all the buildings which were part of the court tumbled down. He seemed to have become a giant and with his enormous black shoe he kicked the tumbled-down buildings and this made them stand up again. So he really put them right.[28]

Melanie explained to Richard that the judge was his father, who was sometimes kind but other times terrifying when Richard wished to steal his father's penis or his mother's breast—hadn't Richard been accused the previous day of picking roses? The charge that he destroyed the court buildings represented his desire to attack his parents and then to restore them to their original condition. His feeling that he was a giant meant that he contained within himself a giant-mother and a destructive monster-father; we might add that he also introjected a giant superego that procured for him not only the impression of being Hitler but also the feeling of omnipotent thought and the idea that he might be stronger than Hitler so he could fight him. The black Hitler-shoe suggested that he created and destroyed the buildings and subsequently put them back together, just as he had demolished his parents and then attempted to rebuild them.

The next day Richard offered some free associations concerning the inexplicable guilt that had caused him much anxiety in this dream: he was also being accused in the dream of breaking a window, which he had actually done a few days before in the playroom, but this misdeed was associated with his identification with Hitler and with the German plane, which had destroyed the conservatory in his family's home and which had frightened Bessie, the cook-poisoner.

Klein's case notes indicate that her interpretive work focused on Richard's excessive splitting and idealization. The analyst believed that Richard was attacking his father's penis, which he imagined was persecuting the inside of his mother's body as well as his mother herself, and which he believed was causing her pain. Mr. Smith, who represented Richard's father in these stories, was therefore transformed all too rapidly, sometimes into a good guy and sometimes into a bad guy. At the same time, the child distinguished between the father and the mother, idealizing the one and making the other into a bad object—and vice versa. In the same way, Richard, within his own self, manifested splitting-and-idealization in such a way that his bad part, "Hitler," attacked and invaded his good parts. The analyst synthesized her painstaking work with her young patient as follows:

> The fight against external foes . . . brought out persecutory fear of them which he attempted to counteract by manic defences. However, the fact that the fluctuations between

what he felt to be good and bad in himself and others were less rapid, was bound up with greater synthesis between the good and bad aspects of the analyst and his mother on the one hand, and of the good and bad father on the other. Such processes of externalization and synthesis of the objects include greater integration of the ego and an increased capacity to differentiate between parts of himself and his objects. Such processes of externalization and synthesis of the objects included greater integration of the ego and an increased capacity to differentiate between parts of himself and his objects. Steps in integration and synthesis, however, stir up anxiety although they bring relief. This was shown in the drawing of the aeroplanes (Forty-sixth Session) where he appeared as both the German and the British plane, which implied a greater unconscious insight into his having simultaneously destructive and loving impulses.[29]

Melanie Klein gradually shifted from the term "ego" to the term "self," which she eventually used "to cover the whole of the personality, which includes not only the ego but the instinctual life which Freud called the *id*."[30] Klein's notion of the self—which is not the same as the psychic phenomenon that, in the eyes of other partisans of the ego or the self, is acquired and slowly solidified during the entire development of the child's psychic apparatus—is present at birth and predates splitting. The Kleinian self represents the essential unity of the subject, which must be understood as what Klein considered to be a fundamental heterogeneity: at once meaning and the drive, capable of absorbing parts taken from the id or the ego, from bodily images and sundry objects as well as from irreducible concretizations. Richard's analysis reflected such an amalgamated and yet unified conception of what Klein called the "self." The case study of Richard— more so than the case studies of Fritz, Hans, Trude, Rita, Peter, Dick, or anyone else—reveals the dynamic yet diverse unity of the psychic apparatus: thanks to the analyst, a *subject* (if we can use that term without being too theoretically anachronistic) emerges who is made and destroyed through crises between the superego and its object.

For Richard, the "concretizations of the superego" functioned as external and persecuting objects that prevented him from thinking in any way other than through manic excitement. His speech was reduced to a feverish logorrhea. When the young patient was confronted with an interpretation, his speech and his thought would begin to change. Richard asked Mrs. Klein if she enjoyed their work together, as if he were trying to understand the meaning of the analytic activity as well as the way the psychic truths unveiled by the analyst had afforded him a sense of gratification that was different from the persecutory excitation that had come before: "Richard was silent for some time and deep in thought. Then he said he would like to understand what psychoanalysis really was. It seemed such a secret to him. He would like to get to the 'heart of it.' "[31]

Another of Melanie Klein's interpretations focused on Richard's feeling of triumph when he seduced—as he believed he had!—his mother as well as Mrs. Klein (he would sleep in his mother's quarters and could see his analyst on Sundays), just as he thought he could use his pencils to kill Hitler! Klein embellished this interpretation by stating that the naval battle between the English and the Germans, Japanese, and Italians "went on internally and not only externally,"[32] that the child allowed himself to kill his mother when he believed that she debased herself by succumbing to his seduction as if she had forgotten the boundaries between what is permissible and what is not as well as the boundaries between good and evil, and that he believed the analyst herself attracted him and authorized him to desire his mother as well as herself. As Meltzer has pointed out, Richard's manic state diminished only when interpretation addressed the most essential point, which was "the contempt of the object and the contempt in the transference for this Mrs Klein, whose bag and clock were the rocks behind which he could hide and attack everybody."[33]

The interpretation of the hostilities that fascinated Richard and their rebirth in the child's inner world made it easier to tone down the superego and to work through Richard's splitting. At the same time, the depressive feelings that accompanied the love for the lost object (Mummy, the analyst) could be consolidated until they dominated manic excitation and eventually colored the components of the superego with benevolence and gratitude. In fact, Mrs. Klein, who adopted during this phase of the analysis the functions of a constantly evolving superego, experienced some of they ways it changed in the final weeks of the analysis: during the thirteenth week of treatment, Richard asked Klein if she herself contained a bad father-Hitler, or, on the other hand, if she was content with her grandchildren, her good husband, or a good penis inside her. The trust Richard placed in his inner good mother and in the good father grew in pace with the trust he placed in Mrs. Klein:

> I had already interpreted that one part of his self, felt to be good and allied with the good object, was fighting his destructive part combined with the bad objects. But his ego was not strong enough to deal with the impending disaster. I would conclude that the engine which he put behind my bag (which had in his analysis often represented myself) stood for his destructive impulses which he could not himself control and which were to be controlled by the analyst—ultimately by his good object. This good object was also felt to be the restraining and therefore helpful super-ego.[34]

The goodness that Richard rediscovered and re-created expanded his psychic space and enabled him to symbolize both past and present conflicts. He became less vulnerable to being "dismantled" by the intrusions of a superego that was as tyranni-cal as it was "incarnate" and "concretized" in the form of real per-secutors who were not imagined: Bessie and Cook, Hitler, his mother, his father, and the analyst herself during the beginning of treatment. The law court no longer had to haunt his dreams, not with Richard's holding himself out as a grotesque giant donning colossal black shoes. The "heart" of psychoanalysis (or, rather, the heart of the psychoanalyst) was about to get the better of the "castle," with its superego-like walls that Richard had drawn to designate the "law court."

In truth, it appears that the raw, even cruel, simplicity of Klein's interpretations was able to consolidate Richard's psychic space, perhaps because the therapist never separated herself from the *goodness* that combined, in her mind, tactful listening and a relentless effort to understand what cannot be understood by linking her patient with her clinical reasoning. James Gammill, who proved in the end to be Klein's most loyal disciple, has said as much: "[Klein] emphasized that one had to understand not only each young child's specific vocabulary, but his personal style and mode of expression as well in order to formulate interpretations that were most likely to be understood and put to use. . . . In addition, she believed it was not enough for the patient to feel understood, for he should also realize what had made such understanding possible."[35]

What Melanie Klein sought was not a mountain of theories (or metalanguages) but a way to understand—and then to understand the how and why of understanding. Such a goal can be accomplished when the cognitive superego cooperates with the drive-based logic of the analyst, but perhaps it can also be the logic of the patient's own suffering, provided he has the luck to have an analyst who is able to stick with him as long as Melanie did.

It turns out—as "the case of Richard" proves beyond cavil, perhaps because of Klein's careful notes and the details they provide—that although Klein still appears to us to be too systematic and simplistic, it was because she showed us that desire itself is incredibly foolhardy. When anxious desire proves incapable of working through its own sadistic excesses, it redirects those excesses toward introjected objects that are entirely dissociated and reversible and that generate a superego that appears grandiose and protective—but that in reality is minuscule and destructive. From that point on, futile law courts inhabit us for real and stay inside us concretely, resulting, for example, in the exhausting series of poisoning Mummies-Bessies and of bombarding fathers-

Hitlers. But Richard's Hitler is only an Ubu, and the horrible trial inflicted upon the child is no more than a circus of internal sado-masochistic reversals. Jarry, for one, has already put Ubu down. But Melanie did not join him. With good (serious? maternal?) intentions, Klein had the courage to reveal the silliness of it all. For her, moreover, Ubu is not outside, but truly inside: Ubu is us and Ubu is you. Who could not fault her for making it so clear?

HOW CAN WE AVOID BEING ALONE?

Not content with being incredibly foolhardy, our inner world is also wholly solitary. Even if the superego cannot take all the blame for this, Klein, at the end of her final work, "On the Sense of Loneliness,"[36] still contends that "the harsher the super-ego, the greater will be loneliness."[37] And yet it is not the mere fact of being isolated, but the *inner* feeling of being alone—even in the company of friends or lovers—that Klein attributes to two essential factors that are no stranger to the early and tyrannical super-ego at issue here.

If the initial preverbal relationship with the mother is gratifying, it establishes a degree of contact with the unconscious of both the mother and the child that is so complete and so gratifying that nostalgia impresses it into the psyche. Speechless though it may be, this contact affords the sensation of being understood, a sensation that is so all-encompassing that it enhances the depressive impression of having suffered an irreplaceable loss. The context of the ensuing psychic evolution is so desirable that anxieties readily surface. Paranoid-schizoid anxiety, which emerges beginning at three months of age, and depressive anxiety, which emerges later, ravage the ego and seek support in a superego that mandates a return to the absolute communication providing a "foundation for the most complete experience of being understood."[38] The integration of the ego, which is aimed at alleviating these anxieties, occurs gradually through the depressive position—but it remains incomplete, which is the second reason behind the sense of loneliness: "Since full integration is never achieved, complete understanding and acceptance of one's own emotions, phantasies and anxieties is not possible and this continues as an important factor in loneliness."[39]

The hope of rediscovering total understanding by reunifying the ego's split-off and misunderstood parts can thus be expressed by the fantasy of having a twin, as Bion has suggested. This hope can also appear in the form of an idealized internal object that deserves unwavering trust. But when the integration of the parts of the ego remains inaccessible, the feeling of nonintegration or exclusion surges forth, and we become convinced "that there is no person or group to which one belongs."[40] Or instead, one can defend oneself against too great a dependence on the external object by thrusting oneself upon the internal object, with the result, in some adults, that they reject any sort of amicable exchange.

A nostalgic, serene, and autumnal tone imbues Klein's final work, which touches on the paranoid-schizophrenic and manic-depressive symptoms of isolation and which concludes by describing an experience common to us all. By the end of this essay, the dramatic portrayal of solitude is transformed into an omnipresent feeling of forlornness that almost proves to be a clear understanding of our condition as beings who are separated and rejected from a paradise that was also a hell—albeit a hell that our superego never ceases to idealize so it can convince us more easily that we are banking on the impossible.

From paranoid-schizoid and manic-depressive loneliness to the present feeling of loneliness that carries traces of it, the early and tyrannical superego softens and transforms into a "good" superego. Such a superego always prohibits the destructive drives and arouses the depressive and paranoid anxieties that persuade us that neither unification nor communication among our split-off parts is possible. For better or worse, however, such a superego also allows the process of integration itself to unfold, which in turn allows us to know, at a minimum, why we experience joy and suffering. In the end, the sense of loneliness becomes the expression of the "urge towards integration, as well as the pain experienced in the process of integration," both of which stem from "internal sources which remain powerful throughout life."[41]

Melanie Klein, who in no way resigns herself to this view, concludes that loneliness is indeed our unavoidable destiny, but that it also affords us an opportunity. To concede as much does not make us happier, but it certainly makes us calmer because we are truer and, perhaps, more welcoming while at the same time never ceasing to be alone. Once we are alone, we can share the analytic understanding of our solitude. The draconian superego succumbs to the ideal ego, which Melanie rarely discusses but which emerges upon the reappearance, during the final pages of her work, of the "good breast" and its internalization: "The internalization of a good breast . . . is a foundation for integration which I have mentioned as one of the most important factors in diminishing the sense of loneliness."[42]

THE CULT OF THE MOTHER
OR AN ODE TO MATRICIDE?
THE PARENTS

The Kleinian universe, as has been stated to excess, is dominated by the mother. The omnipotence of this archaic figure is threatening and terrifying. Is the mother so pernicious that we have to abandon her and hasten her death? Is she unable to transform herself? And even if she is not, what does she become? Does the requisite abandonment of the mother constitute a journey toward the father, as Freud and Lacan believed? Or does it set the stage for subsequent reunions with a good mother who is finally restored, gratifying, and gratified? That is more likely because, in the eyes of our author, there is no birth without a witch and no baby without envy. And only the analyst—preferably a female one or at least a man who assumes his own femininity—is able to convince the newborn, who remains inside us forever, that it is possible to encounter fairies who deserve its gratitude.

Such systematizing visions of Klein's work are not entirely inaccurate. The modest place, at best, that Freudian theory accords to the mother encouraged his successors, including Klein, to be dogmatic in the other direction. And yet, by placing too much emphasis on the mother, whom the founder rejected, one runs the risk of forgetting the father. In fact, what role does the father play in Klein's theory? One of the first to formulate that question was Klein's own daughter Melitta Schmideberg—who posed the question in anger.[1] Other detractors of Klein's followed suit. Still, the psychoanalyst's mind was far more complex than that.

The celebrated breast is never alone, for the penis is linked with it in fantasy. This view, which is hammered home beginning with Klein's early articles in *The Psychoanalysis of Children*, is stated explicitly in *Envy and Gratitude*. Although envy emerges as soon as the breast is present, it also attacks the penis that is associated with it:

> In the vicissitudes of the first exclusive relation with the mother, . . . when this relation is disturbed too soon, the rivalry with the father enters prematurely. Phantasies of the penis inside the mother, or inside her breast, turn the father into a hostile intruder.[2]

In other words—and I have already emphasized this point—from the beginning of Klein's clinical experience, which was based on her analysis of Erich/Fritz and of Hans/Felix, she posited the existence of an archaic Oedipus conflict that is manifested from the child's first night terrors. Such frights reflect repression, and repression exists only in the Oedipus conflict! As a result, although the Oedipus complex does not truly exist before the onset of the depressive position during the sixth month of life, the rivalry with the father emerges prematurely in the proto-Oedipus complex. This notion of prematurity, which appears to contradict the Freudian Oedipus complex that emerges at a later point, can nevertheless be reconciled with universal Freudian theory, and in particular with the thesis—of which Klein deduces the immediate consequences—of an oedipal rivalry that is phylogenetically constituted based on the murder-and-assimilation of the father of the primal horde. But in that case, is the penis *already* inside the breast or does it appear there only *afterward*?

In a 1924 speech to the Salzburg congress, Klein clarified her position: her conclusion, based on her analysis of Rita, was that the father's penis *as such*—and not inasmuch as it may be confused with the inside of the mother—is a coveted object that can only *succeed* the mother's breast. Early oedipal drives combine the oral and the vaginal: children desire intercourse as an oral act in which the mouth and the vagina are both receptors, a desire that facilitates the displacement of oral libido onto the genital.[3]

Still, it is with the depressive position—when love and hate eventually become one, when the ego can lose Mummy and rediscover her in its fantasies in the form of a whole object—that we become aware of what Klein termed "the relation to the second object, the father" and can put him in the context of "the other people in his surroundings"[4] (brothers or sisters). This secondary function is hardly flattering, but it is effective all the same. The initial stages of the Oedipus conflict led Klein to posit the existence of *two parents* in the childhood fantasy, in the sense of an imago of the "combined parent figure."[5] In *Envy and Gratitude*, Klein returned to this theme and expounded upon it:

> Among the features of the earliest stage of the Oedipus complex are the phantasies of the mother's breast and the mother containing the penis of the father, or the father containing the mother. This is the basis of the combined parent figure, and I have elaborated the importance of this phantasy in earlier writings. The influence of the combined parent figure on the infant's ability to *differentiate between the parents*, and to establish good relations with each of them, is affected by the strength of envy and the intensity of his Oedipus jealousy. For the suspicion that the parents are always getting sexual gratification from one another reinforces the phantasy—derived from various sources—that they are always combined.[6]

Excessive anxiety, however, can result in an inability to dissoci-
ate the relationship with the father from the relationship with the
mother, which in turn can generate mental confusion.

When a boy's jealous feelings rise to the surface, they are
focused less on the original object (the breast–the brother) than
on his rivals. The boy redirects his hatred toward his father, who
is envied as if he possessed the mother, and here we see a case of
classic oedipal jealousy. With the girl, in contrast, "the mother
becomes the chief rival."[7] Female envy of the father's penis, which
Freud considered paramount,[8] is secondary in Klein's view: it is
important only insofar as it reinforces female homosexuality:
"This is essentially a flight mechanism and therefore does not lead
to stable relations with the second object."[9] When envy and
hatred toward the mother are strong and stable, they are redi-
rected toward the realm of the father; or, in the alternative, they
split off in such a way that one parent is simply detested and the
other adored. As for the rivalry with the mother, Klein believed,
unlike Freud, that it is not love for the father that forms the basis
for this split but always the envy toward the mother that stems
from "the mother's possession of the father and his penis."[10] The
father, or, more precisely, what he is reduced to, is no more than
a possessor of the mother. We see this affirmation return throughout all of Klein's work, including in her final text, *Envy and Gratitude*. In addition, and very significantly, Klein uses the term
"appendage" in this context:

> The father (or his penis) has become an *appendage* to the
> mother and it is on these grounds that the girl wants to rob
> her mother of him. Therefore in later life, every success in
> her relation to men becomes a victory over *another woman*.
> This applies even where there is no obvious rival, because
> the rivalry is then directed against the man's mother, as can
> be seen in the frequent disturbances of the relation between
> daughter-in-law and mother-in-law. . . .
>
> When hate and envy of the mother are not so strong, . . .
> an idealization of the *second object*, the father's penis and
> the father, may then be more successful.[11]

Despite this final hypothesis—a tentative one at that—of a possible idealization of the father, it is the woman's hatred toward the mother that endures, even under the influence of the father's love. On that basis, female friendships and homosexuality both operate as a quest for a good object that eventually replaces the envied primordial object.

The envy of the breast is what underlies the other manifestations of female pathologies: "In a number of cases I found that frigidity, occurring in different degrees, was a result of unstable attitudes to the penis, based mainly on a flight from the primal object."[12] Translation: if the woman flees the penis, it is because she fled the breast; she will be unable to feel pleasure and she will be frigid because experiencing pleasure is primarily a matter of pleasing herself with the breast that contains the penis.

For the man, concomitantly, homosexual guilt toward the woman is rooted in his feeling that, by hating the mother, he abandoned her too early, a "feeling of having turned away with hate from the mother and betrayed her by making an ally of the father's penis and of the father." This "betrayal of a loved woman"[13] can inhibit male friendships, and the ensuing guilt can inspire the woman to flee, which itself can lead to homosexuality.

A PRIMARY FEMININE PHASE

Although Klein's conception of the early fantasy accords a central role to the breast, it includes a penis inside that breast. Even more important, by recognizing that oral drives are combined with genital ones, the dynamic of the fantasy encourages the ego to desire intercourse as an oral act of sucking at a breast that includes the penis, and then the penis in the image of the breast. This perspective, which applies to both sexes, means that both sexes experience a *primary feminine phase*—which is among the more striking of Klein's analytic observations.[14]

The primary envy of the breast, which is replaced by an oral or receptive envy of the penis, causes the boy to experience an envy of femininity and/or maternity. Hanna Segal describes the process as follows:

> For the little girl, this first oral turning to the penis is a het-erosexual move paving the way to the genital situation and the wish to incorporate the penis in her vagina. But at the same time it contributes to her homosexual trends in that, at that stage of development, the oral desire is linked with incorporation and identification, and the wish to be fed by the penis is accompanied by a wish to possess a penis of her own.
>
> For the little boy this turning to the penis of his father as an alternative to his other's breast is primarily a move towards passive homosexuality, but at the same time this incorporation of his father's penis helps in his identification with him and in that way strengthens his heterosexuality.[15]

Klein, who is more emphatic than Segal in her own observa-tions and countertransference, proposes the following:

> In this phase [i.e., the "feminine phase"] the boy has an *oral-sucking fixation on his father's penis,* just as the girl has. This fixation is, I consider, the basis of true homosexuality in him. This view would agree with what Freud has said in *Leonardo da Vinci and a Memory of his Childhood* . . .
>
> In the phantasy of the boy, his mother incorporates his father's penis, or rather, a number of them, inside herself; side by side with his relations to his real father, or, to be more precise, his father's penis, he develops a relation in phantasy to his father's penis inside his mother's body. . . . He wants to take by force the penis which he imagines as being *inside his mother* and to injure her in doing so. . . .
>
> This result of the boy's development [i.e., heterosexual-ity] depends essentially on the favourable course of his early feminine phase. As I earlier emphasized it is a condition for a firm establishment of the heterosexual position that the boy should succeed in overcoming this phase. . . . The boy

often compensates the feelings of hate, anxiety, envy and inferiority that spring from his feminine phase by reinforcing his pride in the possession of a penis. . . . Thus and only thus, by sublimating his feminine components and overcoming his feelings of envy, hatred and anxiety towards his mother, which originated in his feminine phase, will the boy be able to consolidate his heterosexual position in the stage of genital dominance . . .

In both sexes the anxiety-situations relating to similar events inside the mother's body, constitute the most profound danger-situations. Fear of castration, which is only a part—though an important part—of the anxiety felt about *the whole body,* becomes, in the male individual, a dominating theme that overshadows all his other fears to a greater or lesser extent. But this is precisely because *one of the deepest sources to which disturbances in his sexual potency go back is his anxiety about the interior of his body.*[16]

Klein's notion of a primary feminine stage has been creatively developed by contemporary analysts. Florence Guignard, a careful reader of the later theories of Bion and Winnicott, thus distinguishes between two realms of intimacy that fall into rapid succession during the first six months of the *infant's* life: the "primary maternal" realm, which generates the drama of the fantasies originating in intrauterine life and in castration, and the "primary feminine" realm, which consists of fantasies of seduction and the primal scene.[17]

In the "primary maternal" realm, the newborn establishes his initial link with the world based on his powerless omnipotence, whereas the mother contributes the narcissism of her heartfelt passion and her maternal masochism. The "primary feminine" realm, on the other hand, organizes the earliest female identifications in boys as well as girls, as Klein understood it, around greed toward the naked breast and the early genital desire for the penis that is included in that breast. The union between the breast and the penis is what makes the primary feminine realm "a specific space for organizing the psychic realm."[18] The "libidinal mutual stimulation" that takes places between mother and baby thus lays the foundation for the birth of psychic life as well as the reality principle. Put another way, the child's capacity for psychic activity and thought depends on his primary identification with maternal femininity.

The modern evolution of Klein's work thus attempts to compensate for her lack of attention to the father by defining early mutual stimulation as an "articulation of the desire-to-be-known with the identification with the father-who-knows."[19] Accordingly, the identification is twofold: the young ego identifies at a very early stage with the desire to make itself known (a desire that the woman manifests in the mother), and also with the knowing penetration carried out by the father's penis. If it is true, as Freud believed, that there is only one, essentially male, libido, then the desire for knowledge would be decisively female.[20]

Recent advances by female analysts studying female sexuality have shed new light on Klein's relentless efforts to develop her young patients' thought and to facilitate their knowledge processes. Femininity, defined as a desire for knowledge that facilitates the growth of a psychic inner life in which man and woman encounter each other, is what stimulates—in Klein's view in particular and in the view of psychoanalysts in general—the desire and the ability to overcome inhibitions in thinking. And femininity also develops patients' creativity through the analytic process itself. The message of the ear that the female analyst—and the female of the analyst—lends to the patient who comes to confide his ill-being is not "Act on your desire!" but "Create and recreate your thought by staying in touch with your feminine side!"

FEMALE SEXUALITY . . .

Klein showed an interest in female sexuality at a very early stage in her career.[21] Although she acknowledged her debt to the work of Helene Deutsch, she also claimed that her own view "[went] beyond" that of her confederate.[22] Klein was also an adherent of Karen Horney's, particularly her discussion of Freud's views on female castration and her emphasis on the gradual emergence of a penis envy that follows pregenital investments.[23] Klein further endorsed Ernest Jones's view that women's oral sadism provides a way to forcibly possess the father's penis in order to undertake a relationship of identification with him.[24] Finally, on the theory that one small tribute won't hurt anyone,[25] Klein cited the work of her own daughter, Melitta Schmideberg.[26] Armed with these acknowledged influences, Klein developed her own vision of femininity.

The starting point of her study is clearly Freudian. She cites Freud's "Inhibitions, Symptoms, and Anxiety" (1926),[27] in which Freud himself recognizes that even if women do have a *castration complex,* "we can hardly speak with propriety of castration *anxiety* where castration has already taken place."[28] It is rather bold of Melanie to cite Freud here as she refines her own thought, for she does not endorse Freud's notion that the Oedipus complex in the girl is propelled by the her castration desires and fears.

In Klein's view, the Oedipus complex in the girl emerges through her oral desires, which are closely accompanied by genital drives: the girl desires to take her father's penis away from her mother. To summarize, the female Oedipus conflict does not follow the castration complex, as Freud would have it, even though it is true that she desires the penis and hates the mother who refuses it to her, as Freud understood very well in this instance: "But, according to my assumption, what she primarily wants is not to possess a penis of her own as an attribute of masculinity, but to incorporate her father's penis as an object of oral satisfaction."[29]

As Helene Deutsch had suggested, the penis is thus assimilated into the mother's breast, and the vagina assumes the passive role of a sucking mouth—with the caveat that, for Klein, these fantasies do not emerge upon the girl's sexual maturity but result from her frustrations with the breast from the very beginnings of her childhood!

These early processes, which are manifested under the aegis of oral sadism and then anal sadism, explain why sadism is so predominant in the girl's Oedipus conflict: she engages in "hate-filled phantasies" about her mother's penis-appendage.[30] The little girl fears her mother's reprisals, and, at the same time, fantasizes in a way that forces her to imagine her mother completely annihilated in an act of sadistic intercourse with the father. From that perspective, *female masochism* stems from the fear of dangerous introjected objects, particularly the father's penis, and reflects nothing less than "[the girl's] sadistic instincts turned inwards against those internalized objects"[31] To put it bluntly, the penis introjected in herself is what punishes the female masochist who enjoys suffering.

Because the little girl's destructive drives against her mother are so intense, she invests her urinary and excremental functions more strongly than does the boy: those functions are mobilized into internal attacks against the enigmatic interior of the mother as well as of the girl herself. Women's investment of anality acts "in conformity with the hidden and mysterious nature of that world within her mother's body and her own" Accordingly, "the woman's mode of mastering anxiety remains under the domination of her relation to an inner world, to what is concealed, and therefore to the unconscious."[32] And yet this feminine position provides little protection from anxiety. What is more, although the girl perceives the vagina at a very early stage,[33] the phallic investment of the clitoris relegates this early awareness to second place. In Klein's view, the high incidence of female frigidity proves that the vagina, which is experienced as a cavity that is threatened by sadistic fantasies, is invested defensively and long before the clitoris.

Regardless of what some may have alleged, Klein did not deny that girls experience a phallic stage.[34] She considered the identification with the father based on the introjected penis to be "a process comprising many stages,"[35] one that reinforces narcissism and the omnipotence of thought in the girl, whose virile position is expressed through the erotization of urinary functions. And yet sadism underlies the entire complex of female virility, while scoptophilia and urethral eroticism work to repress female desires per se.

In this context, then, the relationship between mother and

child and the desire to be a mother are not merely an expression of penis envy, as Freud believed, for they also express a narcissistic relationship that is "more independent of [the woman's] attitude to the man and closely connected with her own body and with the omnipotence of her excrements."[36] In Klein's view, the fetus can express the paternal superego: the hatred or fear that the woman will later feel toward her child overtakes the fantasies that liken the penis to bad and toxic excrement.[37] As a result, *reparation*, which is quite pronounced in women, is manifested as a desire to beautify the excremental penis: to create a *beautiful* child, to make oneself *beautiful*, to *beautify* one's home, and so forth. Such specifically feminine acts of sublimation are reaction formations to sadistic fantasies about dangerous feces.[38]

It follows, then, that the female superego, which is formed as a response to this sadistic impotence, is even more severe than is the boy's. Because the girl is unable to edify her superego in the image of her same-sex parent (since the mother's femininity is invisible and her interior is threatening), she structures her superego in a solely reactive way. Thus, "the girl's super-ego becomes raised to very great heights and much magnified." Torn between a powerful superego and the inner world of the unconscious, the woman, in this case like a child, possesses a much less stable ego than does the man. Luckily for her, however, "in her development the woman introjects her Oedipus objects more strongly than the man, which leads to a fuller ego-development . . . and she leans on the powerful super-ego within partly in order to dominate or to outdo it."[39]

Freud, who followed the work of his rather rebellious group of disciples on female sexuality, eventually proposed—after his mother's death in 1931!—a new way of thinking about femininity in his "Female Sexuality," written that same year.[40] Klein responded in the form of a "Postscript"[41] to her own study entitled "The Effects of Early Anxiety-Situations on the Sexual Development of the Girl," which is included in *The Psychoanalysis of Children*. Melanie, who disagreed with Freud's notion of a persistent archaic attachment between mother and daughter[42] and with the notion of "Minoan-Mycenaean"[43] attraction that precedes the Oedipus conflict, categorically refused the Freudian hypothesis of a nirvana among woman, and she emphasized the fundamental ambivalence in women's relations with one another—a relationship she considered to be intrinsically laden with guilt: "[Freud] endeavours to isolate that attachment from the operation of her super-ego and her sense of guilt. This, in my judgment, is not possible."[44]

This consideration of the archaic maternal function, which pervades the primary object of desire as well as anxiety, provides a whole new perspective on women's *endogenous homosexuality*. Not only did Melanie emphasize this point before Freud, but she did so much more emphatically than do Freud's own writings on female sexuality. From the outset, in fact, Klein posited a conflict—rather than an osmosis—between the two protagonists. We know this ourselves to be true: anxiety and guilt are always present from a very early stage, but particularly between mother and daughter. Although the daughter may very well distance herself from her mother so that she can desire her father during the second six months of her life, her love for her father is nevertheless based on her initial—and eternally conflicted—bond with her mother. In the end, the daughter makes her way back to her father, but primary envy surreptitiously infiltrates her Oedipus complex because she refuses to forgive her mother for either the oral frustration that her mother brought about or for the oral satisfaction that, according to her sexual theories about the primal scene, her parents gain from each other through sexual intercourse. As a result, the daughter's resentment permeates—overtly or covertly—her subsequent relationships with the opposite sex. Melanie implies that Freud borrowed this idea from her when he suggested that "many women repeat their relation to their mother in their relation to men."[45] In the end, a woman's object of desire is the other woman, even when such desire is cloaked in heterosexuality: that is what Melanie Klein asserted with greater conviction than did any of Freud's other critics. In a woman's husband you will always find her mother![46]

At the same time, while Freud acknowledged that "we are far from complete clarity" with respect to "the prehistory of the

Oedipus complex,"[47] Melanie posited that men have a *feminine passivity* that is supported through *orality*. Klein paved the way to a study of men's feminine side, which she understood as being either a necessary component of masculine heterosexuality or an incitement to homosexuality. To summarize, Klein recognized an archaic maternal realm that mandates two different types of femininity: women's femininity and men's femininity.[48]

. . . AND MALE SEXUALITY

The mother's interior continues to be the object of her daughter's destructive drives. For a woman, the concomitant of this unconscious operation is that the ordeal of reality, which seeks to discern bad objects, takes place within herself. And as for the boy, whose excremental omnipotence is less developed, he invests his penis from a very early stage:

> His penis, as an active organ, is used to master his object and
> . . . it is accessible to tests by reality. . . . This concentration
> of sadistic omnipotence in the penis is of fundamental
> importance for the masculine position of the boy.[49]

As the organ of penetration, the penis becomes, for the boy, the organ of perception. Like the eyes or the ear, the penis penetrates so it can know, and it facilitates the ego's epistemophiliac drive as well as its journey along the path to knowledge. The penis engages in a penetration that is as destructive as one could imagine, but this sadism is accompanied by fantasies of reparation. Hence, after destroying the object through the sexual act, the boy (through fantasy) and the man (through his sexual experiences) are drawn to restoring that object through love.

The choice of male homosexuality is rooted in an attempt to absorb into the woman all that is terrifying and unknown: the ego protects itself by abandoning the woman for good. Such protection comes at a psychic cost, however. Even if the homosexual man's unconscious comes out of this process divested, pacified, or even beautified, it runs the risk of eradicating his inner world:

> In his homosexual attitude this significance is extended by his narcissistic choice of object to the penis of another male, and this penis now serves as a counter-proof against all his fears concerning the penis inside him and the interior of his body. Thus in homosexuality one mode of mastering anxiety is that the ego endeavours to deny, control or get the better of the unconscious by over-emphasizing reality and the external world and all that is tangible, visible and perceptible to consciousness.[50]

Klein radically redefines Freud's thesis of a social bond founded on a homosexuality among brothers: she sees such a bond as a secret confederation of brothers who band together against "parents combined in copulation,"[51] particularly against a father abusing the mother. Klein also believes that the bond originates in masturbatory fantasies with sadistic overtones that the boy shares with an accomplice.[52] The relationship between brothers, which at first protects the parental couple, reverses itself and reveals its paranoid character. On the one hand, the overinvested penis proves to be a persecuting object made in the image of the father's penis and of the patient's own feces. On the other hand, the precariousness of a good and helpful maternal imago encourages the instability of the ego.[53]

The bad object introjected into the masculine ego can help explain both sexual impotence and alcoholism. With the alcoholic (note that Klein is paying tribute once again here to the work of her daughter Melitta Schmideberg), drinking at first destroys the internalized bad object and assuages persecutory anxiety, but, because all internalization is ambivalent, it quickly loses its ability to soothe and eventually takes on the meaning of the bad object itself.[54]

And yet, as we complete our portrait of male sexuality as Melanie Klein saw it, we should also keep in mind that Klein in no way ignored the boy's rivalry with his father during the phallic period, and that she emphasized that the boy needs to tolerate his aggressiveness and to identify with a good phallic image of the father:

> If he has a strong primary belief in the omnipotence of his penis he can pit it against the omnipotence of his father's penis and take up the struggle against that dreaded and admired organ. . . . If his ego is able to tolerate and modify a certain quantity of destructive feeling against his father and if his belief in his father's "good" penis is strong enough, he can maintain both his rivalry with his father (which is essential for the establishment of a heterosexual position) and his identification with him.[55]

THE "COMBINED" OR COUPLED PARENTS

Klein's notion of the role played by the father and the mother in the child's evolution or in psychosis was discussed at length by the Anna Freudians and later, in a different way, by Lacan and his own supporters. I will return later to Klein's theory of symbolization, which will help us examine, from a different perspective, the gaps in her work with regard to the oedipal triangle, and in particular to the symbolic function of paternity.

Paradoxically, it is important to note that Klein's relegation of the penis to "second" place and, more important, to a function as the mother's "appendage" did not prevent her from basing her theory of splitting on the presence of the penis in the object (the breast) and from conceptualizing the first psychoanalytic model of sexuality founded upon the *couple*. Klein's theory is supported not by the father himself—not even by the father of the primal horde (Freud) or the Name-of-the-Father (Lacan), nor by the mother herself (whatever the power of her breast as a source of anxiety, but also as a way of harnessing that anxiety, which makes it into a central part of the ego and the superego), but by *both parents*.

The two parents are at first "combined" in an act of sadistic intercourse. The lack of distinction between the two partners brings an aggravated sadism, even a mental confusion, to the new ego—which is precisely what generates the imago of the "combined parents." On the heels of the depressive position, however, the young ego learns to distinguish between the two partners by separating the two distinct objects, and then the two total objects (the mother and the father, the woman and the man). This separation lessens envy and facilitates the working through of splitting. The split-off elements can then become integrated with genital sexuality. From that point on, the ego (or the self) learns to choose a dominant mode of sexual identification with the same-sex parent.

It is as if the Kleinian universe functioned—despite her cult of the maternal and particularly in the light of the Oedipus conflict as it emerges during the depressive position—as a dual system: woman *and* man, mother *and* father. It is true that this intuition was never sufficiently supported by a cohesive theory of *language* and the *primal*—a theory that is indeed lacking in Klein's work, which created a gap that has been identified by both her successors and her critics.[56] Still, these initial steps toward a two-sided paradigm prove to be rich with unexplored possibilities in the realm of psychic bisexuality as well as its ethical and political consequences.

Although Klein based her theory on the dyad of the *combined parents*, such a dyad is not merely the product of empirical observations on the part of a mother anxious about her own children, nor is it just a respectful way of recasting the notions of the Jewish patriarch that Sigmund Freud was. In fact, and in anticipation of the Oedipus complex, Klein set forth an original and creative conception of symbolism. From the beginning, Klein's tribute to the mother recognized both the parents and made the couple into the heterogeneous source of the bisexual autonomy of the self: she allocated (some) space for the father in her conception of the proto-Oedipus conflict, and afforded him an even greater role in the depressive position. And yet in Klein's view, the cult of the mother, which is paramount, is transformed into *matricide*. The loss of the mother—which for the imaginary is tantamount to the death of the mother—becomes the organizing principle for the subject's symbolic capacity.

It is worth remembering that the breast, whether good or bad, emerges as the first structuring object only after it has been devoured and destroyed. The mother as a whole object mitigates the exaggerated sadism of the paranoid-schizoid position only once she is "lost" during the depressive position. When the child is weaned—and thus has separated himself effectively—from the breast, he turns away from it and "loses" it. In fantasy life, of course, separation or loss is tantamount to *death*. Paradoxically, as we can see, *the cult of the mother is, in Klein's view, a pretext for matricide*. And yet accepting loss *through love* allows for the development of the depressive position.

Both the cult of the mother and matricide play a saving role. From all appearances, however, matricide is far more than just the cult of the mother: without matricide, the internal object cannot be formed, the fantasy cannot be constructed, and reparation, as well as the redirection of hostility into the introjection of the self, is foreclosed. Kleinian negativity, which, as we shall see, guides the drive to intelligence by way of the fantasy, chooses the mother as its target: in order to think, one must first lose the mother. The paths toward this loss diverge: splitting leads us on the wrong track, whereas the depression that follows the separation and/or death is much more befitting. In the end, a pure positivity—it, too, innate—serves as the very capacity for love. And yet this grace depends greatly on the vagaries of envy or, rather, on the capacity to rid oneself of envy toward the mother—or, to put it more bluntly, to rid oneself of the mother altogether.

In the history of art, and Western art in particular, Medusa's head—an image not only of female castration, as Freud rightfully observed,[57] but also of the loss of the archaic mother that the child absorbs during the depressive position—emerged just as the West was discovering psychic interiority as well as the individual expressiveness of each person's face. This primary beheading (Medusa's lost head and sliced-off head) was followed by more eroticized figures. Some of these figures manifest man's phallic-symbolic power (such as the beheading of St. John the Baptist as he announces the coming of Christ), and others manifest the power struggle between men (David and Goliath) or between woman and man (Judith and Holofernes), and so forth.[58] The "beheading" of the mother, understood as both a "putting to death" and a "flight" to be taken both with the mother and against her—is a necessary precondition for the psychic freedom of the subject: that is what Klein had the courage to proclaim, in her own way and without equivocation.

As I have already noted, Klein's later works, particularly *Envy and Gratitude*, emphasize the child's innate capacity for *love* or *gratitude* that reinforces effective mothering. When this love for the mother buttresses the capacity for reparation that is an integral part of the depressive position, doesn't it erase the tendencies toward matricide that characterize the child's archaic positions—the positions that appear to dominate our author's earlier writings? Some critics have endorsed such an interpretation, while others see this shift in Kleinian thinking toward love as being a variant of *caritas*, even the germ of a new form of socialism.[59]

And yet this oblative tone does not overcome the negativity that dominates Klein's listening to—and interpretation of—the unconscious. Because the death drive is forever, reparation and gratitude are but temporary crystallizations of negativity as well as its dialectical resting points. The capacity for gratitude must be forever cared for and protected—and such assiduous attention, which in modern culture appears to be the exclusive domain of psychoanalysts, demands that we constantly heed the destructive anxiety that works tirelessly by forcing love and gratitude into envy, if not by annihilating them through the fragmentation of the psyche. As for reparation itself, it is by separating from the mother, to which the self was once linked through an initial projective identification, that the self learns to engage in reparation. At that point the self can rediscover the mother, but not as it once knew her. On the contrary, the self never stops re-creating the mother through the very freedom it gained from being separated from her. The mother is a woman who is always renewed in images and in words, through a process of which "I" am the creator simply because I am the one who restores her.

Pity and remorse, which accompany the reparation of the lost object, carry the trace of the imaginary and symbolic matricide that reparation constantly evokes. In fact, the fear and anger common to the state of war that links me, in the paranoid-schizoid position, to Mummy-the breast are followed by a compassion for the other that Mummy becomes through the depressive position. And yet this compassion is no more than a scar of matricide: the ultimate evidence, if any were needed, that the imaginary reconciliation with the mother, which "I" need to be and to think at the cost of a putting-to-death that is excessive and of a matricide that becomes futile but that leaves me a memory that "haunts" me. It inhabits "my" dreams and "my" unconscious, and it appears on the surface of words to the extent that "I" set out in search of lost time.

AN *Oresteia*

Just as the myth of Oedipus illuminates Freudian theory, Klein focuses on the myth of Orestes after diagnosing the matricidal fantasy in her clinic and after unearthing its underlying logic.

In fact, in "Some Reflections on *The Oresteia*,"[60] Klein highlights a different sort of logical process that reflects subjective autonomy—though without ever denying the importance of Freud's Oedipus. In the ancient Greek play, the murder of Orestes's mother grants him freedom, though at the price of a depressive remorse that symbolizes the endless hounding of the Erinyes. Klein's essay, which is somewhat disorganized and which she never completed, was published posthumously despite its gaping holes. It appears that she wrote it around the time of "On the Sense of Loneliness," which was also published after her death. As we have seen, Klein's reflection on solitude concludes with a tribute to the integration of the "good breast." These two published legacies reflect an antinomic crossroad in Klein's thought: the tension between the reparation of the mother and a reconciliation with the object, on the one hand, and the loss of the mother or her being put to death and symbolization, on the other. These are two inextricable sides of the complex process known as the individuation of the self.

Klein's study of *The Oresteia* addresses three aspects of Aeschylus's work from the perspective of her theories. She begins by describing Orestes' fate. Orestes is the son of Agamemnon, who sacrificed his daughter Iphigenia to the gods so that the Greeks might embark on their war vessels immobilized by Neptune's wrath. Orestes kills his mother, Clytemnestra, to avenge his father, whose murder she had encouraged to avenge the death of their daughter Iphigenia. And Orestes is also the brother of Electra, who indulged in passions no less matricidal, though they were more restrained in comparison. It was Electra who demanded that Clytemnestra be killed at the hands of Orestes. Klein could not help but see her own clinical universe in Aeschylus's implicitly incestuous and explicitly murderous imbroglio, as hers was a world in which libido allows itself to be absorbed into the death drive. Such are the consequences of putting Clytemnestra to death: matricide clearly led to Orestes' guilt, but he acquired an immense freedom and a preeminent symbolic capacity along the way.

In the final pages of her *Oresteia,* Klein tells us that the ego seeks whatever means are necessary to create symbols that can become an effective outlet for its emotions, but she also asks herself why it is that we have symbols at all. The answer is simple: it is because the mother is insufficient—precisely because she is incapable of satisfying the child's emotional needs. Get rid of your mother, for you no longer need her: that would be the ultimate message of symbols were they able to explain to us why they exist. And then Klein proceeds to recall one of her earliest writings: her study of little Dick and of the difficulties he had in acquiring symbols and attaining thought.[61]

Does Orestes' drama serve to introduce Klein's reflection on the birth of symbols and her tribute to symbols? Or does this mythological detour explain that the symbol is the murderer of the mother? Or, in the end, is Klein implying that the symbol is the most effective murderer of the mother? It is clear that any such murder, as depicted and encouraged by the psychoanalyst, is but an imaginary one: the point is not to kill one's mother, nor is it to kill anyone else, at least not in reality: "No reality situation can fulfil the often contradictory urges and wishes of the child's fantasy life."[62]

Crimes and other aggressive actings out are merely failures of the symbol; they represent a failure of the imaginary matricide that, by itself, paves the way to thought. On the other hand, the creation of thought, and then the exercise of the sovereign freedom that has the potential to give birth to a work of genius, reflect a successful matricidal fantasy.

The antihero Orestes, an adherent of matricide if there ever was, displayed a devotion to deicide that was just as unrivaled. Unlike Oedipus, a man of desire and repression and an accomplice to the gods, Orestes was an avatar of Jupiter. Oedipus, a creator and a destroyer of enigmas, embodies the profile of the believer. To believe in the father, in the gods, or in knowledge: the differences among them are not as dramatic as some have claimed, for all manifestations of belief absorb both the desire to experience pleasure and the desire to die. Orestes, for his part, is the antison and the antihero . . . precisely because he is antinature. Klein rightfully explains that killing the mother-nature is tantamount to rising up against God: murdering the mother results in guilt, she wrote while reflecting on the depressive position, which itself creates remorse. Here, however, the analyst goes a step further and deduces that the mother, who is feared because she inflicts punishment, is the "prototype of God."[63]

Such an interpretation is not far removed from Sartre's own reading of *The Oresteia*, a reading that informs his play *The Flies*: there, the son who murders his mother is radically deicidal.[64] Yet if Klein is promoting her nonbelief here—just as the mother of Fritz/Erich was said to be an "atheist"[65]—she is also making it clear that her version of matricide bears not a hint of nihilism. To rid oneself of the mother becomes the sine qua non for accessing the symbol.

Indeed, it is when this access to symbolization is lacking that the dark side of Orestes emerges: where we find that side is also where the failure of Oedipus—of his desires and his repression—shall be. The subject returns to splitting and to the destruction of the soul in which psychosis hinders the psychodrama of the neuroses and breaks the psychic realm into bits. Isn't it true that Klein's patients who displayed traces of *The Oresteia* are the precursors of today's gratuitous killers, of the mindless robots without a soul, and of *A Clockwork Orange*? Today, some of these fragmented personalities find refuge in art exhibits and other schizoid manifestations whose minimalist obscenities are welcomed by publishing houses claiming to be "avant-garde." Psychoanalysts, for their part, sense the failure of Orestes as well as of symbolization in the *new maladies of the soul* that take refuge in the merchants and other players who populate our new megalopolises.

And yet Orestes also displays a more reasonable side. The philosophical agenda that accompanies Klein's genius strives to rehabilitate those features in order to discover within them the ultimate preconditions for thought—that is, within the very space that harbors the advent of psychic space and intelligence but that also accumulates the dangers of its suffocation. When the gods are tired or otherwise compromised, all we can do is to reflect upon these fertile sources—to care for them, preserve them, and foster them.

Alongside these acerbic interpretations, Klein's ode to matricide is a plea to preserve our symbolic capacity. The mother of psychoanalysis considered symbolism, the exclusive domain of humans, to be an uncertain miracle that is always already threatened and whose fate clearly depends on the mother, though only as long as "I" can get beyond her. The gist of what Melanie-Libussa's daughter is saying here is that, although the mother is omnipotent, we can—and we must—make do without her and that we are all the better for it. That is the message—a symbolic one it turns out—of the Kleinian "crime."

We can thus understand why some feminists have praised Klein for being the modern creator of the myth of the mother-goddess, while others hold her in contempt for the very same reason: isn't it intolerable to envy one's own mother? Still others reject Klein because they believe she encourages matricide.

Perhaps the only people who truly understand Klein are the female authors of detective stories, though they neither read her nor need to read her: such authors share her unconscious knowledge that when "I" talk about murder, it is not because "I hold a grudge" against men who carry the phallus or because "I" wish to

extricate myself from them—at least those are not the only reasons. Instead, it is because, whether daughter and mother (or
daughter or mother), "I" know the sort of envy of which "I" must
rid myself—the overwhelmingly sadistic desire to work through,
lose, and in a sense *kill*—so that I might acquire a baseline freedom to think. The detective story seems *true* to the extent that it
surpasses the sort of popular literature that recounts the lowbrow
dramas and rather vapid charms of an eventually transgressed
repression. Such queens of pulp fiction dive into a catastrophic
psyche that is no longer a soul worthy of that name. Acts of splitting and dismembering (as Klein understands them), reversals,
acts of envy and ingratitude, and incarnated phantoms that recall
the concrete objects and tyrannical superego of Mother Melanie
all haunt these spaces, which are exposed and then explored and
exhibited with the sweetness of a relatively serene mourning
process. The queens of pulp fiction—and we should emphasize
the feminine nature of this vernacular expression, as if it were self-
evident or commonplace—are depressed women who have reconciled themselves with being put to death, who remember that
in the beginning was an envious sadism, and who never stop cur-
ing themselves from the sadism they describe.

I imagine that these women display the quiet violence of the elderly Mrs. Klein, who herself might have written pulp fiction had
she been given the opportunity to possess a mother tongue and if
she had not become a primary detective—also known as a psychoanalyst. And an analyst she was, in any event, and without a doubt,
even when she appeared to forget that enigmas still remain and
when she rushed to apply a ready-made body of knowledge that she
had developed in her earlier investigations. Still, even when she
pushed the templates of her systems too far, she laid anxiety bare—
and, as with Richard—she did so with a perfect aim and a magic
touch in order to trace more effectively the labyrinth of thought.

7

THE PHANTASY AS A METAPHOR INCARNATE

THE REPRESENTATIVE BEFORE REPRESENTATION

No matter how far back Klein reaches into childhood, she always discovers a fantasizing ego. A sundry entity made up of verbal and nonverbal representations, sensations, affects, emotions, movements, actions, and even concretizations, the Kleinian phantasy is a wholly impure theoretical construct that defies the purists as much as it fascinates clinicians, particularly those who specialize in children, psychosis, or the psychosomatic disorders. And yet Melanie Klein never explicitly reconciled her various approaches to the term *phantasy*—in fact, it was an article written by her disciple Susan Isaacs that pursued that subject and rendered it credible.[1]

As a way to highlight the originality of Klein's concept in the context of the famous Controversial Discussions that shook up the British Psycho-Analytical Society between 1941 and 1945,[2] Susan

Isaacs proposed the spelling "phantasy" in order to denote the psychic activity preceding the repression that interested Klein and to differentiate the phantasy from the daydreams, conscious or repressed, that psychoanalysts have traditionally placed under the rubric of "fantasy." In Isaac's view, "phantasy is (in the first instance) the mental corollary, the psychic representative, of instinct. There is no impulse, no instinctual urge or response which is not experienced as unconscious phantasy."[3]

Freud believed that fantasies did not begin before the second or third year of life, and he in fact conceived of fantasies in terms of his model of the dream. In *The Interpretation of Dreams*, Freud proposed a model of the psychic apparatus that describes it as a "locality" and compares it to a "photographic apparatus" that produces an image.[4]

Between the twin markers of perception and motivity, the psychic apparatus is made up of three types of memories: unconscious memories (the deepest and oldest ones), preconscious memories (the verbal and intermediary ones), and conscious memories. The dreamlike reverie known as the fantasy has what Freud considers to be a *regressive* character: the stimulation regresses to it and follows a retrograde path such that, rather than moving toward an extreme motivity, it approaches sensory extremity. "We call it 'regression' when in a dream an idea is turned back into the sensory image from which it was originally derived."[5] Although Freud emphasized that *vision* and the *visual* memory are particularly appealing to unconscious thoughts and thus enable them to be expressed, he never forgot that the *totality of sensory domains* is what is mobilized in the dream and, by extension, in the fantasy. Freud even expressed regret that his own dreams "are in general less rich in sensory elements than I am led to suppose is the case in other people."[6] Perhaps that explains why his notion of fantasy does not really incorporate these sensory elements.

By staging our unconscious desires, Freudian fantasies are fantasies of *desires* (*Wünschen*), with the first desire being the hallucinatory investment of the *memory of gratification*. To those fantasies Freud adds "primal phantasies"[7] that are more enigmatic and that contain prehistoric truths that the individual does not necessarily experience himself, but that unconsciously reappear in him to fill in the holes (as well as the fantasies of the primal scene, of castration, or of seduction).

The richness and multilayered meanings of Freud's insights here have been extended in various ways. Lacan was drawn to the visual side of the fantasy; he developed, through his notion of the mirror stage, an optic model that encompassed his own theory of the fantasy—which he claimed was faithful to Freud's—and implicitly disagreed with Klein's theory of the fantasy during a seminar devoted to a critique of her work.[8] Lacan considered the eye to be the symbol of the subject, one that emerges *before* the birth of the ego. He described the onslaught of fantasies that spawned Klein's interpretations in her case study of little Dick[9] as "grafts"[10] that functioned through the analyst's speech: Mrs. Klein's "signifier," which proposes equivalences (of the sort "the train is your father"), is what stood the subject Dick in good stead and allowed him to *see* his unconscious desires and to travel down the path of speech.

This Lacanian critique is helpful because it illuminates one of the ways in which Klein's method is effective: Lacan highlights the effect of verbalization on the unconscious fantasy. For a child who understand language but who does not yet know how to speak—that is, a child who has *language* but not *speech*—the analyst's naming of his fantasies helps him shift from a mental universe based on *identities* (the identity of the father and the train, as suggested by Dick's playful actions) to a universe based on similarities (the similarity between the father and the penis, as was believed and put into words by the analyst)—and thus places the child in the realm of the imaginary.[11] In treatment, this shift in domain (from *identity* to *similarity*) occurs with the help of the analyst's speech. In Lacan's view, Klein's speech had the effect of facilitating Dick's access to play, which until that point had remained rudimentary at best; Klein also exposed him to the domain of the symbolic, that is, to the domain of the thought that she articulated. The imaginary and the symbolic were therefore able to rise to the level of the young patient's drive-based real—in the same way that, in the mathematical logic of the optical realm, the real and the imaginary become one, which must be stated explicitly. Though this visionary critique is thorough and appealing, it says nothing about the sundry nature of the fantasy, at least not in the context of Klein's own conception as she projects herself onto her own *regressive* unconscious before giving it a sort of name—in a mythical way, it turns out, and in a way that is heavily laden with the drives.

It is true that the term *projection,* as it is used here, reflects the optical excess that Lacan correctly highlighted as part of his emphasis on the role of the *eidos*—of the idea—in the appearance of the drive in the fantasy, a role that had been neglected by his predecessors' naïve empiricism. Lacan's refocus on the metaphysical foundations of representation comes at the cost, however, of retreating from the world of the Kleinian fantasy/phantasy.

"At first," as Susan Isaacs puts it, "the whole weight of wish and phantasy is borne by sensation and affect."[12] It is true that if we read closely, as does Jean-Michel Petot, the first analyses of children that Klein recounted in *The Psychoanalysis of Children,* we will be inclined to agree with Isaacs's conclusion. The unconscious or preconscious fantasy is present in all psychic activities and behaviors, so much so that the fantasy is an "active presence of fantasy scenes."[13] Such a fantasy is, strictly speaking, bound up with motivity, taste and food aversions, the sharpness of the perception (particularly the visual perception) of the primal scene, the image of the body, voice-song-and-speech, sporting activities, concert-show-and-film attendance, educational and intellectual activities, neurotic symptoms, and, in the end, the entire organization of the personality. Not only is the totality of psychic life *impregnated* with fantasies, but in the children whom Klein listened to and analyzed, the fantasy—that is, the fantasy that precedes repression—is *united* with psychic life because this fantasy and this life, "the representatives of the earliest impulses of desire and aggressiveness, are expressed in and dealt with by *mental processes far removed from words* and conscious relational thinking."[14]

This brings up one of the most difficult problems in psychoanalytic theory, one that Klein's clinical approach addressed creatively without theorizing the concept as such, thereby leaving it to her successors to explore a subject that is the focus of current psychoanalytic inquiry: what is *psychic representation*? Or, put another way, what are *the* psychic representations?

Because Klein returned to the "whole weight of sensation and affect" in the primary fantasy, she could justly boast of her faithfulness to Freud's thought. Isn't it true that Freud, a few pages after he compares the psychic apparatus to a photographic apparatus in his *Interpretation of Dreams* (1900), outlines the regressive "trace" of sensation? Similarly, the Kleinian "phantasy" includes by implication the memory traces described in "A Note upon the 'Mystic Writing-Pad' " (1925)[15] without being identical with them, and her "phantasy" adds such traces to the "photographic apparatus" in the sense of a model of psychic representation. Still, as compared with the amalgam of *diverse domains of representation* that define the Kleinian phantasy (sensations, affects, gestures, actions, verbal and nonverbal representations, and even the concretizations themselves to which fantasies and psychotic suffering are sometimes reduced—and that is just the beginning), Freud's notion of the "representation" of the drive in the psychic apparatus connotes a meaning that is far more "diplomatic"[16] than is Klein's. Put another way, the Kleinian phantasy includes elements that emerge before representation or without it altogether, elements that her followers would seek to conceptualize. Lacan, for his part, adopted a decidedly Greek approach by shifting psychic representation toward the appearance and toward the visibility of the *eidos*. Psychoanalysis today focuses on this clinical and conceptual exploration of the transverbal archaic realm that Melanie brought to our attention, a realm that belies ideal or visual representation.[17]

It is true that both Isaacs and Klein use the term *fantasy*, a term whose etymology clearly evokes appearance-presence-and-vision, but both women distance the term from its Greek etymological and metaphysical origins and saturate it instead with the reality of drives and with such primary "contained" contents as greed and envy. What is more, the *sensation of a drive* in the psychic apparatus is automatically associated with the fantasy of an *object* that is appropriated to it, with each incitement of the drives having its own corresponding fantasy (the desire for food, for example, is associated with the affect of hunger and the breast object). From the moment of birth, the drive engages in a binary expression: sensation/affect[18] and the object both *coexist*, and the presentation of the object clings to sensation. The Kleinian phantasy is the mechanism of this juncture, of the drives' destiny to be both inside and outside: it is an "object-seeking" drive.[19]

Fantasies are not content simply to incite the drives, for they also play a defensive role by producing feelings of gratification that are independent of reality—and that may even deteriorate reality. Such feelings reinforce the omnipotence of the ego and allow it to defend itself against its own destruction (in this sense, the fantasy of being attacked by the "bad" breast is a defense against the feeling of destroying oneself by attacking the "good" breast).

Because of this protopresence of the fantasy and this protopresence of the ego, the destiny of the drive is not circumscribed by the conditions of an external reality. This brings up a central feature of Klein's theory: with regard to psychic life, fantastical fear and anxiety have a greater impact than does the *real* separation between mother and child, regardless of whether such separation is enduring, dramatic, or neither of the two. The fantasy—by representing not reality, but the duo of "drive *and* internal object" and "sensation/affect *and* object," and by anticipating the future while overestimating the threats that future poses—transforms *deprivation* into *frustration*. From that point on, a degree of negativity informs the fantasy-like activity, one that goes through several stages before it accesses the capacity to symbolize through language and thought. According to the whims of the object relation, such reinforced negativity generates a *series of fantasies*: sadistic, paranoid-schizoid, manic, and depressive fantasies that pave the way for an optimal representation of the drives by working through them, that is, by integrating split-off objects and the reinforcement of the ego. In Klein's view, the fantasy is still wholly bound up with the constants of the unconscious: anxiety, greed, and gratitude.

Is the fantasy a metaphor? It most certainly is, in the sense that it replaces one object by another or condenses one object into another. Still, Melanie Klein was not enamored of the simple rhetorical trope of the metaphor, nor was she drawn to plays on words. Instead, she preferred the axis of similarity that provides a space for the sort of metaphoric substitution that occurs in the fantasy (for example, the "train" as a replacement for "papa" and the "penis"). The therapist posited, in fact, that a comparable anxiety of destruction comes on the heels of a repressed libido: the same sort of anxiety latches on to "papa," the "train," and the "penis" and permeates the entire sequence or condensation of the series of objects and words that are fungible in the child's imaginary. This logical process stems from the omnipresence of an Oedipus conflict in which the desire for the mother and the feelings of rivalry toward the father are fused together by the death drive.[20]

Furthermore, when Melanie Klein interpreted her patients' fantasies—in both children and adults—she was simply describing to them the Oedipus myth as embellished by a primordial and destructive sadism. As a result, the meaning of the fantasy that she "grafted" upon them is not a random "signifier" that symbolizes the more or less dichotomous chaos of drives by introducing them into the tripartite structure of linguistic signs. On the contrary—and this point is important—the goal is to inscribe the fantasy in an *oedipal container* that surrounds the autonomy of the subject as well as in the prevalence of the *death drive*, whose ambiguity never failed to impress Klein because it is clearly destructive but also, under certain conditions, highly constructive. It should come as no surprise, then, that the theorist does not speak of "primal fantasies": no matter how diverse Kleinian phantasies may be as they respond to the various "positions" that they reflect, they are intrinsically "primal" and are brought about by an extremely early Oedipus conflict and by the permanence of the death drive.

Interpretations by the analyst herself, which are bound up in transference and countertransference, are an integral part of the fantasy under analysis. Interpretation is the upper psychic face of the fantasy—its symbolic elaboration into a *myth* or a *body of knowledge* (as myths are our archaic bodies of knowledge, and our bodies of knowledge concerning human essence can never be completely separated from myths). In the end, in fact, through the uncanny encounter that occurs in treatment between the child's fantasy-play (or the adult patient's associative fantasy) *and* the analytic interpretation moored in the Oedipus complex and the death drive, the fantasy adopts all the features of a metaphor *incarnate.*

"PRENARRATIVE ENVELOPES" BETWEEN ANXIETY AND LANGUAGE

Recent studies inspired by cognitive science appear to confirm Klein's hypothesis of a proto-fantasy in the baby in the sense of a quasi-narration that articulates the drive and desire and that hones in on the object (the breast, the mother) to ensure the survival of the phobic and sadistic young ego.

In children under a year old, it is true that one can observe "generalized event representations," "story schema," or "cognitive affective models" that, from the beginning, adopt the form of a "prenarrative envelope."[21] Such an envelope reflects a subjective reality that is primarily affective and that displays the logical properties of the drive: desire (or motivation), an aim, its realization, an unraveling in time, repetition, an association of memories, a line of dramatic tension tantamount to a primal story, and so forth. As an emotional, physical, and already subjective experience that bases itself on drives that function in an interpersonal context, this prenarrative envelope is thus a mental construction that emerges from the "real" world; it is an "emergent property" of thought. Under this framework, various "centers" tasked with controlling a host of mental processes (sensations, the needs of the drives, motivity, language, place, time, and so forth)—also known as parallel distribution processing, or PDP—are able to coordinate themselves at a higher level by integrating with a unified event whose structure is similar to the structure of narration.

Just as generative grammar theory posited the existence of

innate linguistic *competence* (with a limited matrix for each utterance: subject-verb-object) that is manifested later on in the form of grammatical *performances* that follow the rules of a given language, our current understanding is that a basic, if not innate, narrative structure begins to take shape from the moment of the newborn's first drive-based interactions. From that perspective, "prenarrative envelopes" are accompanied by "cognitive representations" that are neither a pure experience nor a pure abstraction but intermediaries between the two. The fantasy, then, is a cognitive representation of a narrative envelope experienced in real time.

This theoretical insight is quite appealing, but we must keep in mind that the analytic experience that it draws upon also reveals that the fantasy (and thus the narrative envelope itself) is inscribed in an emotional context that must precede any realization of the fantasy sequence. More specifically, the fantasy acts in this way through the oral-anal-genital destructive drives to which it is inextricably linked. Put another way, the prenarrative sequence that characterizes the formal logic of the fantasy depends on the possibility of expressing—or of not expressing—this destructiveness. On the one hand, the child manifests such destructiveness, and on the other hand, the mother recognizes it through its conduit, which is the death drive. The famous case study of young Dick demonstrates this point brilliantly.

Kleinian and post-Kleinian clinical practice, which has proved that a narrative thought is contained in the protofantasy, is founded not upon the locus of early narrative logic but on the locus of the *primary anxiety* that is a precondition for thought, provided that the object acknowledges it and rejoices in it (by way of the mother, or, even better, the analyst).

We also witness such *excessive anxiety* when we encounter modifications in the canonical narrative scheme, whether they be in a patient's free associations or in a novelist's technique. At the same time, moreover, the psychoanalytic experience shows us that the protofantasy, as a "prenarrative envelope" of an "emergent property" requires the *speech of the other* before it can become a *fantasy*. Although it is true that Klein emphasized the preverbal and affective side of the narrative envelope known as the fantasy, she also linked it—through the very intervention of the analytic framework—with the analyst's verbal interpretation, which in turn, through the help of the analyst's own words, guides prenarration toward the narrated fantasy itself. Indeed, the narrative that consists of the therapist's named fantasy, which interprets the protofantasy enacted by the child, raises the child's emergent thought to a third level: a level that shall be termed *symbolic*, one in which primary anxiety, recognized and restored as such in the narrative of interpretation, encounters optimal conditions for the child's own narration to prevail before other forms of thought even enter the picture.

Although the notion of the Kleinian phantasy as a metaphor incarnate allows us, as we have seen, to appreciate the uniqueness of both the childlike fantasy and the psychotic fantasy and to appreciate their heterogeneity—its representations and "concretizations"—this notion also presents risk. And they are significant ones: in analytic treatment, the danger is in underestimating the metaphoric meaning of the fantasy—to see only the reality of substantiated objects and to ignore the role of metaphor, that is, to ignore this imaginary metaphoricity and to remain stuck in a psychological realism. In that case, the analyst would succumb to the symbolic equations of psychosis and might even run the risk of encouraging psychosis itself because he has deprived himself of the necessary means to transform those equations into an effective symbolization.

The Controversial Discussions[22] highlighted these pitfalls, and a close reading of the Kleinians' rebuttal suggests that both Melanie and her followers were cognizant of this possibility. The Kleinians distinguish between the patient's imaginary and the analyst's imaginary, the latter being quite fruitful, in their estimation, because it is the privileged material of analytic work as practiced with varying degrees of grace in the space between the boundaries of psychotic concretizations, and because it reflects predisposition to adapt to a normative reality. The Controversial Discussions also appear to have arrived at just the right time to usher in this enlightenment, an enlightenment that would not have occurred without the intervention of the debates—even if these dangers still endure, and even if many practitioners still confuse the domains of the real, the imaginary, and the symbolic, which Lacan later distinguished with much fervor.[23]

Other analysts have taken the precaution of distinguishing the various interpretive domains of analytic treatment in the light of the regressive psychic movement toward the drive and the senses. This demand for rigor is reflected in the work of Bion, who supported an analytic theory rooted in a metaphoric language that describes psychic reality. Because Bion feared that such a language might itself induce people to confuse the domains, he relied on such abstract notions as L, H, and K: "(1) X loves Y; (2) X hates Y; and (3) X knows Y. These links will be expressed by the signs L, H and K."[24] Motivated by a similar concern, Winnicott emphasized that psychic phenomena are processes, a notion he insisted upon to the point of abusing the gerund form: being, living, dreaming, fantasizing. . . . At root, however, both men remained loyal to Klein's conception of a primary—if not primitive or primal—psychic functioning that is manifested in the mental experience of the baby and of the psychotic through such terms as Winnicott's "primitive retaliation" and Bion's "nameless dreads," or through what they both considered to be formlessness or a "thing-in-itself."

Did the confrontation with this fantasy-like primary universe result from the psychoanalyst's regression? Did it stem from a theoretical deficiency that was compensated for by the imagination of the therapist, who became troubled by the enigmatic functioning of a baby or of a psychotic who resists verbalization? Or, on the contrary, did Klein's empirical forays reflect the intrinsic need for analytic listening because the fantasy is the one true object of every analyst? It is only by accompanying the analyst's own fantasy with an image of itself that the analyst can guide the patient, always incompletely, toward psychic truth and encourage the patient's encounter with reality. That process does not, for all that, inspire a skepticism about the knowledge of the human experience but, rather, the certainty that the imaginary is the very locus of truth, without which truth would be bound up with repression.

On the other hand, those who try to ignore the fantasy—either by vitiating it by contracting it or by undervaluing the imaginary—are doomed to be unable to hear the unconscious material whose only means of appearing is in the fantasy itself. At best, such analysts can listen to the material in their clinic, but they will resist it through their religiously purified theories. It is worthy of note that it was women (Klein, Isaacs, and Heimann) who had the courage in this debate to emphasize the role of the fantasy in the process of knowledge, while men such as Bion, Winnicott, and, in his own way, Lacan were left using the symbolic to curb the imaginary. Not only did Klein work *on* the imaginary (of the child) and *in* the imaginary (of the analyst), but her work was so deep and intense that the interaction between the two imaginaries (the child's and the analyst's) as they focus on bodies and their acts can only give the impression that we are digging into our guts in the manner of "an inspired gut butcher," as Lacan once quipped.

Perhaps we should seek a more empathetic approach to Klein's fantastical forays into fantasies. By placing herself as close as possible to *frustration*—rather than to *gratification*, Klein did not fail to substantiate the unconscious, which from a certain perspective she could be accused of doing. On the contrary, she reclaimed this anamorphosis of the body into the mind, of sensations and affects into signs, and vice versa—an anamorphosis in which the word "imaginary" remains far too one-dimensional, but also one for which Christianity has invented the term *incarnation*. "Melanie Klein was able to give life to the unconscious, and metaphor absorbs its incarnate features."[25]

And yet Klein rejected the idealist and idealizing tendencies of the version of Christianity that uses the logic behind incarnation to repress the body and sex in the name of spirituality. In its place, she revived flesh within the word, and she privileged the body of drives and passions within the imagery and symbolism that weave patients' fantasies together.

Among all the tributes to the genius of Christianity that have accompanied the advent of its third millennium, one tribute has been ignored: by situating itself in the space in which the Word is turned into flesh, and vice versa, the Christian experience has embarked on a journey to the end of night in which words and things become one. Is this a mystery of the unintelligible or rather an acknowledgment of psychosis? Because Christianity was established on the frontier between the two—a frontier that it subsequently reflected upon—it can lay claim to a certain universalism and can subsume the other religions. Psychoanalysis may well be the only thing that acknowledges this challenge to Christianity, for psychoanalysis is based on a model of the psychic apparatus that incorporates sexuality and acts through transference love.

What is known as Freud's "Copernican" revolution does not reside solely in the wound that Freud struck at the heart of man-God by ousting our mastery of consciousness through the unconscious logic of desire. Even more radically, psychoanalysis seeks to inscribe language and thought in the sexual drive, including in its biological substratum. The Kleinian phantasy hastens this recasting of the dualism between body and soul. By positing that flesh-and-soul are forever linked in the heart of the human being, psychoanalysis surpasses its strictly clinical and sometimes excessively ideological strains. Even if it is difficult for us to admit, psychoanalysis partakes in an indispensable strain of modern thought that has endeavored, for more than a century, to effect a gradual and yet audacious dismantling of metaphysics, beginning with its dichotomous categories (body and soul, subject and object, space and time, and the like). From that perspective, the way Klein listens to the fantasy and then interprets it appears to reflect this deconstruction of metaphysics that is of particular interest to the post-Catholic debate between psychoanalysis and metaphysics. We still must acknowledge, however, that the myth of Christian incarnation has already attempted to reorganize metaphysical dualism: the body of the Man of Sorrow is a soul, and the soul is a body in the dynamic of transubstantiation. By rendering Freud radical, Klein relies on all of her therapeutic sense to transform this myth and its deconstruction into care and respect for the other. The fantasy seems indeed to be both the object (the patient's fantasy) and the Archimedean point (the analyst's fantasy) of this experience.

Despite these formal psychoanalytic and philosophical advances, however, we still have a long way to go before we can describe how the analyst's verbalized fantasy, which is shared through transference and countertransference, encourages the subsequent modification that transforms the prenarrative envelope into a named and playful fantasy. Through the narrative recounted by the child, it also frees up the internal logic of narration—as well as the internal logic of nonnarrative, scientific, and theoretical manifestations.

DO WOMEN HAVE AN AFFINITY FOR THE ARCHAIC?

To the extent that the fantasy is the psychic *representative* of the drive, which we have already seen, it is important to understand that the term *representative* as the Kleinians use it, has a dual meaning. In the first instance, the fantasy is a representative of the drive because it is a "transposition"—or rather an "outgrowth"—that precedes the idea and language and that corresponds to the Freudian term *Repräsentant*. Only then does the representative become an ideal representation that corresponds to the Freudian term *Vorstellungsrepräsentant*. We have also seen that Klein's phantasy, more so than Freud's or other analysts' notion of the fantasy, is sensitive to—and even privileges—the primary meaning of preverbal representation.

This interest in what is primary and what is organic is not the exclusive domain of Melanie and her disciples. Throughout the history of psychoanalysis, a number of female therapists have highlighted the way organic experience informs psychic life: think of Eugenia Sokolnicka and Marie Bonaparte, just to name the most prominent analysts in France, as well as the modern psychosomaticians who followed them. Although this is not an exclusively female theme, women's interest in the organic, which is accompanied by their strong countertransferential impulse, is worthy of our attention.[26] If we keep in mind Klein's contributions to the understanding of female sexuality and the fantasy, and if we reevaluate the contributions that have succeeded her, we can better understand why female sexuality—and not just the female body subjected to the ovarian cycle and to maternity—fosters women's affinity for the archaic. And we can also understand how this attraction, provided it does not get too bogged down in a facile and unfortunately all too common organicist complacency, can serve as the driving force for an analysis conceived as psychic rebirth.

At first, the little girl is attached to her mother and seduced by her mother. As the child's mother-container and the father's wife-lover, this initial presence is inscribed in the girl through an Oedipus conflict that I shall term "Oedipus I." Freud considered this primary attachment to be a lost archaeology that is almost inaccessible, much like the Mino-Mycenaean period before ancient Greece, an attachment that is experienced as a sort of idyllic, self-sacrificing osmosis. And yet we now know, thanks to Melanie Klein and subsequent observers, that Oedipus I, as a consequence of the death drive, is heavily laden with an anxiety and aggression that taints the effects of dependence and reassuring protection with the fear of corporeal and psychic catastrophe for both the daughter and her mother. Oedipus I, which is always forthcoming although it lacks speech, is dominated by sensation: mouth to nipple, mouth to mouth, skin to skin, and sounds and smells that bathe the "between-women" that leave indelible traces, for better or worse. Oedipus I is at first consumed with orality, and then with anality along with urethral drives and an early perception of the vagina that results from an ambivalence toward the woman who is not yet an object, but an *ab-ject*, a magnet of gratification and repulsion. At the same time, when the mother's care is optimal, this sensory intensity is turned into an act of sublimation that appeases the erotic and thanatotic goals of the affects while treating them with great tenderness. As the zero degree of an act of sublimation that will return in the form of female sexuality's tendency toward amorous or aesthetic idealization, sensuality, along with affects filtered into tenderness, can serve as a starting point for repression. Such repression is a symptom of hysterical excitability, which means it is a malleable repression ridden with sensuality, if not sentimentality.

Through the depressive position, the little girl is able to deem the absence of the mother to be a lost whole object. During the phallic phase, the girl changes objects and lays the foundation for her "Oedipus II." What Klein neglects to mention about this process, of course, is that the little girl identifies with her father just as the boy does, although the girl does so in a different way—a way that evinces a type of splitting.

On the one hand, the girl identifies with the father as a Phallus, as a symbolic occurrence that exerts power on the mother through its absence and presence just as it contains a visible and detachable object: the penis. The little girl sees a penis on her own father or perhaps on her brother, and the penis itself becomes an object of desire that is no longer an object inside the mother but an external object of desire for both the mother and the daughter. As the daughter detaches from the mother, she projects hateful feelings toward the female parent—a castrated mother—who did not deprive her of that organ. By tainting the link to the mother with depression, this devaluing of the female encourages the abandonment of the mother as an object of desire in exchange for phallic identification.

In the girl, phallicism is preceded by her love and envy of the mother during Oedipus I. At this point, during the phallic stage, and motivated by the detachment from the mother that accompanies the depressive position, this phallicism appears under the form of an *investment of signs and thought.* The girl appreciates the function of the father, whose authority goes beyond the sensory realm of daily life, and she learns as a result to see her male parent as the primary referent of invisible power, the power of thought. The phallic stage thus orchestrates a surprising encounter between the perception of the father's symbolic authority, the symbolism of language, and the male organ's characteristic qualities of being detachable, "guilty," susceptible to loss, present and absent, turgid and flaccid, and so forth. The logic of the symbolism based on presence and absence and on the binomial 0/1 tests itself out in the realms of eroticism as well as of representation, with the penis becoming the support for this meaning-generating difference, that is, the organic factor in our psychosexual computer. The child becomes a subject once she separates herself from the object: it is here, during the phallic stage of the Oedipus complex that solidifies the depressive position, that we can properly speak of an "object" for a "subject," as all objects signify a subject. At the same time, the father's function is submitted to authority and absence, and the phallus's function is submitted to the battle between power and castration. The result for the subject is that the phallic stage joins sexuality and thought in a way that melds together the unity of its structure as a structure of desire and inquiry and as a quest for libidinal gratification and thinkable curiosity.

Still, although the little girl plays along with the game of this phallic identification—a game that is so decisive for her becoming a subject—she, unlike the boy, feels distant from its dynamic. The girl, for her part, lacks the penis that provides a focal point for the phallic encounter that structures the thinking subject: the clitoris offers only a small-scale equivalent of the penis, and, whatever pleasure it may give her, it remains invisible and unrecognizable. Accordingly, in the phallic-symbolic world that brings on the depressive position, the little girl—the woman— remains an exile. She projects herself onto that world, but she "does not belong to it": she does not believe in it, or, rather, she *pretends* to "belong to it" and to believe in it. She experiences all this "belonging" or "belief," of course, as a sort of masquerade, costuming, disguise, and state of nonbeing. A stranger to the phallic-symbolic universe, she relies on her memory, which becomes increasingly unconscious because it is repressed, of Oedipus I, a Mino-Mycenaean memory of love-and-hatred toward the maternal *ab-ject*. Estranged from the realm of fathers and the communal social bond that is a symbolic bond, she is the "eternal irony of the community" that Hegel described, a more or less avowed nonbeliever, surely a mystic, loyal *and* disloyal. And, because she often experiences her ambiguous appearance through her sadomasochism, she is also a stranger to the phallic-symbolic law of the fathers, one of which she partakes without ever being a part.

That said, and even as the girl remains with the phallic-symbolic side of things in order to become a *subject* who speaks and thinks like the others (and often even more rigorously than boys, inhibited as they are by their rivalry with their fathers), she changes objects. Although the girl is a subject of the phallic law and of language and thought, she chooses the penis as an object of desire. Her choice is no longer the mother who contains the penis (as was the case during Oedipus I) but the penis of the man himself (which marks her Oedipus II). Heterosexuality is the consequence of this *new* choice, one that the girl acquires if she is able to get beyond her envy of her father and to detach herself from her Oedipus I. During Oedipus II, then, the girl desires to take her mother's place, that is, to reap a child from her father just as her mother had once obtained a child from him.

Oedipus I (love-hatred for the mother who possesses the penis), followed by the dual movement of Oedipus II (phallic-symbolic identification *and* a desire for the father's own penis): what Freud called psychic bisexuality, which he believed was more pronounced in women than in men,[27] is shaped *in* and is explained *by* the ambiguity of the changes in psychic posture that occur throughout the woman's development. This complex movement helps explain the uncanny maturity exhibited by certain women who manage to achieve psychic bisexuality, in contrast to the immaturity of men who remain attached to their mothers. But it also helps explain the psychosexual difficulties that most women experience and the multiple failures that keep them inside the excitability of hysteria, the throes of depression, or, most commonly, frigidity. Freud, who remained baffled by all this, asked, "What does a woman want?" It is true that, from the maternal *ab-ject* through phallic-symbolic identification and to the change in object that makes the woman choose the father instead of the mother as an erotic partner, one might very well ask, "Where might we find a woman's object of desire?" Melanie never posed this question, as she believed that female desire, more than any other desire if such a thing were even possible, is dominated by anxiety.

Motherhood forces the woman to confront a new way of experiencing the object: the child, her first real presence, is neither an *ab-ject* (the Mino-Mycenaean mother) nor an object of desire (the penis/phallus), but the *first Other*. Or at least the child is capable of being such, as he encourages his mother's tendency toward sublimation that was already enhanced by the symbolic side of the phallic phase through its inhibiting the goal of the drive and directing it instead toward language and culture. From that point on, the child becomes a harbinger of an alterity that provides female narcissism one last chance to abandon its focus on the self and the mother and to devote itself instead to the Other, that is, to the joys and sorrows of motherhood. It is true that the mother runs the risk at this point of closing herself off in the omnipotence of an androgynous matron (because she has captured the father's penis to make *her own* child, and even more so if that child is a boy!) who imagines herself to be fulfilled for the first time through the power that she exerts over her weak child—a child who will no doubt enable her to finally become "actualized." But she may also find herself forever weakened when she finally discloses her psychic bisexuality (which is nothing less than her incompleteness, the opposite of androgyny) by constantly experiencing her vulnerability with respect to the Other that she has delegated to the world, an Other who is separated from the start and is inherently impossible to master: her child, her love. The piteousness of this maternal mind-set should not prevent us from acknowledging its civilizing tendencies: this compassion toward the Other that allows the drive to renounce its goal of separation and to grant itself not an other goal, but *an Other*: simply put, a concern for revealing the Other. The child is the first other, and the experience of motherhood is its requisite appendage. It is an interminable experience that is utterly lacking and, for that reason alone, utterly sublime.

As the woman fulfills this maternal function, she comes back to her memory of her archaic bond with her mother as well as to her Oedipus I: she recalls her dependency on the other woman and her rivalry with her, and she recalls sensory communication and its primary sublimation, which make eroticism and anxiety its paramours. Motherhood—and, more broadly, the paternal function—form the basis of the caring attitude that transforms the erotic-thanatotic drive, that fundamentally sadistic desire that flings us toward the other, into the solicitude whose only goal—and it should not have any other goal—is to *allow one to live* in peace.[28]

Among all the therapists of human misery, the psychoanalyst is the one who most shares this maternal vocation, for he hears psychic pain in the suffering subject. The soul that emerges in the psychoanalytic experience, far from being an abstraction, is a soul of the desiring and hating body. To hear that soul, the act of listening must make itself a paramour of desire and anxiety, though by de-eroticizing the analysand who transports such desire and anxiety in order to create an *Other*: the patient is my "different," a different who lies at the edge of the very indifference that allows him to *think about* his truths rather than to merge with them. As a constant creation of alterity, psychoanalysis is also an alchemy that transforms anxious eroticism into tenderness. A tenderness with respect to what? To the truths of the Other in which I project myself and yet extricate myself, because those truths are other. As a man of science of law, Freud spoke not of "tenderness" but of "benevolence," and Melanie, for her part, invoked the sublimation that frees up intelligence and that explicitly formulates the logic of the drives that allows access to thought.

In this dynamic, a female analyst who does not censor her own female sexuality remains consumed by the psychic bisexuality mandated by both Oedipus I and Oedipus II. Such an analyst activates within herself—and hears in her analysand—a complex mixture of both the mother's sensuality and the eroticism/thought imposed by phallic identification as well as by its transformation into a feminine position that takes in the father's penis in order to obtain a child. The maternal archaic—the archaic of her own relationship to the maternal *ab-ject* and the archaic of the motherly role she plays for her child—allows her to access the complexity of psychic life as well as the space between drives and words, between thought and the sense. When a woman so constructed listens to or "thinks about" her patient, she is neither applying a system nor making a calculation. The logical process behind what has emerged as a phallic and symbolic computer, with its 0/1 grid, does not dominate here; instead, a striking imaginary coloring permeates our knowledge of transference and countertransference. Only then can the analyst be reborn and enable her analysand to be reborn. Psychic experience as a rebirth requires such access to all the domains of the psychic apparatus, including the transverbal maternal realm.

Does this force a regression to the archaic? It would be more accurate to call it an access to the translinguistic primary realm. A psychoanalyst—whether male or female—who claims to restore the psyche not as a system or structure but as the *psychic life* of the Other, is necessarily confronted with the feminine, even with the maternal inside him or her—the feminine and the maternal that the Kleinian phantasy constantly exposes the analyst to because of its heterogeneous configuration as a "metaphor" incarnate. Melanie's forays into the archaic laid bare this necessity, and her most creative students understood it as well: were Bion, Winnicott, Tustin, and others not watchful for the feminine and the sensory in them, as well as in us?

THE IMMANENCE OF SYMBOLISM
AND ITS DEGREES

In light of the early emergence of the ego and the superego, as well as the Oedipus conflict and incarnate fantasies, we now view the infant's psychic universe, as Klein conceived it, as being consumed from the start with a sort of primary symbolization, however rudimentary it may be. As much a generator of social bonds as it is defensive and inhibiting, such symbolization is destined to be modified before it reaches the level of what we call, in the strict sense of the word, a thought. In some people, that level is reached only with the help of psychoanalysis. Using some of Freud's essays as a starting point, Klein revived the notion of a rudimentary presence of a symbolization of the drives, so much so that she appears to have broken ranks with the founder, even though neither she nor her disciples ever stopped mentioning their link to the legacy left by that master. Such loyalty-combined-with-innovation, a constant in Melanie Klein's work, appears most prominently (often implicitly more than explicitly) with respect to symbolism and its stages, a concept that the Kleinians would later attempt to flesh out.

Klein's case study of Dick is helpful in tracing this evolution.

Dick was a four-year-old boy who was, in casual parlance, "slow." He could barely speak, seemed indifferent to the presence or absence of his mother and nurse, displayed no emotion when he hurt himself, had great difficulty manipulating knives and scissors, and had the intelligence level of a fifteen- to eighteen-month-old child (to the extent that one can have faith in such evaluations). The analyst described what both she and Dick's mother considered to be his "strong negative attitude,"[1] as "negativistic behaviour alternating with signs of automatic obedience."[2] Unlike the sort of neurotic child who is somewhat inhibited in his play but who is nevertheless capable of symbolizing relationships with objects (a child, say, like Fritz[3]), Dick displayed no affective relationship with the objects around him; he "called out" to no one, and his relations to his surroundings "were not coloured by phantasy."[4] The analyst diagnosed him as having schizophrenia (which she argued was more common in children than was typically believed), based on his display of "an inhibition in development" rather than "regression."[5] Contemporary clinicians would most likely see autistic features here, but, as Klein pointed out, her goal was not to commit herself "on the subject of diagnosis."[6] Most important for our purposes, in fact, is to follow the intensity of Klein's observations: the conclusions she draws about Dick's mental state and development, but also the more basic notions about the genesis of symbolism that she derives from this case.

Klein, who as we know was a student and analysand of Ferenczi's, adopted Ferenczi's view that at the heart of symbolism is *identification*, which is essentially the young child's effort to discover, within every external object, his own organs and their function. Ernest Jones had posited that the *pleasure principle* is what enables such identification to occur, an identification that is itself a precursor to symbolism. The *similarity* between the identified inside and outside is founded upon the *similar pleasure* that both of them generate. Klein distanced herself from Jones's view, however, as she claimed that it is not pleasure but *anxiety* that helps unleash the identification mechanism:

> Since the child desires to destroy the organs (penis, vagina, breasts) which stand for the objects, he conceives a dread of the latter. This anxiety contributes to make him equate the organs in question with other things; owing to this *equation*, these in their turn become objects of anxiety, and so he is impelled constantly to make other and new *equations*, which *form the basis* of his interest in the new objects and of symbolism.[7]

We should keep in mind the term *equation*—Hanna Segal subsequently differentiated between the old ones and the new ones by granting them a specific role in the two-stage symbolization process that she elucidated.[8]

In the primal and prominent sadism displayed by certain subjects (such as Dick), then, one can detect rudiments of symbolism that are ineffable and that can impede those subjects' access to the activity of the imaginary. Dick, for example, "had almost no interests [and] did not play."[9] Only the analyst could sense the rudiments of his sadistic fantasies—as we have seen, Winnicott spoke of "primitive retaliation" and Bion "nameless dreads." Melanie's approach was more biblical: she believed that states of battle and retributive justice dominate the universe of primary violence imposed by the death drive, even more ruthlessly so when that drive is excessive. A skeptical reader cannot help but wonder if Klein is mistaken here or if she was perhaps simply dreaming of herself. Or was it Dick who confirmed her hypotheses? And if so, what is the meaning of such a "confirmation?"

Melanie Klein's second conclusion invites only more questions: "The sadistic phantasies directed against the inside of [the mother's] body constitute the first and basic relation to the outside world and to reality."[10] In other words, if these fantasies are successfully manifested in language and play, they will create a fantasy-like reality with the external world, an "unreal reality" that "gradually" prepares for "a true relation to reality."[11]

In Klein's view, then, it is possible to distinguish between two degrees of symbolism, as reflected in her analysis of Dick. First, a *primary symbolism* of the drives that is rudimentary but that already obeys the logic of "equations" is borne out by Klein's 1946 conception of the mechanism of projective identification.[12] Second, a *symbolism of the named fantasy* uses the verbalization furnished by a third party (the analyst) as a way to establish an early means of negating anxiety (its *Verneinung*, its retrenchment, and the beginning of its repression) as well as a concomitant construction of a "true relation to reality" that replaces the "unreal reality" that the child had thus far found to be overwhelming. In 1934 Klein will link this logical thought process, which she laid out in painstaking detail, to her discussion of the depressive position, in particular to the way that position turns "equations" into the "symbol proper."[13]

What led Klein to begin drawing these conclusions in 1930? Dick resisted play and was indifferent to his surroundings. She concluded that it was important to change technique and first to overcome "this, the *fundamental* obstacle to establishing contact with him."[14] Relying heavily on her earlier work, particularly with Fritz, Melanie insinuated herself as if *she* were *he*: she decided to "graft," as Lacan put it,[15] Dick's presumed but silent fantasy onto the boy by formulating it herself:

> I took a big train and put it beside a smaller one and called them "Daddy-train" and "Dick-train." Thereupon he picked up the train I called "Dick" and made it roll to the window and said "Station." I explained: "The station is mummy; Dick is going into mummy." He left the train, ran into the space between the outer and inner doors of the room, shut himself in, saying "dark" and ran out again directly. He went through this performance several times. I explained to him: "It is dark inside mummy. Dick is inside dark mummy." Meantime he picked up the train again, but

soon ran back into the space between the doors. While I was saying that he was going into dark mummy, he said twice in a questioning way: "Nurse?"[16]

During the third session, Dick started looking at objects with some interest. The analyst detected an aggressive posture and offered him some scissors, but he was unable to use them. Melanie then tore off some pieces of wood attached to the car, "acting on a glance which he gave me," at which point Dick threw the destroyed car aside and said, "Gone." Klein remarks, "I told him that this meant that Dick was cutting faeces out of his mother."[17]

With extraordinary clinical insight, Klein associated the privative or negative sense of being "gone" with anal eroticism and the destruction of imagined fetuses inside the mother's body as being identical with excrements. The child emerged from his hiding place and immediately displayed a burgeoning curiosity for other toys, for the bathroom, and so forth. Everything is eternally linked, and equations multiply into other equations. Not until Klein's loyal disciple Hanna Segal did someone sort this whole mess out . . .

What was going on in the analyst's mind, and thus in the mind of the child?

In view of Dick's apathy, Klein hypothesized that he understood language even though he did not express himself. Accordingly, she decided to assume the role of the speaking subject, which implies that she believed Dick possessed two forms of linguistic competence: both a passive familiarity with language and a fantasy-like presymbolism, that is, an infralinguistic capacity to fantasize that accorded with the fantasies communicated by Melanie's speech. What Klein presumed to be preverbal fantasies were hardly innocent ones: they were oedipal fantasies (the same ones she observed in neurotic children who played and spoke, fantasies in conformance with Freud's paradigm), but in Dick's case, they were intensified with a violent sadism.

Based on what she knew about her young patient, Melanie offered the hypothesis (which will be later deemed a function of countertransference) that the mother's body incited enormous fear in Dick because he desired to attack it to empty it of the father's feces and from the feces that represented other children. In Dick, Klein believed, oral sadism (to which was linked urethral, muscular, and anal sadism) had become intensely exaggerated and had been replaced early on by genitality. This sadistic-and-genital joining with the maternal object (Dick had troubles nursing and suffered from early digestive problems, rectal prolapse, and hemorrhoids, and he had trouble learning to control his bowel movements) was aggravated by his mother's depression and, more generally, by the lack of love in his family, which was compensated for only in part by the affection his nurse showed him. Yet once she discovered that the child masturbated, she reprimanded him and made him feel guilty. Klein interpreted that guilt as an inhibition of sadism: Dick was incapable of expressing any sort of aggression and even refused to chew his food. "Dick's further development had come to grief because he could not bring into phantasy the sadistic relation to the mother's body."[18]

Melanie's ear picked up on the fact that Dick's oral desire for the penis had emerged early on as a major source of his anxiety:

We came to see this phantasied penis and a growing feeling of aggression against it in many forms, the desire to eat and destroy it being specially prominent. For example, on one occasion Dick lifted a little toy man to his mouth, gnashed his teeth and said "Tea daddy," by which he meant "Eat daddy."[19] He then asked for a drink of water. The introjection of the father's penis proved to be associated with the dread both of it, as of a primitive, harm-inflicting super-ego, and of being punished by the mother thus robbed: dread, that is, of the external and the introjected objects. And at this point there came into prominence the fact which I have already mentioned, and which was a determining factor in his development, namely, that the genital phase had become active in Dick prematurely. This was shown in the circumstance that such representations as I have just spoken of were followed not by anxiety only, but by remorse, pity and a feeling that he must make restitution. . . . Side by side with his incapacity for tolerating anxiety, this premature *empathy* became a decisive factor in his warding-off of all destructive impulses. Dick cut himself off from reality and brought his phantasy-life to a standstill by taking refuge in the phantasies of the dark, empty mother's body.[20]

Melanie Klein first attested to the child's desire for his father by seeing it as a combination of the young boy's feminine position as he assimilated the man's sexual organ with his mouth, on the one hand, and his oedipal desire to kill the rival who was his father, on the other. From that she concluded that Dick had reduced his mother to the space "between the doors" where it is "dark."[21] As she put it,

He had thus succeeded in withdrawing his attention also from the different objects in the outside world which represented the contents of the mother's body—the father's penis, faeces, children. His own penis, as the organ of sadism, and his own excreta were to be got rid of (or denied) as being dangerous and aggressive.[22]

The analyst formulated, in the first instance for *herself*, the fantasy of this cannibalistic aggression toward the-mother-and-the-father and restored it for the child through the verbal and playful mechanisms that she thought he was able to engage in. What she did was to make Dick understand that the darkness between the doors *was not* his mother, but merely *resembled* her—that it was a "signifier," as Dr. Lacan would later put it. In response, Dick began to acquire the capacity to signify and began to experience a world of similarities and *significance* and not of identities—a world of games and speech:

It had been possible for me, in Dick's analysis, to gain access to his unconscious by getting into contact with such rudiments of phantasy-life and symbol-formation as he displayed. The result was a diminution of his latent anxiety, so that it was possible for a certain amount of anxiety to become manifest.[23]

So are these sadistic "rudiments of phantasy-life"[24] present, but just not expressed as fantasies? Melanie expressed them herself: the trains are daddy and Dick, the station is none other than a mummy to be penetrated, to wreck the car is to destroy mummy by removing dirty objects from her tummy—she recites the very pages from the psychoanalytic bible that credits Freud and Klein herself for such opinions. Yet it is clearly these verbalizations, and nothing else, that freed Dick from his hiding place (from the "between two doors" that Melanie did not refrain from interpreting as a "black tummy"). And so Dick began to *call out for other people* (the nurse, to start with); he *looked for* toys; and he *washed himself* in the bathroom, which continued to be his mummy's body as well as his own. The world began to exist, as if it were created by the series of equations that arose out of the exchange between therapist and child. Dick could finally glean something out of the experience: the unnameable real had become a comforting imaginary. And this had occurred with the help of the analyst's speech. But would just anyone's speech have sufficed?

Certainly not. To begin with, there has to be a *third party*—in the sense of a different person, a stranger to the osmotic dyad—which is itself too self-contained or "empathetic" (as Klein puts it)—that the child had thus far engaged in with a disappointed or depressed mother. Neither the nurse nor the father nor any other person could have offered such words.

But that alone was not enough. This maximal alterity of the "subject-presumed-to-know"—the analyst—is realized through a speech that has a very specific content: a speech that tells and retells an oedipal myth with unusually aggressive connotations and that describes an oedipal sadism that targets "daddy in mummy's body." Dick desired to eat daddy in mummy by way of an Oedipus conflict that coveted the father's penis itself, especially as it was the noble "signifier" of the "Name-of-the-Father." That is what Klein was talking about with her "brute instinct." Still, the violence of the analyst's speech, which unknowingly took refuge in the signifier (though not to the point of ignoring the cannibalistic drive), is what unleashed Dick's oral and genital sadism: it was denied for what it was, but in the end it turned into psychic curiosity and thought.

One could always assume[25] that any sort of discourse would have sufficed because discourse, regardless of its form, uses the peaks and valleys of the signifier (with the alteration between presence and absence driving the very motor of the sign) to orchestrate the banging of the two doors between which the child was hiding. That would be an eminently unwise proposition, however, because what Melanie heard was not a random signifier, let alone an empty one, but the oedipal sexualization and the intense burden of the cannibalistic death drive: "Eat daddy" interchanged with "Tea daddy." By acknowledging these phenomena in transference and by grafting them onto Dick's play, the analyst got the child to acknowledge his anxiety and to represent it in the open space of transference itself, which is nothing less than the space of this particular interpretive speech.[26]

Dick was thus freed from his morbid oedipal anxiety because it was exposed to him by the Other. He became able to represent it to himself, even to hallucinate it, though not in the sense of a *hallucination of gratification* (which is the original Freudian connotation of the word hallucination) but a hallucination—a fantasy, it turns out—of *frustration*. "I cannot penetrate mummy and kill daddy inside her; that makes me frustrated; it's a game; it's just a game with Mrs. Klein; I play, therefore I think, therefore I am"—such would be the trajectory of the Kleinian syllogism as manifested in the link between play and interpretation.

The *verbal* recognition of oedipal anxiety introduced "difference" into the psychic apparatus. A breach of sorts shattered the osmosis that froze the child's fearful fascination with his mother. The verbalization of anxiety-on-top-of-pleasure is what sanctioned the ever-threatened state of entropy between mother and child. Interpretation created a gap in the lack of differentiation that accompanies the early identification based on pleasure and displeasure, an identification that existed between the mother and the child. As a result, the child could avoid the risk of a disintegrated ego and organism. The analyst's speech was a scansion that punctuated the ineffable hallucinatory continuity that had engulfed Dick.

To speak, as Klein does, about what Dick *hallucinated* he *had done* with daddy-mummy is not the same as to make it into a fantasy awaiting an audience. Solitary and unnameable, this silent fantasy gave the child a crippling sense of gratification. The analyst's words soothed her young patient's anxiety and aggression by offering him a chance to distance himself from them through speech and play. What the Other *said* endeavored to remove the dyads good/evil and identification/projection that underlay the ineffable fantasy—the rudiments of symbolization—of his "unreal reality" removed from the world. In its place, the fantasy was granted the status of a veritable psychic experience. It is true that the experience became a *psychic* one in the sense that it could be communicated between two complete and separated persons, between two subjects (Dick and Mrs. Klein) who acted outside the scene of the fantasy itself, although they were capable (and because they were capable) of transmitting the scene between them. That is what enabled Dick to enjoy a certain autonomy— and it is what instilled in him an "authentic reality" that carved out a space for the imaginary life of play. Before Dick's analysis, these *transpositions* were inhibited by *equations*: he could not enjoy them and did not express his fantasies. After Dick's analysis, the transpositions finally emerged because they were influenced by the symbols in the analyst's speech that also provided a place for the child. These *identities* were transformed into *similarities*, and they developed into a playful curiosity—and in the end an intellectual curiosity—about reality.

By intervening in two ways—through the *speech* of a third party and through the *recognition* of sadistic oedipal anxiety— interpretation soft-pedaled the defenses and splitting that to that point had formed the basis of the child's psyche. As verbalization came to acknowledge destructive drives, the inhibiting defenses that Dick had formed against those drives became neither as strong nor as necessary. Beforehand, the child had structured himself not on a model of repression but on a model of splitting.

This dual recognition of his aggressive Oedipus conflict *and* of the way his analysis verbalized that conflict modified the status of his fantasies. Put another way, the degree of symbolization that Dick attained afforded him a position as a subject of desire with respect to Mrs. Klein, who gradually replaced the static ego in its paranoid-schizoid passion for mummy.

Klein's accompaniment of Dick here, it would seem, participated in a trajectory of *negativity*, a notion that appears on two occasions in the analyst's case study when she refers to Dick's destructiveness, though she uses the term negativity in a more general sense here than do others and from an empirical rather than a theoretical perspective within the context of her own interventions aimed at driving out her patient's destructive negativity. Klein's goal, in fact, was to uncover Dick's negativism and, by reinforcing it with speech, to raise it to a higher level in which it denies its own status as negativism and transforms itself into a form of self-knowledge. This analysis led to a true evolution in the potential for thinking as well as a chance for a spiraling negativity to reverse itself into a positive form. Because of the destruction endemic to the rudiments of fantasy, negativity infiltrates the space of play (what Winnicott would later refer to as the "transitional space") made of fantasies that are verbalized by the analyst, that are seen as such by the patient, and that have the same effect as a removal of inhibitions that releases a form of playful, cognitive creativity.

A number of contributions by Klein's friends and disciples develop—more theoretically than did her own clinical genius— the logical components of the "work of the negative"[27] that the psychoanalyst had nevertheless pointed out and encouraged in her analysis of Dick in particular. Should we say that it was the work of the negative—that is, the work of the symbolization process—that enabled her to *give birth* through Dick? Because she made the child into a *creator* of symbols rather than a simple *user* of symbols?[28]

These studies lavish attention on the various features of the negative as reflected in the young child. Klein's disciples, as they returned to notions first advanced during the Great Controversial

Discussions of 1941–1955, emphasized the manifestations of the death drive in the experience of the young ego: "the force of death," "cruel suffering," "opening the floodgates of aggressive anxiety," "a desire for retaliation," "hostility," "a hatred that precedes love," "ordeals," "defenses against anxiety," "primary narcissistic anxiety," "a defiance of the object," "despair," and so forth. And yet, without being satisfied with these realist affirmations, these authors emphasized that this perceived negativity reflects a psychic reality that is intrinsically fantasy-like and thus "subjective," and that this subjectivity is by necessity a subjectivity of the observed object (the child) as well as of the agent of observation (the analyst).[29]

From that perspective—and this is the Kleinians' second important contribution—the Kleinians tried to set forth a theoretical foundation for the *stages* of the creation of symbolism and judgment, beginning with the fantasy and proceeding through the constitution of reality and of our knowledge of reality. Two of Freud's works, which received little attention at the time by the (Anna) Freudians themselves, provided a starting point for their own work: the section on "*Fort*" and "*Da*" in "Beyond the Pleasure Principle" (1920) and "Negation" (1925).[30] To summarize, through a concerted effort by a group of female Kleinians—for at that point all of the most important theorists were women—we have learned about the successive stages involved in getting beyond the fantasies of projective identification and thus unveiling the symbol proper, which is "felt to *represent* the object," as Hanna Segal put it.[31]

KLEIN ON NEGATIVITY

Susan Isaacs[32] elaborated upon Klein's thinking about the shift between the rudiments of symbolism and symbolism itself in the light of Freud's commentary on "*Fort*" and "*Da*." In rereading Freud, Isaacs painstakingly noted the degree to which the child identifies the presence or absence of the mother with the back-and-forth motion of the reel: the child plays this game by expressively uttering "o-o-o-o" ("*Fort,*" the German word for "gone") followed by a jubilant "*Da!*" (the German for "There!"). After having mastered the game, the child manages to find a way to make himself disappear: he crouches down in front of the large mirror that reaches down to the floor until his own image disappears, which is followed by a "long-drawn-out 'o-o-o-o.' "[33] Isaacs concludes that the emergence of language is preceded, though not in a linear way, by a generic continuity in which the mastery of the presence or absence of the object, which culminates in the mastery of the appearance or disappearance of the baby's own image, is a sine qua non for understanding language—which itself develops well before the active use of language.[34] Her conclusion serves as a good introduction to what will become Lacan's "mirror stage," but here it is portrayed as a process of a heterogeneous negativity consisting of movements, fantasized acts, and verbalization, and only then of scopic images.

In her commentary on Freud's "Negation" (1925),[35] Susan Isaacs develops in more detail the way the symbolic capacity is moored in an early corporeal and fantasy-like experience. She notes the following about Freud's essay:

Even the intellectual functions of judgement and reality-testing "are derived from the interplay of the *primary instinctual impulses,*" and rest upon the *mechanism* of introjection . . . : he also shows us the part played in this derivation by *phantasy.* Referring to that aspect of judgement which asserts or denies that a thing has a particular property, Freud says: "Expressed in the language of the oldest, that is, of the oral instinctual impulses, the alternative runs thus: 'I should like to take this into me and keep that out of me.' That is to say, it is to be either *inside me* or outside me." The wish thus formulated is the same thing as a phantasy.[36]

Isaacs goes on to conclude that, from the perspective of Klein and her disciples, what Freud called "picturesquely . . . 'the language of the oral impulse' " or, in other contexts, "the 'mental expression' of an instinct"[37] is the fantasy in the sense of "the psychic representatives of a bodily aim."[38] In Isaacs's view (which she supports with references to various cases studies on children that I have previously mentioned), an early, ineffable symbolism is founded upon "oral impulses, bound up with taste, smell, touch (of the lips and mouth), kinaesthetic, visceral, and other somatic sensations" because those drives, more than any others, are associated from the beginning with the experience of sucking and swallowing, of "taking things in."[39] As Isaacs puts it,

> The visual elements are relatively small. . . . The visual element in perception slowly increases, becoming suffused with tactile experience and spatially differentiated. The early visual images remain largely "eidetic" in quality—probably up to three or four years of age . . . : intensely vivid, concrete and often confused with perceptions . . . : for long intimately associated with somatic responses.[40]

Later in the developmental process, the visual begins to "predominate over the somatic," and the bodily elements "largely undergo *repression*," while the visual elements geared toward the outside world, themselves easily purged of sexuality and emotion, become an "image" in the strict sense of a representation "in the mind." The ego "realize[s]" that external objects exist and that their images are in "the mind."[41]

Paula Heimann,[42] for her part, focused on the repetition compulsion as a privileged manifestation of the death drive that was less "mute" than Freud believed.[43] She thus highlighted the continuity *and* the difference between, on the one hand, the "hallucination"—a means of primary symbolization and a model of fantasy as well as a source of thought[44]—and on the other hand, a thought in the strict sense of the word that is capable of perceiving reality once the ego extricates itself from the id.[45] After pointing out the similarities between the two processes (as evidenced by the genius of language that is reflected, for example, in the German word *Wahrnehmen* or in such words as *comprehend* and *apprehend* that describe an effect of perception), Heimann herself came back to Freud, who rooted judgment in "the rejection of stimuli." Put another way, perception is not merely reception, for it already comprises a sort of judgment that "functions as a barrier" against stimuli.[46] That is what is reflected in the mechanism of Freud's *Verneinung*: the patient can name sexual stimulation or confess to it only if he denies it (On: "You ask who this person in the dream can be. It's *not* his mother." We emend this to: "So it *is* his mother."[47]). The analyst, however, detects a more somatic and primary negativity in the language of taste itself. In that vein, Paula Heimann cites, as does Susan Isaacs,[48] the same passage of Freud's "Negation."

One can only admire the efforts on the part of Klein's compatriots to root her originality *in* Freud's work by developing a legitimate theory of thought that arises out of Freud's founding texts. The originality of their own work is quite striking, and we can better appreciate both its boldness and its limitations by comparing it with Lacan's own analyses ten years later.[49]

The Kleinians' focus was on the experience of the drives underlying vision: on the *Ausstossung* or *Verwerfung*, to use Freud's words, that precedes the scopic hold and that prefigures the *Bejahung* of judgment that takes place before the gaze and immediately through *taste*.[50] From the beginning Klein's disciples drew attention to two asymmetrical (as Jean Hyppolite would say) stages of symbolization: the fantasy anchored in the drive, and then the judgment of existence focused on reality. At the same time, the Kleinians did not set forth the conditions for true symbolicity (although Hanna Segal took a step down that road in her 1957 article), nor did they examine philosophically the character and the preexistence of the symbolic function in human beings. It was clearly in the wake of *Developments of Psychoanalysis*, which was published in 1952, and in a spirit of sneaking up on the "proponents of the new psychoanalysis,"[51] that Jacques Lacan and Jean Hyppolite attempted in 1954 to fill in the Kleinians' gaps through a display of remarkable intellectual bravado that brought philosophy into the analytic field. They did so, however, by setting aside the domain of *primary* symbolization, which they considered to be "mythical," and by questioning the omnipresence of the early Oedipus conflict so they could reformulate Freud's

Oedipus complex through their newfound theory of the Name-of-the-Father.

Hyppolite, the Hegelian, appears closer to the Kleinians in that he detected an "asymmetry"[52] in Freud between the *concrete attitude* of negation (*Verwerfung* and *Ausstossung*, which are prominent in the negativism of psychosis) and the *symbol* of negation. Hyppolite explains how, for Freud, the intellectual realm is dissociated from the affective one, although the affective realm is only "mythical"[53] because human beings are inscribed from the beginning in a "fundamental historicity."[54] Thinking emerges long before that point, in primary symbolization, but it does not appear there as such. An asymmetry is also present in the inner workings of a judgment of attribution ("this *is* good or bad") and a judgment of existence ("this *exists* in reality outside the scope of my representation," which reflects the distinction between representation and perception and between hallucination and reality). The judgment of existence presumes that "I" rediscover in "my" memory (and thus that "I" attribute myself to "me"—who thus becomes a "subject") a representation that *belongs* to an object and that *de-sign-ates* an absent object for the subject that "I" have become. Put another way, the judging subject cannot exist without a lost object: by relying on memory, "I" can signify the object only as it is—lost for the "ego" who, as a result of losing the object, is held out as a "subject." The interaction between the judgment of existence and the judgment of attribution forms the basis of intelligence, in the sense of a symbolic thought that is distinct from the imaginary or from the fantasy.

Thought always emerges under the aegis of the *Verneinung* that negates primary negation. A "negation of the negation"[55] is thus the essence of such thought, which is distinct from the hallucination, though it arises out of its foundations: it is a "dialectical" negation. *Verneinung* "might be the very origin of intelligence,"[56] but the realm of the intellect reflects a different sort of negativity: a "suspension" of the content of what has been repressed "for which the term sublimation is not inappropriate."[57] What Hyppolite is proposing here is a reading of Freud that accords with the Kleinians' views on the birth of the symbol proper. Hyppolite posits that affirmation through judgment is the *equivalent* of *Verneinung* (affirmation is its "Ersatz"[58]), whereas negation through judgment is the *successor* (*Nachfloge*) to the drive to destroy (*Destruktionstrieb*). Two mechanisms are at work here— "equivalent" and "successor," though the latter is better defined as a "suspension": "instead of being under the domination of the instincts of attraction and repulsion," the repressed content is "taken up and used again in a sort of suspension,"[59] which generates "a margin of thought . . . an appearance of being in the form of non-being."[60]

Lacan's reading, which has Heideggerean undertones, is uninterested in such degrees of symbolization. Instead, Lacan suggests more generally that "the primordial condition for something to emerge from the real and to present itself to the revelation of being"[61] is realized through *Verneinung*. Alongside this philosophical perspective, and in a more psychoanalytic vein, Lacan emphasizes *anal* ejection—which is a medium of externality and of the formation of an object from the outside—and offers the archetypal example of the Wolf Man (along with his female identification through the passive investment of anality). Lacan revives the *oral* domain so dear to the Kleinians, most curiously, through the case of the Brain Man. Lacan borrows this other clinical case from the analyst Ernst Kris. The patient, a plagiarizer, felt compelled to eat brains. During his first analysis, he was the analysand of none other than Melitta Schmideberg, Melanie Klein's own daughter![62]

Lacan's epistemological lucidity, which sets forth his views on the role of the symbolic in constructing the subject, emphasizes language and verbalization. Not only is it speech that, particularly in psychoanalysis, structures the subject and reconstructs his perceptual memory (whose archaic nature is manifested in the hallucination in which it loses the very capacity to speak, the "disposition of the signifier"), but in the concrete form of the psychoanalytic cure, everything that lays claim to a first perception can have only a mythic character.[63] By choosing as its focus the symbol, without which nothing *ek-sists*, and by remaining wary of the mythic-imaginary, this view nevertheless runs the risk of forgetting the outposts of symbolization that the Freudian text had wisely highlighted and that the Klcinian school explores by lending all its weight to the imaginary incarnate. The Kleinians did so by emphasizing their work with the patient's imaginary—but they also emphasized their work with the analyst's imaginary and thus created the first clinical approach to transference that is inseparable from countertransference.

All the same, many analysts, both Kleinians and others, continue to confuse the domains of the knowable imaginary and of knowable reality. The Lacanian line of thinking, which distinguishes between the real, the imaginary, and the symbolic precisely so they can be joined together, thus represents a considerable step forward. Before Lacan, however, the Controversial Discussions had already contributed a great deal, albeit from a more empirical or clinical perspective, toward clarifying the distinction between the use of the imaginary in the cure, on the one hand, and the consideration of an objective and knowable reality, on the other.

The effect of the analyst's fantasy on the formation of the analytic object (whether it be the patient's associative discourse or, even more powerfully, the archaic, unnamed, and presumed fantasy), has come to be called countertransference, as we know. Klein herself appears to have had some qualms about this notion,[64] but it is not the least of her school's accomplishments to have drawn attention to the dynamics of countertransference all the same. Credit for this is due to Paula Heimann's work during the Controversial Discussions of 1941–1945. During a highly scholarly debate that culminated in some crucial epistemological arguments, Marjorie Brierley criticized Heimann on the following grounds:

> If we persist in equating mental functions with our subjective interpretations of them, we forfeit our claim to be scientists and revert to the primitive state of the Chinese peasant who interprets an eclipse as the sun being swallowed by a dragon.[65]

In response to Dr. Brierley, Heimann courageously offered a different rationale for psychoanalysis, one that was not so far removed from the position advanced by the Chinese peasant: "What *we* are studying is *not* the solar system, but the mind of the Chinese peasant, not the eclipse but the belief of the peasant concerning the eclipse."[66]

In 1950, and in a later work as well,[67] the same Paula Heimann endeavored not only to justify the advent of countertransference and its interpretation for the patient as being indispensable to the analytic cure but to consider such countertransference to be a symptom of intuition and empathy as well.[68] The analyst was consumed with patients' projections before she recognized her patients' projective identification. But she also recognized her own identification—precisely in order to get beyond it. In truth, it is by enacting her own unconscious reserves that the analyst can rid herself of a mode of listening that stems from the superego or simply from the conscious and thus adopt the celebrated and yet enigmatic "benevolent listening," which operates from a distance, of course, but which is rooted above all in identification, intuition, and empathy.[69]

Finally, although Hanna Segal's article entitled "Notes on Symbol Formation" does not reach the philosophical depth of the French debate, it contributes an essential ingredient to Klein's theory of the symbol, as manifested brilliantly in the case study of Dick.

Under the weight of projective identification, as Segal points out, a part of the ego is identified with the object, such that the symbol and symbolism become one. Under these conditions, there is no symbol proper to speak of, but only a "symbolic equation"[70] (the rag *is* mummy; which is still not "the rag *looks like* mummy" or "the rag *takes the place for me* of the mummy whom I lost and who is no longer there"). Put another way, the internal object replaces the *equivalent* external object. This archaic logical process is also characteristic of the thought process of the schizophrenic who tries to deny the ideal object and to control the persecuting object. Still, the depressive position and the work of mourning allow us to experience the loss of object, and to form an internal psychic reality, as we have seen, as something separated from the lost object and different from it: the *equation* breaks down and *signifiance* emerges. Only then do we see the symbol, a product of a *psyche* that evokes a *lost reality* that for that reason alone is recognized as being truly real. The continuity of the sublimation-symbolization, fantasy-thought, and splitting-repression process is thus assured, as the process is focused on the potential for loss. From this new perspective, "symbolic equations" no longer appear to be simple regressions but, rather, play a role in a "genetic sequence" as primitive symbols, as a primary symbolization that is contemporaneous with the beginnings of life and that precedes the emergence of the signifier/signified/referent that structures the matrix of thought in the end.

The careful way in which the Kleinians and the post-Kleinians have traced the evolution of symbolism still leaves open the question of the role of the father, which Melanie always underestimated. This lack encourages and demands a more elaborate clinical and theoretical framework for this "true" symbolic function that follows the "equations." Didn't the Kleinians neglect the role of "primary identification" with the "father of personal prehistory" from the time of the earliest relations with the rudiments of objects? Doesn't primary identification with the father play a role from the time of the "equations," before the process of symbolization through the depressive position? Doesn't the phallic ordeal of castration, manifested differently but inevitably for both sexes, impose its own indelible imprint on the reinforcement of this transition between identity and similarity, equations and symbols, and fantasy and thought? These questions must be left unanswered here; they invoke the most pressing problems of psychoanalytic study today.[71]

THE POST-KLEINIAN APPROACH TO THE ARCHAIC AND THE PRIMARY

In the wake of Klein's work and by focusing on the clinical approach to psychosis and autism, several of Klein's disciples have developed a theory about the archaic states of symbolization. Some have considered these states to reflect the existence of a primitive or primal symbolism. As dangerous and philosophically foolhardy as such a notion may seem, the clinical research that supports it is quite reassuring. Following Hanna Segal, for example, W. R. Bion returned to the evolution of the symbolic capacity in the young child, but he worked his way back before the depressive position and described the primitive thought that marks the paranoid-schizoid phase: in his view, projective identification is the first form of "thinking."[72] He considers it to be a preverbal thought that is strictly private and that is made up of links among various sensory impressions, of "ideographs pertinent to the sense of vision," "a primitive matrix of ideographs." The ego and the object transform these sensory occurrences into "alpha elements"[73] that are rendered "suitable for employment in dream thoughts, unconscious waking thinking, dreams, contact-barrier, memory."[74] The alpha elements are the same as the elements of preverbal thought that are attacked by a person's psychotic part, the part that destroys the very capacity to "unite" by imposing splitting and fragmentation. This results in elements that are not linked together and that can be used only in projective identification—what Bion refers to as "beta elements"[75] or "the thing-in-itself to which the sense-impression corresponds."[76] The beta elements are comparable to the "bizarre objects" that characterize psychotic fragmentation as well as hallucinatory images, a source of terror. The attacks are visited not only upon the object (as Klein believed), for they also target—and may even prefer—thought itself in the sense of a process of linking. As Bion revisits Klein's conclusions about the shift from the paranoid-schizoid position to the depressive position, he describes a transformation from disintegration to integration that is at the core of what he calls "learning from experience." Bion believes that this transformation and the object enable the person to "feed on" sensory and emotional occurrences by "assimilating" them as if "digesting" them—with the result that "thinking" is nothing less than "linking."

At the root of this linking activity is a hallucinatory experience or "emotional experience" that recalls the child's encounter with the breast. We hear echoes of Klein's theory here, even though

Bion offers an original approach of his own. Bion presumes the existence of an *innate preconception* of the breast, a knowledge a priori of the breast that evokes Kant's notion of a "knowledge wholly a priori." This sort of a "thought as no thing"[77] that awaits being filled up by the breast is destined to be replaced by the *nonrealization of the breast*. Put another way, the baby experiences the need for a real encounter to take place within the interaction between mother and baby as a negative—as frustration—in the context of the a priori of a breast that is already there. Freud posited an initial real gratification through the breast that was followed by a moment of hallucinatory wish-fulfillment. Bion, for his part, reversed this order by positing an already-there, a transcendental occurrence of the drives that was originally granted a preconception that is itself innate in the object: a "thing-in-itself." The union between pre-conception and nonrealization generates "protothoughts"[78] that have the features of "beta elements": to wit, a sort of alliance between the bad breast that is encountered in reality and the need for a breast experienced as a "thing-in-itself." Only then comes the "realization of the breast," or the real experience of the breast through the interactions between the baby and the mother.

From that point each baby finds his own way of combining his capacity for tolerating the frustration endemic to his thought and his real experience, satisfying or not, of his mother's care. The ensuing level of his own envy and hate will be either excessive or tolerable accordingly.

Bion also presumes, as a modification to Klein's notion of projective identification, that the child can project onto his mother what he does not like about himself. This primitive mode of "realistic"[79] communication is comparable to the experience created by the baby that enables him to exert a degree of control over the stimulation that originates from the outside world, whereas he remains defenseless against the internal stimulation from his drives. Bion believed that the youngest children experience "the mother's capacity for reverie,"[80] which is capable—or incapable—of absorbing "beta elements" and of transforming them into "alpha elements," thereby ensuing optimal conditions for the child to differentiate between a *stimulation* and its *representation*. That is what gives rise to the environment required for the emergence of an abstraction of the breast, of the idea of the breast, of the "representation of the breast as a 'thing-in-itself,' " the true symbol of autoerotic gratification or secondary narcissism.

We can now appreciate the extent to which Bion enhances the notion of the omnipotent Kleinian phantasy, which has been often criticized for not being sufficiently attentive to the reality of the maternal environment, to the reality of the intervention—both conscious and unconscious—of the mother. The mother acting also as a lover, according to a notion advanced by French psychoanalysts,[81] is capable of a reverie that is sufficiently receptive and sufficiently distant, perhaps even suppressive of the hold that the mother and the child have on each other, to facilitate the emergence and development of the child's symbolism. The integration of the ego during the depressive position organizes the "alpha elements" into a "membrane" or a "contact barrier" that forms a basis for the distinction between conscious and unconscious. Symbolism operates as an antidepressant apparatus that inhabits the quantity of stimulation and facilitates the transformation of beta elements into alpha elements. A *contained*, which reflects impressions of the digestive system, is projected onto a *container*, which is the object that contains (at first, this object is simply the mother) and that is structured in the end as "an apparatus [that makes] it possible to think the already existing thought."[82] Created in the mother, this apparatus for thinking the thought facilitates the formation of an analogous apparatus in the child, such that it becomes possible for the baby and his Other to communicate psychic and existential occurrences (love, well-being, a sense of security, and so forth).

Although Bion's notions reflect an oversimplified distinction between the affect and representation, and although they remain locked within a mystical conception of a psychic reality adorned with a hallucinatory receptivity and "the suspension of memory, desire, [and] understanding,"[83] his work has considerably enriched our understanding of psychosis.[84]

Finally, the clinical practice of autism has modified or refined

Klein's theory in several important ways. It has been observed that autistic children are incapable of projective identification because they do not distinguish between outside and inside and do not appear to engage in a relation to the object. Is that an autoeroticism before the onset of the object relation?

Donald Meltzer offers a different perspective on the autistic child. For him, such children are exhibiting not defenses against anxiety but a true "onslaught of sensations" that results from both "inadequate equipment" (neurological deficiencies) and a "failure of dependence." For these children, the breast is like a sheet of paper, what Klein calls an "object," but it is two-dimensional and thus lacks the three-dimensional quality necessary for the "geography of the fantasy." What Meltzer and his followers theorize is even more violent than Klein's primitive splitting: an early segmentation of perceptual capacities within psychosis. Meanings are disparate and varied, the attention Bion wrote about is suspended, time does not flow, and, concomitantly, the self has the feeling of "breaking into pieces."[85]

Esther Bick, for her part, speaks of a *binding identification*: the child's fear of losing his identity is so great that, in order to glean an identity for himself, he latches onto his mother. From that perspective, clinicians have explored the subject's primary life that occurs well before projective identification, and have proposed a true phenomenology of the early bonds, which in this case take the form of a narcissistic identification centered on the psychic function of skin.[86]

A group of psychoanalysts working in France has also received attention recently for their work on autism based on these post-Kleinian advances, some of the most prominent being Annie Anzieu, Cléopâtre Athanassiou, Bernard Golse, Geneviève Haag, and Didier Houzel.[87] A new continent of psychoanalysis has thus emerged in the wake of the Freudian discovery, one that could not have taken hold without Melanie Klein's genius. Through the work of her followers, moreover, Klein's innovations, which, it must be said, occasionally fell victim to dogmatism, offer an exceptional fecundity and diversity, and the clinicians specializing in autism and in infantile psychosis are able to link Klein's initial forays into the subject with their own creative approach to listen-ing to ill-being that they practice every day.

From that perspective, other clinicians, beginning with Frances Tustin, have conceptualized an autism that is endoge-nous, primary, or normal. This autism is a primitive state of undifferentiated autosensuality, a sort of "extra-uterine gesta-tion" that is replaced by the narcissistic stage, which begins by presenting an idea of a self separated from the outside world. Tustin revives Freud's notion of a narcissistic stage, but he devel-ops it, in the wake of Klein, by closely analyzing the relationship between mother and baby that emerges in it, a relationship that is already based on objects and that is subjected to separation trauma. Some babies are unable to tolerate such separation; they experience it as a "projective explosion" of urine, gas, feces, saliva, and other substances that are linked to the absent nipple, which forces the infant to confront a terrifying world that is no more than a "black hole." The mother is summoned to contain this explosion and to introduce discontinuity in order to move toward symbolization. If she fails to do so, the child can express himself only through increased use of "the sensations of his own body" to flush out emptiness and hostile black material. A veri-table mourning of the "primordial sensation" becomes necessary, a primitive reflexivity of the body that is established by the mother or the therapist.

This new version of an autistic primary symbolism common to all subjects is manifested in "normal," nonautistic psyches in the form of a tendency toward a quiet retreat from the world, an escape to the primary that challenges all forms of subjectivity without being truly narcissistic.[88] On the contrary, in fact, the introduction of the negative, once the child is able to formulate it, indicates that he has entered a three-dimensional world fol-lowing his two-dimensional experience. In that sense, Tustin interprets Klein's case study of Dick by emphasizing the point at which the young patient hurled a toy and said, "Gone." Dick had recognized the loss of the object in the presence of a third party, introjected unpleasant affects, and introduced this ordeal into the internal psychic world of speech: the symbol and the psyche are constructed as a "third world" that soothes the child, precisely because it can be shared through language.[89]

Finally, among the many extensions of Klein's thought, we should keep in mind the contributions made by someone who ranked among Klein's most loyal followers before he joined the "Independents."[90] D. W. Winnicott, who was analyzed by Joan Riviere and James Strachey and who was the analyst of Eric Clyne, Melanie's son, was able to ward off the strange desire on the part of this mother and this leader of a school to supervise Clyne's treatment herself![91] Although Winnicott resisted the idea of a death drive and of innate envy, and although Melanie cooled to him as a result, he was able to retain a creative closeness with the Kleinian legacy and to outline one of the most daring variants of psychoanalytic thought. Winnicott's sensitive clinical approach to the early years of childhood and to psychotic suffering earned him both a broad audience and renown beyond the specialized realm of psychoanalysis. In his effort to hone in on the relationship between mother and child and on the creation of the particular brand of symbolism that it generates (or hinders), Winnicott proposed calling that bond a "transitional state," which he believed was at the root of all our creative potential. I will limit myself here to illustrating just a few key moments in the transitional by citing the language that he himself used during a series of lectures addressed toward students of social work:

> In the day-to-day life of infancy we can watch the infant exploiting this third or illusory world which is neither inner reality nor external fact, and which we allow to the infant although we do not allow it to the adult or even to an older child. We see the infant sucking fingers or adopting a technique of twiddling the face or murmuring a sound or clutching a piece of cloth, and we know that the infant is claiming magical control over the world. . . . These terms imply that there is a temporary state belonging to early infancy in which the infant is allowed to claim magical control over external reality, a control which we know is made real by the mother's adapting, but the infant does not yet

know this. . . . Out of these transitional phenomena develop
much of what we variously allow and greatly value under the
headings of religion and art and also the little madnesses
which are legitimate at the moment, according to the prevailing cultural pattern.[92]

Is it a transitional object that the child created—or that he
found in the mother? Is it both found and created?

I would put it this way. Some babies are fortunate enough
to have a mother whose initial active adaptation to their
infant's need was good enough. This enables them to have
the illusion of actually finding what was created (hallucinated). Eventually, after a capacity for relationships has been
established, such babies can take the next step towards
recognition of the essential aloneness of the human being.
Eventually such a baby grows up to say "I know there is no
direct contact between external reality and myself, only an
illusion of contact, a midway phenomenon that works very
well for me when I am not tired. I couldn't care less that
there is a philosophical problem involved."[93]

This disarming Winnicott was able, in the face of Melanie the
warrior, to deftly absorb our most primary fantasies, and, by paying tribute to the baby in us, to stimulate our desires for freedom
in religion, in the arts, or elsewhere. We are grateful for his conception of freedom that has Kleinian overtones but that is also
original in its Protestant inspiration.

Because the liberation of my desire is preceded by its elaboration and sublimation, at the end of my analysis I find myself in
a state of perpetual *rebirth*. In Winnicott's view, birth presumes
that the embryo has acquired a biological and physical life autonomy that is capable of extricating itself from the encroaching
environment and of avoiding being traumatized by the violent
act of birth. This fundamental independence is, in some ways, a
precondition for the "inner psychic reality"[94] that Winnicott
considered to be our most precious and mysterious freedom,

inasmuch as we are *beings,* as opposed to actors or *doers.* Winnicott detected this interior in "the capacity to be alone," a subject Klein took up in her own way,[95] as well as in the *voting booths* of democracies. He tried to revive the principle of freedom that characterizes the living elements in analytic treatment itself: analytic work uncovers the "false selves" that are constructed as defenses against invasion from the outside, and it rehabilitates our endemic interiority. Authentic inner life must nevertheless be perpetually re-created, for it is an endless process that only then makes us free.

In Winnicott's writings, the adjective *free* is used as a synonym for an "inner life that must be perpetually re-created," one that operates in tandem with an external life that must always be internalized. In Freud, the word *free* essentially signifies a resistance to the twin tyrants of external reality and the desires of the drives. After Klein and Winnicott, the term has come to mean something else: *free* means to internalize the outside, provided that this outside (the mother, to begin with) allows for play and allows itself to play.[96] In sum, at the end of an analysis that has been terminated but that remains infinite, and because we have revealed freedom at the cost of our desires, we find ourselves not only mortal but "full of birth," to come back again to Hannah Arendt's idea, in the sense that we are capable of creating a psychic inner life that is to be forever replenished.

Was the sensitive pediatrician too quick to dispose of philosophical questions? Even if he was, he tempered the violence of Klein's work in order to propose a way of caring for children—and thus for the human beings that they become—that combines the wisdom of English empiricism and the bold innovations of Melanie Klein.

Klein, for her part, did not ignore the "transitional space" of creativity, for she did not confine herself to the primitive forms of sublimation that were endemic to the savage fantasies of her patients who were psychotic or inhibited children. She broadened her inquiry to include works of art that allowed her to flesh out the permanency of primitive logical processes, which she treated with the dignity of a contagious and cathartic creativity.

CULTURAL ACTS OF SUBLIMATION:
ART AND LITERATURE

In 1929 Melanie Klein, still in Berlin, read a review in the *Berliner Tageblatt* of Ravel's opera *L'Enfant et les sortilèges*, which had just been performed in Vienna. The German translation called it "The Magic Word" (*Das Zauberwort*), which is none other than "mummy." Melanie painstakingly reviewed the story of the opera and saw within it—thanks to "the profound psychological insight of Colette,"[97] who wrote the libretto—the sadistic anxieties of a six-year-old boy. His anxieties inhibit him at first, but they become a source of generosity in the end.

At the beginning of the tale, the little boy is restless, does not want to do his homework, and becomes angry with his pestering and threatening mother. The maladjusted lad breaks dishes and objects, torments a squirrel and a cat, screams, plays with the fire in the fireplace, breaks a grandfather clock, pours ink on the table, and so forth. All of a sudden, the mistreated objects come alive and seek revenge. The child steps back, becomes consumed with despair, and hides in the garden—but there too he is pursued by terrifying insects, frogs, and other animals. He also comes across the wounded squirrel, and, without thinking about it, bandages the squirrel's leg and mumbles, "Mama." "He is restored to the human world," our analyst observes before penetrating more deeply into the psychology of the neurotic young boy. "I refer to the attack on the mother's body and on the father's penis in it."[98]

Colette and Ravel thus illustrate the early sadism that precedes the anal phase, that is, at the very moment when the oedipal tendencies emerge! In ontogenetic development, these tendencies are followed by a genital phase that puts an end to sadism. At that point the child became capable of pity and love, as evidenced by his behavior toward the squirrel. In 1934, as we know, Klein would attribute such solicitude toward the "whole object" to the advent of the depressive position. In 1929 though, she limited herself to commenting on the insights offered by Colette, who observed that the young boy's sadism was unleashed by oral frustration:

didn't the mother forbid the child from "[eating] up all the cakes in the world" and didn't she threaten to feed him only "tea without sugar and dry bread"?[99]

We are as far as we could be from Proust's tea and savory madeleine. As we recall, our little Marcel experienced no frustration with the world of taste, for the kiss from his mother as he lay down to bed was the only thing that brought him a grievous memory of such frustration. Is that why Proust's masterpiece never describes the future narrator's sadism? Although our taster from Combray loves to denounce the nastiness of other people—the Baron de Charlus, Mme Verdurin, or the Guermantes—he shields himself from any suspicion of violence on his part. In Ravel's work, on the other hand, a cannibalistic anxiety imbues desire, and Colette's intuition presages the analyst's insight as she portrays infantile logic and the *sortilèges*—or spells—of the unconscious.

At the same time, Klein sees the artistic creation as more than just a diagnostic tool. The work of art can also serve as an initial—and perhaps even an optimal—way of caring for other people. Is it more effective than interpretation? That question is implicit in another article that the analyst discusses in the same essay: Karin Michaelis's "The Empty Space," which recounts the story of Ruth Kjär. This wealthy and independent woman, a gifted interior designer, suffered from depression and complained that, "There is an empty space in me, which I can never fill!"[100] Her melancholia got much worse after she married. One day, Ruth's brother-in-law removed and sold a beautiful object, one of the paintings that adorned her home, which left an empty space on her wall. This reification of emptiness only heightened her despair (we should note that the agent of her frustration was her husband's brother, a painter). Following this incident, nothing seemed to be able to halt her ever worsening depression, until one day Ruth decided to replace the painting. Although she had never painted before, she created a magnificent picture. Her husband, and then her brother-in-law, expressed their awe and disbelief. To convince them as well as herself, she went on to paint a series of pictures—"masterly" ones![101] After her initial effort, she first painted a life-size portrait of a dark, nude woman, then her younger sister, and finally a portrait of an old woman and her mother. "The blank space has been filled."[102] The archaic frustration—which stemmed from her mother, which she relived in her marriage, and which was focalized in the loss of the painting—was "repaired" by a creativity that supplanted her depression.

Early on, then, Klein proposed the notion of a "reparation" that was concomitant with the loss of the object in the depressive position, a notion that she would elaborate upon in 1934: "The desire to make reparation, to make good the injury psychologically done to the mother and also to restore herself was at the bottom of the compelling urge to paint these portraits of her relatives."[103]

The sadistic desire to destroy the mother, which was at the unconscious foundation of Ruth Kjär's melancholia and which was transformed into a feeling of frustration, was replaced by reparation. The work of art functions as an autoanalytic activity that absorbs guilt as well as the acknowledgement of guilt. As the work is created, anxiety is diminished, and the artist's personal success increases the confidence of the depressed person whom he conceals through his capacity to love and restore the object as a good object. Accordingly, the creator deems unconscious hatred to be less frightening and threatening. In the end, the recapitulations of success integrate the repaired object with the ego, such that the melancholic man or woman no longer needs to exert an exhausting degree of control over the Other but accepts instead his or her object of desire of love as it is. From that perspective, the work of art provides a way to re-create the harmony of the inner world and to maintain tolerable relations with the outside, if not to experience love with other people (through marriage, in this case), despite the enduring conflicts that stem from the upheavals of childhood.

In line with her schematic approach that applies her theories to aesthetic objects in order to find "illustrations" of those theories, Klein also analyzes Julien Green's novel *If I Were You*.[104] The subtitle of Klein's study is entitled "A Novel Illustrating Projective Identification." The hero, a young worker named Fabien Especel (or, playing around with the signifier, "*espèce-elle*"?), who is unhappy and unsatisfied, orphaned by a father who squandered the family's money, makes a pact with the devil that allows him to be transformed into other people. Melanie Klein traces with great delight the complex maze of the "projective identification" through which Fabien successively becomes M. Poujars, Paul Esmenard, Fruges, Georges, and finally Camille. The frustration and aggression that he experiences during these transformations, which are tinged with a homosexuality that the analyst does not hesitate to detect underneath the masks, nearly disappear upon his discovery of a good maternal image—the baker—that revives for him the loving life of his early childhood.

It is as if Fabien takes on the identities of other men because he is unable to identify with his father. He loves them—temporarily—and is disappointed in each instance as he seeks to adopt a passive feminine position toward them.[105] The restoration of the archaic mother takes place through a fantasy: having entered a church filled with candlelight, he imagines the baker pregnant with all the children he made for her. Because of this positive vision, the hero reconciles himself with his "sinful" thoughts and overcomes the envy and greed that secretly consume him.[106] Is this a conception of Christianity as a reparation of the Virgin Mother who abates the incestuous fantasies of the son? From that point on Fabien renounces an ineffective solution to his anxieties that consists of a distraught flight into his projective identifications, which are as disappointing as they are exhausting because he tries to gather up his projected parts. In the analyst's view the final scene of the novel depicts this tension and this impossible reunion very well: as Fabien lies in bed with a fever (wasn't his pact with the devil a hallucination brought on by a fever?), Fabien-Camille moves toward the door of his home. But the reunion of his split-off parts never takes place.

In fact, the hero dies with the words "Our Father" on his lips, which suggests that he has reconciled with *his own* father. Still, his final double, Fabien-Camille, whom the sick boy believes he hears near the doorway in anticipation of giving him his identity back, is not really there. No one is there, in fact, as his mother points out. At the same time, a certain reunion has taken place: the reunion of a son dying after a coma with . . . his mother, who, he has finally recognized, loves him.

> As a result of overcoming the fundamental psychotic anxieties of infancy, the intrinsic need for integration comes out in full force. He achieves integration concurrently with good object relations and thereby repairs what had gone wrong in his life."[107]

The reader of Klein is still hungry: the mechanism of reparation certainly does not exhaust the creative process, no more than do the themes of falsity and of perversion, sadomasochism, or profanation, which appear in Julien Green's novel but which are not addressed by our psychoanalyst-turned-literary-critic. The naïveté of Klein the essayist is juxtaposed with the perseverance of Klein the theorist as she reveals the details of the logic behind what she has discovered on the couch: projective identification and its replacement by a reparation process that is wholly dependent on the experience of loss.

Still, what Green recounts is not the death of a mother (as the child's sadistic fantasy would have it, in Klein's view) but the death of the son. Is that the secret of the writer-son and homosexual, his version of the sacrifice that imbues the Kleinian template? His goal is to preserve his mother, to never lose her, and to let her live by making himself into a creator, though at the cost of a certain death of the self. Fabien's death could also be considered an abandonment of sexual identity: neither man nor woman, man and woman, nothing, neuter, everything. And all of this occurs so that the writer-son might re-create all the identities, identify with them all, and project himself everywhere. And, in the path of the infinite reparation that describes the engagement in the imaginary, so he can try to settle his debt to a mother to whom reparation has thus been made, but even more so his debt to a hated father. It is an endless payment, an inconsolable payment, a payment to the death.

Klein's text is replete with important questions, but it limits itself in a scholarly fashion to being an ambitious and cautious illustration of psychoanalytic theses, those that became the theses of *her school.*

Melanie sought to preserve her young patients' capacity to sublimate-symbolize. When art and literature effect a dynamic that is comparable to the ordeals of psychic survival that she has described, she enjoyed holding those texts up to the mirror of her theory, which she polished herself while sitting in her analyst's chair and listening to her analysands. Along the way, literature benefited from being in the spotlight, though it also jealously retained its enigmas. The analyst, for her part, solidified her concepts and reinforced her clinical practice by returning to the sundry details of the confessed and acknowledged fantasies that make up what is known as a cultural imaginary.

All the same, might we describe her critical approach as displaying a theoretical pretension that profanes the subtle flesh of the work of art? I am more inclined to detect some humility—no doubt in crude form but noble in the end—on the part of a woman who dared to shed some light on the world of artistic illusions. She did so without ever doubting that such illusions, like fantasies, are inevitable and necessary. In her own way, was Klein not a creator as well, with her own projective identifications with her patients and in her imaginary, *fantasy-like*, interpretations? "If I were you," she thought as she interpreted. Was it Melanie or was it the final disguise, this time a successful one, of Fabien?

The version of psychoanalysis that Klein has bequeathed us is an experience of the imaginary that does not lay claim to beauty but that seeks to know itself without ever denying the imaginary proper.

FROM THE FOREIGN LANGUAGE
TO THE FILIGREE OF THE LOYAL
AND DISLOYAL

A FOUNDER WITHOUT A TEXT

In 1925 Melanie Klein learned English from Alix Strachey in preparation for delivering papers in England: "I've taken the plunge & am to teach Melanie English—anyhow the Fach-department. For this purpose I propose going thro' *Little Hans* . . . with her; she is to read him aloud, & then we are to discuss him in English."[1]

The distinguished Londoner was impressed by her student's understanding of the English language, but because Klein's accent was horrible, the two of them decided that she should continue her studies with a formal teacher.

From the moment Klein moved to England in 1926, she formulated her thoughts in English, although she often returned to her mother tongue so she could remain in contact with her emotions and share them with other people. When her son Hans died, for example, Klein poured out her feelings to Paula Heimann in German.[2] It is also likely that the dreams she had about her son's death, which revived many painful memories—her father's preference for Emilie, Sidonie's early death, her cruel loss of Emanuel for which she continued to feel pangs of guilt, her resurgent anguish about her mother's death, her ambivalent feelings toward her husband, Arthur, her despondency following Abraham's death, and her troubled relationship with Kloetzel—were in German. *The Psychoanalysis of Children*, published in German around the same time, was translated into English by James Strachey with the assistance of Alix Strachey, Edward Glover, and Joan Riviere, and then was revised a good deal for the official version of her complete works. Although Melanie's mastery of English improved (during the war, her correspondence with Winnicott was peppered with idiomatic English expressions)—Melanie relied on her anglophone friends when she began to write in English. During the 1930s she received considerable help from Joan Riviere, who substantially corrected and revised her work. She later turned to her secretary, Lola Brook, a Lithuanian Jew married to an Englishman who would serve, from 1944, as Klein's trusted confidante and indispensable collaborator. Brook read, among other works, Klein's "Some Theoretical Conclusions Regarding the Emotional Life of the Infant" with great interest, and she made as many suggestions about style as about the organization of the material. In response, the author thanked her in a footnote.[3] Finally, *The Psychoanalysis of Children* would have never seen the light of day without the help of Elliot Jacques, who became the secretary of the Melanie Klein Trust and who oversaw the publication of her complete works. In every instance, it must be added, the indefatigable Melanie Klein wrote about—and rewrote about—her sessions with her patients, modified her comments and her clinical conclusions, and gradually refined in writing the development of her thought, which is reflected in her archives.

We should also add that Klein's later works are filled with quotations from English literature that are sophisticated to the point of appearing "forced," though they still remain relevant today. And we should further point out that Jean-Baptiste Boulanger, who translated *The Psychoanalysis of Children* into French, considered Melanie's French to be good enough for her to communicate very easily with him as she supervised his translation. At the same time, however, this linguistic cosmopolitanism did not prevent Melanie from remaining "Germanic to the end," as her biographer put it.[4]

Was German her mother tongue? In some ways it was. In fact, Libussa's later letters show that German did not come easily to her.[5] We recall that both mother and daughter were proud that Moriz Reizes, the husband and father, spoke ten languages,[6] no matter how mediocre a doctor he was! But what was Melanie's mother tongue?

Matricide emerges when someone abandons his mother tongue. It was already in play with Melanie's parents, and even more deeply in the migratory fate of those European Jewish families that possessed every language and no language, except Yiddish for some of them, a language that Melanie did not want to learn[7] or even to hear spoken around her. In the aftermath of parental desire, particularly her mother's, Melanie chose to immerse herself in German language and culture, which served as her first symbolic rebirth and a cultural deliverance of the self. Her second break with the past, the one that drove her to Great Britain, accelerated her flight—which became increasingly higher and stronger. In order to contemplate this old memory known as an unconscious and to give a name to the fantasy, must one listen to it from a distance, that is, from another place that can only represent a sort of foreignness? Is such a flight perhaps a way of protecting oneself from the memory by abandoning it *over there*, combined with ineffable childhood sensations in an unfamiliar primitive code? Is it less frightening to hear what is far away through the clarity of a mind armed with so many secondary, mediatized, "estranged" initiations into the archaic and forgotten world of motherhood?

One might read into that fate of being a stranger—a fate through which Melanie Klein's Jewishness was crystallized and disguised as well as nurtured—the elaboration of an old splitting, an ever painful matricide, and an endemic psyche. Because Melanie Klein was able to get in touch with this dynamic, and because she experienced it as being a source of both destruction and salvation, she was able to develop a theory that resonates more directly and more incisively than does Freudian theory with the very splitting that betrays comparable matricides experienced by us all, not only by many intellectuals but, at the end of the second millennium, by ever-growing groups of people.[8]

Human beings are less "identities" than *journeys*, as they are always in transit *between* a memory that is repressed to varying degrees and a conscience that dominates to varying degrees, as Freud was patient enough to explain to us. Freud developed what some have called his personal novel when he proposed that, ever since the glaciation that stacked psychoses onto neuroses, *homo religiosus* has survived in the modern people that we are by journeying surreptitiously into our psychic structures, dreams, and symptoms.

One could imagine that the Freudian vision has been influenced by the renewed loss of a settled way of life that humanity experienced during the twentieth century. Technology and politics have increasingly detached us from our natural habitats and have turned us into nomads once again. To persecuted political exiles are added the migrants of the global economy and the navigators who use satellite television or the Internet. Along with the questioning of authority, the law, and values—which has been interpreted as an attack on the role of the father—the loss of habitat that characterizes our fate undermines the original place, assaults maternal support, and threatens to destroy identity itself.

Sensitive poets and frightened curators have thus made an ode to preserving this place by returning to the origin, the ecology of the habitat, and the protection of the homeland. All of these seek to preserve the possibility of entering into a stable abode, a reliable arrangement, and a primordial, religious meditation on the human experience that is contingent on a space that knows how to space itself out.[9] How can we not understand them, how can we not accompany them when we know that the destruction of this first source of security—the anchoring of our identities, the primary possession of our objects of desire and hatred—which consists of language and the management of a household, would deprive of us what is, for the time being, the ultimate sign of humanity: the possibility to sublimate, and then to symbolize, the biological cauldron?

Other people, Melanie Klein among them, take a different approach to preserving the possibility that we can make sense. Their own goal it to familiarize themselves with the locus of pain itself, that is, with the original uprooting—not to repress it in an effort to hastily rebuild their habitat, but to "inhabit" the dehabitation and the primordial separation—provided the verb *to inhabit* is not too placid to describe the auscultation of the original wound that Klein the psychoanalyst engaged in. Our Melanie was a nomad of sorts: Vienna, Rosenberg, Krappitz, Budapest, Berlin, and London, with several addresses in Berlin and five different homes in London. Her son Eric claimed never to have had a home of his own. And yet this woman enjoyed changing residences, though she decorated them in an ever more luxurious manner. Two contradictory tendencies in Klein's wandering ways penetrated the places she lived as well as her own thinking: first, an opening that threw her off balance and that resonated with the loss of the self; and second, a closing that engulfed and counterbalanced danger. On the one hand, the work of a death drive confronted head-on, and on the other hand, the establishment of such rigid structures as a theory, a school of thought, and a bourgeois household. At the same time, the dominant chord was one of the greatest possible expression, a permanent *unleashing*, and a timeless "nonspace." At that point, however, what can we use to lead us past the cruelty that we suffer and that we maneuver?

Melanie Klein discovered at least two possible solutions. First, she trusted the memory of prelanguage: the secret of lost time can be regained through analytic insight and through projective identification with the patient. "If I were you," she says, and then she follows through on her suggestion. Second, she assimilated a new language: at first the language of the fathers Freud-Ferenczi-Abraham, and also the language of the British, and why not, since they appreciated her and welcomed her: is their civilization not an empire, even an Empire, in light of the globalization now under way? In the end, that is how she created her own code. Having made her way into a world of knowledge, systems, and sharing, she appropriated it, broke new ground in it, and created a body of work that she protected through politics. It is easy to poke fun at the elderly woman, who, as London was being demolished by bombs, could think only of her *vurk*—in German-English, of course. In the end, though, we also respect her.

It is possible to speak of Melanie Klein's existence, which had estrangement at its very core. The foreign language was its visible side—English, obviously, but, even more fundamentally, psycho-analysis itself as a *system* with the ideolect of "Kleinian theory" its crowning glory. We see Melanie the clinician who descended "over there," by way of her phantasy, to the wordless place of inhibited, psychotic, and autistic childhood, and we also see Klein the head of school of thought who spoke, schematized, and super-vised her underlings. The latter Melanie gave rise to her con-densed formulations and her dense writings, which are peppered with well-defined concepts that argue patiently, circularly, and repetitively—but that often engage in flashes of insight whose substance is forced upon us without any forewarning and thus does not stem from the airing of words and rhetorical strategies. It was the journey, then, that joined the two faces of Klein. If we forget that fact, and when she forgets that fact (which happened rarely, if ever), we see only the "madwoman" or the "doctrinaire."

Is it also possible to speak of Klein's text? We read Freud like a body of work that is rooted, as hers is, in the very flesh of lan-guage. But Melanie did not partake of the memory of the Ger-man language; rather, she was a member of a different class of thinkers who worked in an international laboratory and expressed themselves in a universal code. Were these thinkers mutants des-tined to disappear or were they endowed with a foreignness that gestured toward their chosen language (in this case, English)? Did they simply seek to facilitate the tasks assigned to the intellect so they might be better equipped to deal with borderline states and impossibilities? In the eyes of our psychoanalyst, this linguistic estrangement, which is in every respect a foreign way of thinking, may well have seemed paradoxical: is it not the case that the unconscious is structured in the light of a mother tongue (just as, for the Fabien of Green's *If I Were You*, the baker's face reappears in the light of the church candles)?[10] We believe the answer is yes, and Melanie never stopped conveying as much through the sieve of her first language: she returned to German when she engaged in vigorous debates and theoretical formulations.

According to what Klein told us, moreover, she often combined various languages—for her, every language was a foreign language as if it were a dream, as Freud taught her: do you remember the "petits fours/petits frou/*kleine* Frou" from which she derived *Frau Klein*?[11] It is because the mother tongue, from the perspective of the place where Melanie situated herself—from the nonplace where she situated herself—is from the outset a foreign language. There is a foreign aspect to what is familiar, a maternal *uncanniness* that lurks beneath. Is it possible to hear the mother's mother, to go where there is no more "there," no more "she" or "place," nothing but sensory chaos, overload, dismantling, a clinging intimacy, and a catastrophic being? Is it possible to move toward a ruthless love of the mutual stimulation that takes place between mother and baby, the prepsychic realm that would became our latest myth, eventually our last myth? Psychoanalysts are like fish who avoid "depths," Melanie quipped to Jones.[12] Klein, on the other, hand, loved depths—particularly those beneath the mother!

Klein's thought bore the effects of this exploration, of this journey to the nonplace that took her thought apart before putting it back together. On the face of it, Klein's writings include reports of "case studies" that are exhaustive, even oversimplified, and that are accompanied with ready-made, almost forced, interpretations. Her writings became increasingly systematic with time, encouraged as she was by disciples who capitalized on the ease of subscribing to a school of thought, to use it to their advantage, and to pull it in the wrong direction. At the same time, however, the artifice that she constructs crumbles without warning, and we are struck by the truths that shine through. Out of the cumbersome quality of her writings arises an appreciable degree of care that is able to nurse the wound into a new, sensitive skin—and without succumbing to complacency.

Melanie's reasoning itself displays a trace of that skin: she has often been criticized for her ambiguous concepts, which are both things and representations, positive and negative, and which lead nowhere, for no sooner have they articulated a possibility than they turn around and argue its opposite. Is the introjected object a thing or an image? Is the fantasy a sublimation of the drive or a defense against the drive? Does the depressive position indicate a nostalgia for the part object or its ceding to the whole object? Does the depressive position give in to manic defenses that have been present since the schizophrenic position, or does it spawn reparation? Klein's detractors have taken pains to point out, in addition to her abandonment of Freud's Oedipus complex for the sake of "internalized objects"[13] and other clear divergences from his work, her troublesome method of thinking. Marjorie Brierley, for example, takes issue with the Kleinians' endorsement of a "bodily" and "imagined" form of knowledge, which Brierley finds astonishingly subjective and incompatible with "true science."[14]

"A mental mechanism modeled on and corresponding to bodily experience is an imagined action, a mode of imaginary behaviour patterned on foregoing actual behaviour."[15]

Glover, who was far more uncompromising, frankly reached the point of ridiculousness: "Unless one is at pains to correct this 'hop, skip and jump' method, disciplined argumentation is impossible."[16]

So was Melanie unscientific? Her detractors said as much in her time, and even today, American professors desperate for attention would have called her an "impostor" had they known her.

In truth, as Jacqueline Rose has suggested,[17] Klein in no way set out a linear form of thinking to describe the linear development of the child or the unconscious. Klein's logic does not function as a "causal sequence" from point A to point B, but as a *circular effort*. Projective identification is perhaps the most important crystallization of "negativity," which forms a "vicious circle" in the words of Joan Riviere, who shows how projective identification allows the child to experience the relationship between cause and effect:

> "You don't come and help, and you hate me, because I am angry and devour you; yet I *must* hate you and devour you to make you help." This revengeful hate which cannot be gratified increases tension further; and the thwarting breast is endowed with all the ruthlessness and intemperate absoluteness of the infant's own sensations.[18]

Riviere, who was cognizant of the uniqueness of this logical process, and who was even proud to have been involved in its discovery and its therapeutic and theoretical application, sang its praises and sought out its protagonists. In truth, though, is anyone really capable of going down such a path?

With this talk of "mothers" and "gifted intuitive" people,[19] a group to which Klein's disciples decidedly believed she belonged, who "are not scientists, and are almost as inarticulate as babies themselves,"[20] the ironic teasing plugs the wound inflicted by Klein's detractors, although these women also partook of the negativity brought about by the emotional expression of the baby. Indeed, their logic is no more incomprehensible than is "a foreign language"[21]—it guides us toward the inner workings of an individual's life, "to a period not previously explored."[22] The unconscious that Melanie pursues, then, is a stranger: her work exposes us to its radical estrangement, as Joan Riviere pointed out: is it not because the unconscious shows us that we are *strangers to ourselves* that we hold a grudge against it?

One can endorse Joan Riviere's exegesis while parting company with the amateurish enthusiasm she displays when likening Melanie's bold interventions to the "beacon" that is Freudian thought. In truth, Klein's penchant for sharp thinking, which is undisputed, was paired with a perpetual return of the negative and to the negative that functions as a sort of *black hole* at the center of her systematization, and that renders her altogether different from a "beacon." The "black hole" of autism, as Frances Tustin would later describe it. The "black hole" of the fantasy, caught forever in the snares of projective identification. The "black hole" of the archaic internalized object, destined to be abandoned, with the onset of depression and the "black sun" of melancholia, in order, through reparation to work toward a veritable translation of ill-being into veritable symbols. Klein's systems are inherently disrupted through the permanency of the interpretative imaginary, which is nothing less than the intrusion of the negative into reasoning itself: it is the negative of the drive, and then the negation of that first negation, constructed as a formulation that is itself always negative, that always sees the worst—that is, as a transference and countertransference that is exposed without having any recourse to the fantasy of destructiveness and death. Klein's analysand Clare Winnicott, Donald Winnicott's wife, pointed out that Melanie, as an analyst, emphasized "the destructive side" of things,[23] and that it was very hard for her to accept love and reparation.[24] Were Clare's observations a transference effect, or were they the "black hole" of Klein's negativity, which generated dazzling insights but which also hindered them?

The dread of what lies at the origin became, for the stranger and the translator of those origins that Melanie Klein was, a courageous coexistence with the negative. The fate of the negative, which is less dialectic in Klein than in Freud, brings her closer to the limits of what is human, and her journey to these resistances is articulated in a line of thinking that appears less graceful but that in truth is very audacious. And this continues until the pulse of the origins to be lost, the pulse of the maternal to be betrayed, and the pulse of the habitat to be abandoned to allow for a free life by way of an exile into the *symbolic*—that new stranger who is perpetually chosen and conquered—are defensively transformed into a war among women. With nothing to latch onto, emotions became ruthless: witness those exchanged between Melanie and Melitta. In the wake of the mourning of the father, that is, of Freud himself as was the case during the Great Controversial Discussions, analytic thought turned out all the better for it. But the danger still remains: flirting with psychosis can lead to a hysterical psychodrama, and *The Oresteia* can collapse into sorcery and into skirmishes among women.

What we still need to do, then, is return to the laboratory: beneath the depths of the Kleinian code persists her rigorous and relentlessness witnessing of experience. It is incumbent upon us to revitalize its boldness, hesitations, and confessions in order to discern in the warfare led by "mother Klein" the brilliant insights offered by the foreigner. A foreigner who she still remains today in the contemporary analytic movement. Because we are forced to confront the "new maladies of the soul" (borderlines, psychosomatics, substance abusers, vandals, and so forth) when we ignore listening and speech, we end up returning to Klein's children and students and realize how much her work faced indescribable suffering. We absolutely must return to these dense pages—so we can do better than she did. Melanie is there to be surpassed, like a mother, like a real mother. . . . She was so different from the "real" mothers who hold you back, and from the real mother who she was herself.

MOTHER AND DAUGHTER

Melanie gave birth to a daughter on January 19, 1904—less than one year after she married Arthur on March 31, 1903. As if it weren't enough to give her daughter the last name *Klein*—"Little"—Melanie chose the first name "Melitta" for her—"Little Melanie." This doubly diminutive little girl thus had cause for complaint from the beginning, but she decided to wait for the right time to articulate it. When her parents argued, she apparently took her mother's side—a wise choice it turns out, since Melanie, who suffered from the iron rule of Libussa, was always leaving her behind for travels and cures. In the mother's absence, it was the grandmother who looked after the little girl. Libussa was devoted and attentive, but she nevertheless preferred the younger boy, Hans. She suggested to Melitta that her mother was only "an emotional cripple, so ill that she had to desert her daughter."[25]

Still, things went relatively well until the 1930s. By that point Melitta had turned into an intelligent young woman who accompanied her mother to psychoanalytical meetings in Berlin and who had completed her studies in medicine. Her mother was still unknown and, lacking any advanced degree, felt the scorn of the medical establishment. Was she jealous of her daughter? Melanie's biographers have wondered as much, particularly after Melitta's 1924 marriage to the very distinguished Walter Schmideberg, the son of a rich and assimilated Jewish family, educated by Jesuits (like the "better" side of Melanie's own family). Not only did Schmideberg become a captain in the Austro-Hungarian army, but by developing an interest first in the occult, and then in psychoanalysis, he befriended the rich and talented Max Eitingon, who introduced him in turn to Freud. Schmideberg even helped the Freud family financially during their difficult days in wartime Vienna. Could one imagine a more eligible bachelor? But Papa Arthur was opposed to the notion of a marriage to a man fourteen years Melitta's senior, a man rumored to be given to alcohol or other drugs. This disagreement set in motion a father-daughter conflict into motion.

Melitta's entrée into the psychoanalytic world was both sudden and brilliant. It appears that she was analyzed by her mother when she was a child.[26] She subsequently underwent a training analysis with Eitingon, then with Karen Horney, and, once in London, with Ella Sharpe and finally Edward Glover. She earned her diploma at the University of Berlin in 1927 and then left for London, where she wrote her thesis on "The History of Homeopathy in Hungary," which she submitted in 1928. Was Melitta dependent on her mother, relying on her presence so she could carry out her own work? We should note, however, that Melitta dedicated the finished thesis to her father.[27] Beginning in 1930, Melitta regularly took part in the meetings of the British Psycho-Analytic Society and even delivered papers there (and we know that Melanie mentions her daughter's work in *The Psychoanalysis of Children*).[28] In 1932 Melanie saw triumph: her first book was published in England, where it was warmly received. Troubles soon began, however. With Walter's arrival in England, the Schmidebergs bought an apartment, and Melitta increasingly asserted her independence. Her analysis with Edward Glover had pointed her in that direction—a letter, most likely from 1934, communicates what appears in hindsight to have been a declaration of war against her mother.

> You do not take it enough into consideration that I am very different from you. . . . I do not think that the relationship with her mother, however good, should be the centre of her life for an adult woman. . . . [The attitude towards you which] I had until a few years ago . . . was one of neurotic dependence.[29]

The war between the two women was made public in October 1933, when Melitta Schmideberg was elected a member of the British Institute: in her membership paper, "The Play-Analysis of a Three-Year-Old Girl," she attributed the digestive difficulties of her patient Viviane not to "constitutional factors" (as Melanie Klein's theory would have it) but to the attitude of a mother who had subjected her to an excessively strict toilet training. Upon the death of her brother Hans in 1934, Melitta spoke of suicide—and hinted that, as with any suicide, the responsibility for it could be traced to difficulties with the family, to idealization and disappointment. The daughter's vendetta, encouraged by Glover, soon escalated to the point of disturbing other members of the society. Some uncomfortable scenes followed. Melitta shouted rude remarks at Melanie: "Where is the father in your work?" It was a guerrilla war fought with sarcastic asides, indiscretions, and accusations dating back to Melitta's early childhood and to the Kleins' family life.

To make matters worse, in 1938 Melitta went so far as to accuse the Kleinians of committing plagiarism—in a collective work called *The Bringing Up of Children*, which was edited by John Rickman and which included a paper by Melanie on weaning. A committee made up of Jones, Brierley, and Payne investigated the complaint and found it utterly baseless. Melitta's accusations, still backed by Glover, eventually took on the form of a theoretical debate: the two protesters criticized the Kleinians' positions and accused them of breaking with Freudian orthodoxy. Yet beneath the legitimate facade of scholarly debate lurked a virulent settling of scores. Glover was far too attached to his analysand—and perhaps saw her as an opportunity to replace his own daughter (who suffered from Down's syndrome) with a true accomplice. He walked alongside Melitta during an international congress.[30] Melanie generally refrained from commenting on such excesses, and left to her followers the task of waging the theoretical battle—although she always remained behind the scenes to pull strings and to suggest the most promising tactics.[31] She suggested, without ever pressing the issue, that her daughter's aggressiveness could be attributed to psychic difficulties rather than to simple theoretical opposition: "And there is even one very obvious fact which I feel quite sure *should not be mentioned*, nor even hinted at by any of us, and that is Melitta's illness."[32]

And what illness would that be? A schizoid state? After proving herself highly critical of Anna Freud's works, and even attacking Freud directly in a comment on a colleague's book, Melitta tried to bond with her just as the differences between the Anna Freudians and the Kleinians had reached the level of an all-out conflict. She paid a visit to Freud when he arrived in London on June 6, 1939. Melanie, who had sent the master a letter of welcome, was not received and was limited to attending Freud's funeral at the end of September. Melitta participated in a meeting with Anna Freud and her partisans and then lent her "caustic" and "sarcastic" tone to the multiple controversies against her mother.[33] She accused the entire British Society of hostility toward Anna Freud,[34] but Anna harbored no illusions about the true psychological basis for Melitta's attacks.

During the Controversial Discussions, Melitta refrained from aligning herself with Anna Freud.[35] Her hostility toward her mother, as both a person and an analyst, appears to have been the primary motivator here, a motivation tainted with venom but one that nevertheless sparked a fundamental debate about psychoanalysis.

In the end, Melitta incurred the disapproval of many members of the British Psycho-Analytic Society, including even some of the Independents, who themselves were hardly blind followers of Melanie. Evan Rosenfeld, a friend of the Freuds' who had entered into analysis with Melanie Klein, recalled the painful atmosphere that so shocked all who experienced it: "I could only see something quite terrible and very un-English happening, and that was a daughter hitting her mother with words and this mother being very composed."[36]

After Glover resigned in 1944, Melitta left the British Society for all practical purposes (although she did not formally resign until 1962). In 1945 she departed for the United States, where she worked with delinquent adolescents, adopting an approach that recalled psychiatry and social work more than psychoanalysis She was in London again, however, on the day of her mother's cremation: Melitta gave a lecture "wearing flamboyant red boots"[37]—an unmistakable sign, if any were needed, that the two had never reconciled. As for Melanie, she bequeathed the following to her daughter Melitta:

> My gold flexible bracelet which was given to me by her paternal grandmother, the single stone diamond ring given to me by my late husband, my gold necklace with garnets and the brooch which goes with the said necklace, both of which I received as a present on my 75th birthday and I have no other bequest to my said daughter because she is otherwise well provided for and by her technical qualifications able to provide for herself.[38]

In summary, Melitta's important role in Melanie's story is beyond dispute. The matriarch insinuated her daughter into the family connection, her descent from her father's family, and even the professional tribute that was paid to her on her seventy-fifth birthday. But her bitterness quietly permeated her references to "my said daughter," who is "well provided for" and possesses so many "technical qualifications," unlike the said mother . . .

Although Glover had fanned the flames of the mother-daughter quarrel, he tried to be objective: the daughter was less energetic than the mother, he conceded. Melitta was his analysand, but "she had been to a dozen analysts before that" (!); "it was largely by Dr. Schmideberg's instigation that these debates continued"; and finally, "I think they were both, herself and her daughter, prejudiced. On the other hand, Dr. Schmideberg, her daughter, made a very good fight for her spiritual liberty, and she had some of that slightly desperate character which made her come right out in the open."[39]

Like mother, like daughter—or not exactly? Melanie remained implacable: Glover was a "bad analyst," "crooked and unscrupulous,"[40] but could she really be impartial on the subject?

Whether we consider all of this in terms of ego or primary object, of inside or of outside, it was projective identification and envy that prevailed—and spared no one in their path. Melanie was forced to live out the proof of her own theories.

PEACE AND WAR AMONG THE LADIES

A 1988 play by Nicholas Wright, *Mrs. Klein*, exposed a large audience to the analyst's quarrels with her biological daughter and with her symbolic daughters. The story takes place in London in 1934, and the play dramatizes the day and the night in which Melanie Klein was unable to attend her son's burial.[41] Melitta writes Melanie that it was most likely Melanie herself who caused her son's death (a possible suicide). Melanie never reads the letter. Melitta is cast aside for a third woman: a newcomer, Paula, who enters into analysis with Mrs. Klein at the end of the play. That initiates the process of mourning for the son, which in some ways is also a mourning for the daughter. Guilt and depression permeate the drama—which is nevertheless dominated by the power of Mrs. Klein: nothing, absolutely nothing, can distract her from her determination to pursue her work, her *vurk*.[42]

There are no men in this female hell. Mrs. Klein's son is dead, and the three women's past or present husbands—all of whom are either tyrants or sensualists—neither understand their wives nor appreciate the importance of psychoanalysis. The theater exaggerates and caricatures, communicating a folklike Kleinian universe that serves only to reinforce the myths that even the most scrupulous biographers cannot avoid.

"Insensitive,"[43] "ruthless"[44] with infidels, requiring "undivided loyalty"[45]—and let us not forget "paranoid" and "depressive"— Melanie rigidly defended her thought and pounced upon the slightest divergence or the smallest hint of personal or intellectual autonomy. Phyllis Grosskurth's biography traces the details of the numerous seductions, often followed by disagreements, that punctuated Melanie Klein's life and that remained bound up with her analytic career. I will discuss only the most significant of these relationships—those she had with her three favored disciples: Paula Heimann, Susan Isaacs, and Joan Riviere.

Heimann is the play's "Paula," the person who replaces the daughter in Melanie's heart and who becomes the confidante of her depression, then her analysand, and finally her symbolic daughter, a talented collaborator.[46] Shortly before Paula died in 1983, she confessed that she had been so "seduced"[47] by Melanie that she had decided to enter into analysis with her. The rivalry between disciple and daughter rose to new heights when Paula joined Melitta's husband, Walter Schmideberg, in Switzerland, where they established themselves permanently—but continued to receive visits from the daughter of Paula's analyst. What an odd trio they formed: Paula-Melitta-Walter![48] Heimann's official break with Melanie was in 1955, when she discovered the theory of breast envy, but it is possible that she was one of the examples Melanie gave of excessive envy.[49] Was the envy on Paula's part? Melanie described her to Hanna Segal as being the "too destructive" patient. Or was the envy on Melanie's part, as a response to Paula's autonomous thinking? Is Melanie referring to herself when she invokes in *Envy and Gratitude* a putative patient who had borne an intense love toward her sister that was mixed with "paranoid and schizoid feelings"? Envious or not, Melanie Klein dismissed Paula Heimann from the Melanie Klein Trust Fund in 1955, informing her that she had lost confidence in her.[50]

Susan Isaacs was among the group—Edward Glover, Sylvia Payne, John Rickman, Joan Riviere, Ella Sharpe, the Stracheys— who had attended Melanie's 1925 lectures in London. A brilliant child psychologist and the director of studies in psychology at the University of London, Isaacs became the first principal of the

Malting House School, the experimental school in Cambridge. She was won over by Klein's ideas, which she elaborated upon with great skill.[51] Analyzed by Otto Rank and Joan Riviere, Isaacs was particularly supportive of Melanie during the war, when the party chief was staying in Cambridge near her daughter-in-law and grandson—but she also sustained her by preparing several ripostes during the Controversial Discussions. Throughout their lengthy correspondence, Melanie tried hard to respect Susan Isaacs's independence while guiding her with authority. Isaacs claimed to be convinced that it was Melanie, and not Anna, who was the true successor to Freudian thought.[52] Yet it was Paula Heimann who reported Melanie's "malicious remarks"[53] regarding Isaacs to Pearl King. Was the spite Melanie's—or Paula's?

Joan Riviere, too, did not escape the Kleinian freeze. Riviere, a product of the English intellectual haute bourgeoisie who was analyzed by Jones and by Freud himself, the first lay analyst in the British Society, and the translator of Freud, remained fascinated by Melanie. Riviere saw Klein as frustrated and as perhaps stuck in a permanent dream state, but she also perceived that Klein possessed "le feu sacré."[54] Freud admired Riviere's intelligence and probably her aplomb as well, but in his correspondence with Jones, he attacked "the theoretical statements of Mrs. Riviere," rather than those of Melanie herself, whom he pursued through her disciple. Loyal among loyalists, Riviere analyzed Isaacs and Winnicott and wrote the "General Introduction" to *Developments in Psychoanalysis*. She was skeptical, however, of "borderline cases," as Melanie defined them, and she did not wish to analyze them. Still, her reserve did not prevent her from being a highly nuanced theorist on the subject of the "negative therapeutic reaction."[55]

Was this subtle theorizing what made Melanie turn spiteful and injudicious toward Riviere as well (again according to the words of Paula Heimann)?[56] Klein, a theorist of envy, was by all accounts prone to envy herself—an envy toward her mother, her sisters, her sister-in-law, Anna Freud, Marie Bonaparte, Helene Deutsch (she once said to Tom Main, who saw her home one evening, "I think my work will last, don't you? I've done better than Helene Deutsch, haven't I?").[57] At the end of her life, had she reached the conclusion that envy among women was unanalyzable? Could she have said such a thing, in her own slow, heavily accented voice with the hearty laugh that she had acquired over the years? Is female envy unanalyzable, as she asserted with respect to the orthodox Jew and the practicing Catholic?[58] Some of her most devoted followers would refute such a pessimistic hypothesis. Among those who remained loyal to her, the most tenacious and the most useful was Hanna Segal. An analysand, then a scrupulous exegete of Klein's work, Segal never failed to deepen Klein's thought, though she consistently sustained an interpretive spirit free from accommodation. The artist Felix Topolski, who created a sketch of Melanie Klein, remembered the psychoanalyst's arrogance and the rosy complexion of a Viennese woman fond of creamy pastries and conscious of her sex-appeal: Topolski gave Klein the look of a satiated vulture, which took her friends aback. Segal disagreed: for her, the drawing represented the very satisfied expression that Melanie assumed after an exceptionally effective interpretation.[59] Hanna Segal, or the passage through envy: she succeeded where Paula Heimann had failed.

However brilliant the male analysts of the British Society—Bion, Jones, Glover, Rickman, Strachey, Winnicott, to cite only a few—may have been, one has the impression that during this era, the era of Melanie, the destiny of psychoanalysis was decided in a matriarchal universe. R. D. Laing found the Kleinians "humorless"—that is to say "communist."[60] Rickman quarreled with them, Bion was entreated with tears to cite his debt to the party chief, and Winnicott passed into the group of "Independents," distancing himself to the point of "coolness." But the female psychoanalysts, already active in other countries, found themselves in England at the center of impassioned theoretical debates. Newly arrived in a psychoanalytic world that was itself new and full of innovation, they would inevitably fall into excess. The return of repression—here the repression of the feminine—did not come without violence. Beginning with Melanie, were these women acting out the psychodrama of incestuous mother-daughter relationships, or one of unconscious feminine homosexuality?[61] Were they theorists of the primal object exposed to a primary sadism, not recognizing the place of the *phallus* as capable by itself of severing or cultivating the "drives" and the "objects": how could they possibly escape it?

Yet we should be careful not to jump to conclusions here. The "open, Sesame" that was the Kleinians' "internal object" was followed by the omnipotence of the "phallus," which Lacan's successors presumed was capable of clarifying all misunderstandings and of resolving all the dramas of the passions. It is more difficult to engage the clinical and historical details of the conflicts in question. Concrete experimental investigation is much more complex—and also more risky. And—for Melanie, in any event—such investigation invited an unsympathetic scrutiny of her closest relatives.

Analytical technique gleaned at least one nonnegotiable principle from all of this: the line between personal friendships and analytical ties should not be crossed. Otherwise, such "promiscuities" reinforce the passions that are uncovered on the couch and that have no place in worldly or social relationships intended to be more or less civilized. As an explorer of the intolerable, psychoanalysis is—and must—remain "outside the world" as it is "outside time." Might a masculine authority, whether paternal or phallic, have *protected* the psychoanalytic universe of the Kleinians, sparing it these psychodramas among women? Perhaps, but only through repression. The fierceness of certain reactions *toward* Melanie, or *from* Melanie, might have been avoided. What this public unveiling accomplished, however, was to highlight the real objects of the Kleinian inquiry: maternal dependence and matricide.

In fact, beyond the various confrontations among the paranoid-schizoid positions that were latent in these women to varying degrees, it was Melanie's theoretical ambition itself that was revealed in all its unbearable radicalism. Is it possible to reach the limits of primal repression, the point at which the symbolic character of human nature collapses into chaos? The analyst's heartfelt anguish is so clearly necessary, in the voyage to this estrangement, that few among us can tolerate it: few indeed are the analysts who possess enough of an ability to sublimate so they can "dive in" without "drowning."

It should be noted that women joined Melanie Klein in taking this risk en masse. And women also counted among her most prudent adversaries, as we have seen: femininity in itself guarantees nothing. What mattered, for Klein, is the way that femininity is thought and lived. Besides, Freudian psychoanalysis today encounters so much resistance and is so seldom received and accepted, certain media popularizations notwithstanding, that Klein's breakthroughs remain—with the exception of a clinical circle specializing in the treatment of psychosis and childhood—totally unknown. Our "Valkyrie," as her enemies were prone to calling her, emerges as an explorer returning from a journey to the end of night. Melanie Klein ripped off the veil of a culture based on the sacred conversation between mother and child, if not indeed on the Pietà itself, and she allowed us to glimpse the underside of our civilization. *The Oresteia*—indeed, the whole Greek cosmogonic theogony, founded as it is on thwarted couples, which animated pre-Socratic thought and in particular the work of Heraclitus[62]—points the way toward the heart of the modern world, where it encounters new psychoanalytic revelations about our latent psychoses and depressions, revelations that will be forever deemed Kleinian ones.

If it is true, as Freud believed, that the son by himself can sometimes close his anxious gap with woman and can position himself as the unique object of indestructible love,[63] there is no doubt that the gap between mother and daughter is never satisfactorily filled. Melanie Klein took on the challenge of descending into that abyss. After reading her and trying to understand her, we should no longer feel the need to go as far as she did. We are so sure to go beyond her, are we not, simply by virtue of having just read her . . .

THE POLITICS OF KLEINIANISM

FROM THE GREAT CONTROVERSIAL DISCUSSIONS
TO THE INDEPENDENTS

By confronting archaic anxieties, which had received little attention before her, and by winning over the British therapists,
Melanie Klein gained an international audience within the psychoanalytic movement. To her innovative thought and her talent
were added an indefatigable tenacity and an unparalleled ability
to guide her friends, to divide her adversaries, and to regulate
envies and gratitudes—the signs of a powerful woman. Many
people noticed these qualities after Klein arrived in England. Just
after Ferenczi's 1927 visit to London, for example, Ferenczi wrote
Freud, as we recall, to denounce "the domineering influence
which Frau Melanie Klein has on the whole group. . . . Apart from
the scientific value of her work, I find it an influence directed at

Vienna."[1] Did Melanie "mesmerize" the British Society, as some have accused her of doing? Although Klein rose to the status of an "idealized object," did she nevertheless help lower herself into its "denigrated opposite?"[2] From the beginning, both her adherents and her skeptics acknowledged what the former considered her innovations and the latter her doctrinal transgressions. The debate only intensified when Anna Freud began to publish her own writings, which evinced an approach to child analysis that directly conflicted with Melanie's. The first skirmishes took place when the master's daughter attempted to be published in England.

Anna Freud (1895–1982) was thirteen years Melanie's junior. The last of Freud's children and one of his own analysands, Anna did not graduate from the *gymnasium* although she was highly intelligent. She was placed under the guidance of Hermine von Hug-Hellmuth so she could learn child analysis, and she became a member of the Vienna Psychoanalytic Society in 1922. After practicing child analysis for two years, she hurriedly published *The Psycho-Analytic Treatment of Children*.[3] It was important for the daughter and the heir of the inventor of psychoanalysis, whose cancer was already known, to confirm her father's authority. When Anna addressed the Berlin Society in 1927, she contended that the analysis of normal children could be hazardous, which conflicted with Melanie's view that analysis should play an integral role in the education of *all* children. Anna's work essentially argued that the analyst should adopt the role of the child's ideal ego so that treatment could get under way. Of course, such a notion of the analyst as a mentor whose authority exceeds that of the parents themselves was poles apart from Klein's own conception.

The British analysts—Barbara Low (whose support of Anna Freud never dwindled and who wrote a very positive review of Anna's book), David Eder, Edward Glover, Joan Riviere, Ella Sharpe, and Klein herself—pored over the master's daughter's work. Though a diverse group, they unanimously agreed, according to a letter Jones wrote Freud in response to his expostulations, that it was ill advised for Anna to have been "so hasty as to publish her first lectures in such an uncompromising form and on such a slender basis of experience," a decision that risked imposing a "check" on the development of early analysis.[4] Until the end of her life, Anna remained bitter about this denunciation, particularly with respect to Jones, who proved at this point that he could hold his own with Freud.

The antagonism between the two women only deepened. These two intransigent personalities—Anna/Antigone and Melanie/Valkyrie—who came from different cultures, each defended her own notion of child analysis. Their differences soon became quite apparent, at which point Melanie summarized Anna Freud's principles of child analysis, which she found unacceptable, as follows:

1. No analysis of the child's Oedipus complex was possible, as it might interfere with the child's relations with its parents;
2. Child analysis should exert only an educative influence on the child;
3. A transference neurosis cannot be effected because the parents still exert a predominant role in the child's life; and
4. The analyst should exert every effort to gain the child's confidence.[5]

If such principles were adopted, they would in fact contradict Klein's own observations, which many analysts had already accepted as forming the basis of a new analytic technique: the early emergence of the Oedipus complex, the concomitant presence of an aggressive object relation that results in the projection of the death drive, the prior emergence of the superego, the rapid emergence of transference in children and the meaning of its impact on interpretation, particularly in negative transference, and so forth. All of these insights were laid out in Melanie's work—and she returned to them in the English version of *The Psychoanalysis of Children* in 1932.

The Anna Freudians, for their part, objected that Melanie, in addition to advancing the theoretical innovations I have just mentioned, failed to consider the real existence of the mother, interpreting instead the fantasies and innate drives projected by the child. As varied a group of clinicians as Melitta, Bowlby, and Winnicott shared this view to varying degrees, and some of the Independents would try to fill the gaps in Klein's work by referring to Merrel Middlemore's work *The Nursing Couple.*

The contentiousness between the two analysts, which preceded the Freuds' arrival in London in 1939, underlay the dissensions that would later be articulated by clinicians both British and Continental and would be elaborated upon during the famous Controversial Discussions. A broader mindset, a commitment to scientific research based on empirical experience, and a highly democratic impulse that infiltrated the institutional politics of the British Society all helped transform this contentiousness into an unprecedented scholarly debate, as evidenced by the published *Freud-Klein Controversies.*[6]

Long before the Second World War, then, these diverging views hardened and led to fractures inside the very fabric of the British Psycho-Analytic Society. The impassioned quarrel between Melanie and Melitta, which Glover only encouraged, added even more venom to the discussions. Political realities entered the fray beginning in 1938, as many Continental analysts—Balint, Bibring, Edelberg, Hitschmann, Hoffer, Isakower, Kris, Lanton, Stengel, Schur, Stross, Sachs, Straub, and others—escaped the Nazis and settled in England. Their arrival en masse inflamed the brewing crisis. On the one hand, classic Freudianism and Anna Freudianism, which functioned as a hegemony, were confronted in England with a dissidence that was no small matter, as some on the Continent believed. On the other hand, because of both the war and the sudden influx of new immigrants, these practitioners were faced with a dearth of clients, even with unemployment. Who will submit to training analyses? How will we educate psychoanalytic trainees? Are some groups perhaps abusing their power by injuring others? As always, symbolic "power" proves to be economic as well. Behind all these theoretical machinations, a social struggle had started to overwhelm the psychoanalytic field.

Freud died on September 23, 1939. All his loved ones and disciples mourned him greatly. In the dramatic context of the war, moreover, his disappearance inspired his disciples to clarify their master's ideas. Each of them claimed to speak for him, professed undivided loyalty, and in fact sought to appropriate his work in a grand totemic feast during which the sons—under the direction of the daughters—debated among themselves and tried to separate the "pure" from the "impure." The history of psychoanalysis, still an emerging discipline, suggests that its protagonists experienced it, more or less unconsciously, as a religion. Jung's schism with Freud had recently suggested as much, and Lacan's dissidence would do so as well.

And yet in the face of this retreat, the reader may believe that the shake-ups in the British analytic movement during the war, which arose out of Melanie Klein's work as well as her controversial discussions with the Anna Freudians, offer an encouraging example that this sort of religiosity can be overcome. To the violence of conflicts—which were indeed sacrificial, if not sacred—were added a viable work of reflection and a theoretical, clinical, and institutional development. The exchange of new and complementary perspectives opened up the path toward viable psychoanalytic research. Can we really pursue that path today, one that the successors to these pioneers have refined?

For the time being, Melanie dreaded the arrival of the Viennese contingent,[7] whose conformity she rejected: "It will never be the same again. It's a disaster."[8] The Viennese themselves, who found themselves persecuted and vulnerable because of their exile, were prone to feeling that " 'bei uns war es besser' (we did it better in Vienna)."[9] The stage was set for an ever-deepening conflict, a conflict fomented by both Glover and Melitta. Conflict spiraled even more because the analysts of English origin took refuge in the country during the war, while the Continentals remained in London and stuck together during their many days spent in theoretical discussion—at first in the majority, but then in the minority. A "middle group" crept up between the two brigades, and some observers pondered the meaning of the attendant intellectual tempest. One of them was James Strachey, who quite accurately described the "extremism"[10] of the two camps and who wrote the following in 1940, in a bizarre letter to Edward Glover: "Why should these wretched fascists and communists invade our peaceful compromising island?—(bloody foreigners)."[11]

As London was being torn apart and bombarded by Nazi war planes, psychoanalysts, unscathed by the blitz, spent their time arguing about the propriety of Klein's contributions, the exact meaning that Freud sought to give to the "death drive" and the "superego," the nature and early emergence of the "primal fantasies," the "body-ego," "rejection," "negation," the possibility or impossibility of a scientific judgment in psychoanalysis: in sum, they spent their days pondering the price of tea in China.

This "trivial"[12] debate began with some very practical questions: How should we train young analysts? Have the Kleinians not appropriated the majority of the candidates for themselves? An ad hoc committee was appointed that concluded that Melanie had not "manipulated" the young trainees! Irritated, the Kleinians who had once considered breaking away were able to relax for a moment. But the respite mattered little, as the theoretical disputes persevered. Glover and Melitta were uncompromising, Anna Freud showed herself to be more reasonable but still dictatorial and aggressive, Jones may have been simply feebleminded and wily, Ella Sharpe switched sides, Sylvia Payne was fairly objective, while Joan Riviere refused to accept any challenges from the Viennese—and only Winnicott, who was more independent and clearheaded than ever and who hardly ever participated in the discussions—allowed himself to bring up real life: "I would like to point out that an air raid is going on," he once said during a debate on the subject of aggression in psychoanalysis!

The various factions had staked out their respective ground. With Anna Freud were Dorothy Burlingham, Kate Friedlander, Barbara Lantons, Hedwig Hoffer, Barbara Low, and Ella Sharpe, with Melitta off doing her own thing. Continentals, all of them men, and who were less effective than the ladies, also joined the group: S. H. Foulkes, Willi Hoffer, and Walter Schmideberg. The Kleinian camp included reliable woman: Paula Heimann, Joan Riviere, Susan Isaacs, and, for a time, Sylvia Payne, who would soon become an Independent; it also included such men as Roger Money-Kyrle, John Rickman, W. Scott, and D. W. Winnicott. The intermediaries made themselves heard as well: James Strachey, Marjorie Brierley, and others. The majority of the members of the British Society would gradually come from the Middle Group and would express concern about the Kleinians' proselytizing tendencies.

Jones made an invaluable foray into diplomacy, one that approached hesitation and indecision, and he shuttled deftly between the two groups, as evidenced by the following excerpt from his January 21, 1942, letter to Anna Freud: "I consider Mrs Klein has made important contributions. . . . On the other hand she has neither a scientific nor an orderly mind and her presentations are lamentable."[13]

Particularly her presentations on the Oedipus complex and the role of the father, he added, forgetting that he himself had endorsed Klein's notions on those subjects in his 1934 article "The Phallic Phase"![14] In another letter, the society president was none too kind to Anna either: "[Anna] is certainly a tough and indigestible morsel. She has probably gone as far in analysis as she can and has no pioneering originality."[15]

Jones, in fact, was nowhere to be found during the Controversial Discussions. He suffered from a series of psychosomatic illnesses and retreated into the countryside. He miraculously recovered just as the Discussions were ending, though by that point he had surrendered leadership to Glover—and had thus taken away any opportunity Melanie might have had to benefit from his influence. Fortunes changed, however, and Edward Glover, at first the director of research at the institute, felt increasingly put upon by the success of Klein's theory and by the compromise that the two factions were forming. He resigned from the British Society in 1944 and joined the Swiss Society, expressing his dismay at seeing the British Society become "a woman ridden society" and at seeing the "Klein imbroglio" develop—which was really just a way of implicitly acknowledging that his attempts to discredit Melanie had failed.

Anna Freud, who shared child analyst training duties with Melanie Klein, resigned from the Training Committee and began to lead seminars from her home. She had already been accepted as an authority with her *The Ego and the Mechanisms of Defense*, and she organized the Hampstead War Nursery, which remained under her influence.[16]

Their closest rival was the prestigious Tavistock Institute and Clinic, which Hugh Crichton-Miller founded in 1920 to treat those suffering from shell shock, that is, those nervous traumas—shaking, paralysis, hallucinations—that result from repeated exposure to explosives. Under the direction of John Rees, these activities grew to include the treatment of juvenile delinquents in individual or group therapy. Under the influence of Rickman and Bion, Freudian and Kleinian theories came to dominate the work of the Clinic, so much so that it came to be considered one of the bastions of Kleinianism. Beginning in 1946, John Bowlby introduced the Independents' approach as well as family therapy to the Clinic, and Balint contributed his group therapy technique.[17]

Anna Freud, who was highly combative and even "dictatorial" but who was thrown off track by the dissemination of Klein's views, threatened and manipulated until people began to fear she would follow Glover: Could Freud's daughter actually resign from the British Psycho-Analytical Society? Never! What should be done about the mere prospect? The atmosphere could not have been more heated.

Melanie, too, entertained thoughts of breaking away, as some had suggested that she should do. She divided her time between her family in Cambridge and her patients, particularly in Pitlochry, Scotland, where she analyzed little Richard. As she was absent from the beginning of the Discussions, she sent her devotees in her place, who nevertheless remained under her firm and steady control: she supervised every aspect, for example, of Susan Isaacs's work on the phantasy.[18] Klein rarely intervened orally, and Jones occasionally prevented her from speaking,[19] but she issued no shortage of notes and letters. When she presented written texts, moreover, the pages were dense.[20] A militant mind-set surrounded her. The most passionate of her supporters formed the "I.O. (Internal Object) Group" in order to clarify the matriarch's theory and to make it accessible to the Viennese. The "battle group"—Paula Heimann, Susan Isaacs, and the doctrinaire Joan Riviere—grew even tighter.

On both sides, women were the most active, but they never stopped turning to men: Papa Jones and Papa Glover were discussed or invited to the Discussions, and the symbolic authorities Freud and Abraham were often cited, particularly by Melanie.[21] The figure of the father, whether dead or not, clearly hovered over the Discussions, even more so because the Kleinian faction appeared less strong than it actually was, with the result that Melanie's political genius became more impressive than ever imagined. I will give two examples of this.

Just when all hopes of reconciliation had vanished, Klein attempted to compromise with Anna Freud in May 1942. Anna was "very surprised, though very pleased"[22] by this development, and, even if the armistice was far from succeeding, Melanie's idea was clear: she did not want schisms, she held herself out as a follower of Freud, she just needed some time to prove it, whether with Anna or against her, but in any event not against psychoanalysis, for all psychoanalysis is—and can only be—Freudian psychoanalysis. Klein hated the adjective "Kleinian," and with good reason. It was only because of Glover's malicious rumor-mongering that people thought she saw herself as a prophet, even as Jesus. Her determination to innovate *within the context of Freudianism* was a valid conviction and, for that very reason, provided a convincing strategy:

> My greatest experience in this was "Beyond the Pleasure Principle" and the *Ego and the Id* and *what* an experience it was. In a smaller way I saw in my own work [on reparation and the depressive position] repeatedly a new light appear and things altered by it. . . . I think these findings could not have been unworldly to have been made even by Freud and he would have had the greatness, the strength, the powers to present them to the world. I don't want you to misunderstand me. I am not *afraid* of fighting against anybody, but I *really don't like* fighting. *What I wish* to do is to quietly let others participate in something I know to be true, important, and helpful.[23]

And there we have a nice display of insolence with a noble stab at modesty!

In a similar spirit, Klein sent Winnicott a note apologizing for asking him to tone down a resolution he had proposed presenting. By showing consideration for Winnicott, she was preserving more than anything else their shared place in the Freud locomotive. And then she forwarded her comments on Winnicott's proposed text to the other members of the group:

> I think the impression which it might give that Freud is more or less history would not only be dangerous, but the fact itself is not true. Freud's writings are very much alive, and still a guide for our work. . . . Anything which could give the impression that we think that Freud could be put on a shelf is the most dangerous trap we could fall into.[24]

That view could already be termed, as part of an effective strategy, a "return to Freud." That is, to a clearly refurbished Freud!

Melanie was not content with merely summarizing Freud's views as a way to defend herself, for she also attacked those who did not read Freud as she did[25] and solidified her own ideas. It is not true, she said, that she denied the existence of the mother's external reality, and to the extent that she believed that what is perceived is always "colored" by the fantasy, one has to concede "the vicissitudes of the relationships with internal objects" that are "fluid" and not established for once and for all.[26] It is true that the seeds of depressive feelings exist from the beginning of life, but they are limited to the time between the child's third and fifth month during the depressive position. And the father is not present in the child's fantasy before the fourth month.[27] And the love for the mother is not merely libido, but a veritable form of gratitude toward the person whom the child himself dreams of feeding,[28] an emotion that is already highly complex before the depressive position even though it is entirely manifested only with that position.[29] And an immediate sublimation is formed within the relation to the breast, which is a true "bridge" between the infant's paranoid omnipotence and his adaptation to reality.[30]

Klein the theoretician built her castle while Klein the politician maneuvered with great skill, particularly with respect to Strachey's preliminary report on the training of psychoanalysts. As Melanie was not a physician herself, she fought against the discrimination visited upon psychoanalysts who were not doctors, and she advocated a training in psychoanalysis alone as she believed medical training was of no help in understanding mental disorders. To Strachey, she declared her wish to remain "behind the scenes," although she very tactfully suggested that it would be inadvisable to "penalize originality"—the subtext being that the "originality," her own, was on the verge of prevailing. At the same time, she told her cohorts the following:

> We must, of course, avoid giving any ground to feel that we are triumphing and I feel that I can now keep on for a time bearing the situation in which my work is at the same time being appreciated and depreciated, sometimes in one breath by the same people.[31]

The war among the ladies wound up being a peace among the ladies. Several of them had a change of heart: some of the loyalists—Marjorie Brierley, Barbara Low, Ella Sharpe, and Adrian and Karin Stephen (who supported Klein from the beginning)— turned against Melanie with hostility. At the same time, Sylvia Payne, who, along with W. H. Gillespie, had declared herself an "Independent" and who had endorsed Susan Isaacs's work on the phantasy, became disappointed with Glover and abandoned Melanie's adversary for good. Payne was elected president of the British Psycho-Analytical Society in 1944. Klein's theories held their own, even among her adversaries: although Anna Freud did not adopt the depressive position, didn't she begin to speak of "grief in infancy?"[32] Miss Freud resigned from the Training Committee in 1944 and abstained—as did Glover, the Schmidebergs, and the Viennese—from participating in any way in the second series of Controversial Discussions. As a result, "power" reverted de facto to the prewar members of the society.[33] Following a series of theoretical and administrative negotiations, a compromise was struck. These ladies—and these gentlemen—subscribed to the principles of democratic cohabitation. For institutional purposes, the society approved two parallel courses of psychoanalytic training in order to satisfy both the Kleinians and the Anna Freudians. This did not prevent many clinicians—and some of the best ones at that—from feeling a mix of irritation and admiration for Melanie, as did R. D. Laing, Marion Milner, D. W. Winnicott, and Sylvia Payne.

One of the important benefits of these skirmishes among the various psychoanalytic factions was to facilitate a close analysis of the tyrannical logic underlying groups—all groups. One could hypothesize, in fact, that the sectarian functioning and exclusivity that characterized the Kleinians (they were caricatured as "the Ebenezer Church")[34] served as a laboratory for Bion—one that complemented his experience as an military psychiatrist who was the officer-in-charge responsible for rehabilitating victims of shell shock—when he offered a scathing analysis of group functioning.[35] Although his book was based on Kleinian principles, it did not find favor with Melanie, who was analyzing Bion when he wrote it—and her reaction was well founded!

Bion's book incorporates his belief that a group is an entity unto itself and not simply a conglomeration of individuals with which one has a relationship comparable to the infant's relation to the breast (or to the part object). The failure to respond effectively to the demands of this relationship is experienced as an intolerable frustration, which is manifested in the paranoid-schizoid regression that characterizes the members of the group. Although the family grouping, with its oedipal libido, largely remains, as Freud believed, the prototype of the group bond, Bion wisely modified that analysis and contended that group dynamics reflect far more primitive mechanisms, as manifested, in Klein's view, by the depressive and paranoid-schizoid positions. It is true that groups in any form (the religious ones based on a hypothesis of dependence, the aristocratic ones based on coupling for the aristocratic ones, and the military ones based on fight-or-flight) conceal not only psychotic anxiety but defensive reactions against such anxiety as well. The inability to form symbols is not the sole province of isolated cases, as Klein showed with Dick, but "[extends] to include all individuals in their functions as members of the basic-assumption group."[36]

The Controversial Discussions clearly reflected such paranoid-schizoid regressions, and Melanie's personality no doubt reinforced the imago of the fascinating and persecuting breast.[37] But Klein also encouraged, as she did with Bion, the analysis of this phenomenon in the etymological sense of the word: its decomposition through genuine analytic work of an unprecedented depth and clarity, one that applies to the interpretation of all groups, whether they be psychoanalytic, political, religious, or otherwise.

In the end the most important consequence of this "peace among the ladies" was nothing more than to preserve the spirit of inquiry. In addition to forming the group known as the "Independents" (Jones, Sharpe, Flugel, Payne, Rickman, Strachey, Brierley, Fairbairn, Winnicott, Balint, Kluber, Khan, and Bolby[38]), the British analysts sustained an ecumenical movement of substantial psychoanalytic investigation. Since that time this broadening of the mind and this taste for confrontation have been appreciated by all those who consider psychoanalysis to be an active quest. Even more intimately, finally, the upshot of all this has been described by Winnicott, who, in a parallel to Bion's dissection of the group, endorsed a more sober, essentially analytic, alternative: "The Capacity to Be Alone"[39] as the foundation of creativity, and creativity in psychoanalysis in particular. Melanie responded with her own "On the Sense of Loneliness," in which she elaborated upon the benefits of feeling lonely.[40] It is as if she were showing us the way there![41]

LACAN'S ENVY AND GRATITUDE

The first time Lacan referred to Klein in writing was in his essay on aggressivity, which he delivered in May 1948 as a speech to the Congrès des Psychanalystes de Langue Française in Brussels.[42] He likened his own notion of the "imagos of the fragmented body" to Melanie's notion of the "internal objects" of archaic fantasies, and he paid tribute to the aspects of "the phenomenology of the Kleinian experience" that consist of the "fantasies of what is termed the paranoid stage."[43] In appropriating Klein's notion of the paranoid position, Lacan augmented it, defining the ego as an instance of imaginary *méconnaissance* built upon a paranoid structure. The negative transference emphasized by Klein helped Lacan understand treatment to be a controlled paranoia that serves to remedy the ignorance of the ego: psychoanalysis "induce[s] in the subject a controlled paranoia" that is tantamount to the "the projection of what Melanie Klein calls bad internal objects, a paranoiac mechanism . . . filtered, as it were, and properly checked" by the analyst.[44] With a great deal of loyalty to Klein, Lacan traces his concept of the "imaginary," which he was still forming in 1948, to Melanie's own writings: he speaks of "the imaginary primordial enclosure formed by the imago of the mother's body."[45] He also appears amenable to the idea of an archaic superego, though he is less interested in the biological prematurity that supports it than in its cultural dimension as a "signifier." The "persistence in the imaginary of good and bad objects" generates the notion of an early superego, which has a "generic" meaning for the subject; the same applies to the infantile dependence associated with the baby's "physiological misery" but inseparable from his "relationship to his human surroundings." The superego is thus an instance laden with meaning that lies at the "crossroads between nature and culture."[46]

In August 1949 Lacan returned to many of these themes during the Sixteenth Congress of the International Association of Psychoanalysis in Zurich, where he delivered a paper entitled "The Mirror Stage as Formative of the Function of the I."[47] The emphasis that Lacan, beginning with this paper, placed on the visual realm as a signifying organizer of the other sensations in the structure of the subject appears to be inconsistent with Klein's theories.[48] Lacan's piece also pays substantial tribute to Anna Freud, a move that has often been interpreted as part of his political strategy to link himself with the daughter of the "founder." Although Lacan had at least two irons in the fire of international psychoanalysis, one could see this reference to Anna as a way for him to disassociate himself from the outer limits of a Kleinianism preoccupied with the primitive ego. Lacan was seeking a focal point for his own non-Freudian theory of the subject, and he abandoned Melanie while flirting with Anna Freud's surprisingly empirical and restrictive propositions concerning the ego's secondary or defensive mechanisms. In the end, though, Lacan associated both women with the "structures of systematic méconnaissance"[49] in which Miss Freud's ego defenses join the Kleinian phantasy.

While courting Anna, Lacan was also contacting Melanie and even suggesting to her that "the progressive point of view in psycho-analysis,"[50] which Melanie believed belonged to him in the eyes of the French, should have been represented during the first World Congress of Psychiatry not by Anna Freud but by the Kleinians themselves.[51]

Seduction, approbation, and abandonment: was this a game, an ambiguous one to say the least, destined to become a "Freudian slip" . . . or was it a true act of sabotage? René Diatkine, who was in analysis with Lacan, translated from the German the first part of *The Psychoanalysis of Children*, and he entrusted his translation to Lacan. Françoise Girard, an analyst also being treated by Lacan who married the Canadian analyst Jean-Baptiste Boulanger, obtained Melanie's approval to translate *Love, Guilt, and Reparation*. Melanie learned from Diatkine that one half of *The Psychoanalysis of Children* had been translated, but that Lacan was not the author of that version. And yet Lacan told the Boulangers otherwise when he offered them the chance to translate the second half of Klein's work. The first part of the translation, the one that Diatkine handed over to Lacan, is nowhere to be found! Lacan never formally admitted that he had lost it, and Diatkine did not keep a duplicate for himself! In January 1952 the Boulangers had lunch with Melanie and recounted the whole sorry tale to her. Lacan lost all credibility in her mind, and she subsequently aligned herself with Daniel Lagache.[52]

In the meantime the anthology *Developments in Psycho-Analy-*

sis, edited by Melanie Klein, Paula Heimann, Susan Isaacs, and Joan Riviere, was published in 1952—and for Melanie's seventieth birthday, Roger Money-Kyrle put together a Festschrift. This tribute was eventually published in the form of a special issue of the *International Journal of Psychoanalysis* that was edited by Paula Heimann and Roger Money-Kyrle and that included work by fourteen contributors.[53] These publications recapture and elaborate upon the essential features of Klein's thought regarding the Controversial Discussions, and they clearly reflect her desire to renew psychoanalysis.

Two years later, in 1954, and during his Seminar on Freud's Papers on Technique, Lacan returned to the "case of Dick" and offered his own reading of Freud's "On Negation" in response to Jean Hyppolite.[54] As I have mentioned, Freud's essay served as the Kleinians' battle horse during the Controversies with the Anna Freudians, who proved themselves unfamiliar with the work.[55] Lacan thus employed the same strategy that the Kleinians did during their own attempt to recast psychoanalysis. But Lacan failed to credit his sources, and he declined to cite Klein in his discussion of Freudian negativity, except, perhaps, through his indirect reference to Kris and Melitta in the context of the case study of the Brain Man!

Lacan's displacement, incidentally, is significant. The primacy of the signifier eradicates what I have termed Klein's "incarnationism," her ever heterogeneous conception of an imaginary that is at once a thing and an image, a sensation or an affect and representation.[56] Lacan saw himself apart from all this and laid out "developments" and "new directions" of his own—but he also forgot the women who inspired him and avoided confrontation as a result.

That did not keep him from occasionally referring to Klein's work, usually with a respectful tone, as if he had gotten over envy without quite reaching gratitude, suggesting that he sensed deep affinities with Klein's work, particularly with her conception of a primal paranoia and of an early fantasy that structures the ego. From that perspective, he likened Klein's "depressive position" to his own "mirror stage" in the sense that both concepts attest to "the characteristically imaginary nature of the function of the Ego in the subject."[57] And he also paid tribute to "Melanie Klein's genius" in having "reconstructed" the "depressive core" that is ushered in by the death drive.[58]

And yet Lacan pulled no punches when it came to indicating his fundamental disagreement with her, particularly with respect to her failure to acknowledge the paternal function or to create a theory of the subject, and he also objected to Klein's reducing the penis to a role as a mere appendage in her hypostasis of the maternal imago that remained forever foreign to Lacan. In that spirit, he admonished Jones for having endorsed the "utter brutality" of Klein's concepts and for having seen the penis only as a part object and not at all as "the phallus." He also denounced Jones's "failure . . . to include the most primal oedipal fantasies in the mother's body and to account for their origin in the reality presumed by the Name-of-the-Father."[59]

Amid all this envy and ingratitude, "inspired gut butcher" appears to be the most gripping formula. Did I simply hear these words during one of Lacan's seminars that has not yet been published? I was unable to track the phrase down in Lacan's published writings. Is this undiscoverable quotation an indelible symptom of a Klein who eludes our grasp, a symptom that infects those who love her as well as those who hate her, as if she refused to be summed up in a carefully worded phrase (as we have seen, she was a founder without a text)—and was she perhaps satisfied with simply making others speak, dream, and associate? Was Klein an analyst, in sum, from whom Lacan built a little bridge that reached to the Brain Man, to that plagiarist who "borrowed" without acknowledging as much?

It turns out that the phrase can be found in an essay that Lacan devoted to none other than André Gide![60] The phrase appears in the context of Gide's "oddly unsustained attack" (in the words of Lacan himself, who nevertheless took it upon himself to remind us of it!) on Freud, whom the author of *The Counterfeiters* called a "brilliant imbecile."[61] After tracing, as does Jean Delay, the endless maze of Gide's identifications, particularly his identifications with the discourse of a mother who "fills the gap through a passion for

230 / THE POLITICS OF KLEINIANISM

his governess," Lacan addresses the writer's bond with his cousin Madeleine, and eventually likens his imaginary to an "antique theater" replete with "shaking, slips, and repulsive figures," "being shaken to the core of one's being, a sea that enraptures everything." This horrifying female imagery caused nightmares about a "creek that consumes" the young André, and love abruptly turned a corner into what lies beyond death, when it was not into laughter, until a vengeful Medusa, flanked by the Lady of the Troubadours and by Dante's Beatrice, insinuated herself into Gide's and Lacan's visions of a "black hole." It is in this very context that we find Lacan's allusion to Melanie Klein, whose name has been effaced: "Indeed, the child filled this void with monsters—a crowd of monsters known to us, since a diviner with a child's eyes, an inspired gut butcher, has catalogued them for us—projecting those monsters into the womb of the nursing mother."[62]

"Brilliant imbecile" (Freud according to Gide) and "inspired gut butcher" (Klein according to Lacan): therein lies a true "diviner" who speaks volumes about the phobic fantasies of the mother's "guts" in Gide, as endorsed here by Lacan, which the man and the artist avoid through "inspiration"! But there is so very little on Melanie's work itself! Except, perhaps, when the psychoanalyst correctly points out that it is essential, in a clinical sense, to consider the degree to which the child's primary fantasies originate with the mother herself. Lacan invites us to lend our ear to the child who was the mother, that is, to the child that always remains a mother when we analyze the child of the mother.

THE LEFT AND THE FEMINISTS TAKE HOLD OF THE "INSPIRED GUT BUTCHER"

Klein is a truly paradoxical figure. On the one hand, the mechanical popularized view of Klein, which is oversimplified and which sometimes arises out of our author's own writings, can come across as so many lessons drummed into students' heads. The "positions" with the precepts of "reparation" and the "integration of the ego," when reduced to the form of newspaper headlines,

can resemble the sort of sensible advice that educational maga-
zines offer to families. On the other hand, a restless dissidence,
one that emerged during an era of conformity and of planned
transgressions, reflects the sober vision of a human being gov-
erned by a death drive that is readily transformable into creativity
as long as he or she is given a bit of innate luck, a capacity for love,
and a "good enough mother" (as Winnicott puts it in an effort to
counter Melanie's grip over the "internal object").

These two faces of Kleinianism have not failed to attract the
attention of sociologists and other theoreticians in Great
Britain—and they have interested American and British feminists
as well. Melanie Klein is perhaps the only psychoanalyst who,
without ever reflecting herself upon modern history and society
in the way that a Freud and a Reich have done, has inspired political reflections that clearly exceed the immediate scope of her clinical conceptions. Her empiricism and her theoretical awkward-
ness give her work an intrinsically open and multilayered quality
that invites expansive interpretations. But that alone is not
enough to explain her success in the field of sociology, a success
that seems due in part to the attraction that deep psychoanalysis
has for our contemporary world, which cannot be fully understood through ideologies and the traditional philosophies.

For a nonconformist elite, psychoanalysis's uniqueness in being
at the crossroads between empirical utility and speculative daring
destines it to become a new model for thinking about social relations, beyond the family or specific groups, while still respecting
the alternative of being alone.[63] From the "socialist consideration"
inspired by Kleinian psychoanalysis to the agenda of a "good society" attentive to the "inner world" and through a reconsideration
of Rousseauism from the perspective of a social theory based on
Klein's writings,[64] the work on this subject has continued to grow
in the past ten years or so. These reflections would have certainly
surprised even the most ambitious dreams of a Melanie who was
concerned about being useful to society, and they foreclose the
most acerbic criticism from her contemporary detractors who
have accused her of being oriented solely toward the inner world.

Two faces of Kleinianism thus emerge through the sociological extrapolations from her work. Some critics emphasize her theory of the negative and the importance of the death drive and of the disruptive forces that call to mind the image of the antiestablish-mentarian and the rebel when they do not descend into the figures of the paranoid person or the quietly schizophrenic egotist. That sort of reading, which is informed by the French psychoanalysts' interpretation of Klein, has recently come to the fore in writings by several British theorists.[65] Other critics during the past decade, on the other hand, pride themselves on discovering in Melanie Klein a foundation for the social bond by focusing on conciliation and by overplaying what even some Kleinian clinicians themselves have not refrained from exaggerating: reparation, the formation of an object relation and of symbolization to the detriment of violence and anxiety. It is important to note, however, that the supporters of this view run the risk of transforming psychoanalysis into a social safety net—even into a secular religion.

Such risks have not discouraged attempts to theorize a socialism attentive to the inner universe and the depressive self by drawing from Klein as a way to lessen the blows of the globalization we are currently experiencing.

Michael Rustin and Margaret Rustin, for example, believe that Melanie Klein expanded the scope of psychoanalysis by proposing a relational conception of human nature that, although consumed with destructiveness and greed, is profoundly moral. If socialism is to replace waning religions, such a vision could provide a viable starting point. A socialism conceived along those lines would consider modern men and women not as a simple source of comfort but as a clearheaded strain of humanism that is capable of reflecting upon death, destructive sexuality, the infantile realm, and innate differences. To exonerate the importance of the family, to revive emotion and feeling beyond the realm of abstract reason, and to make reparation to the ego's lifelong relationship to a social community are only some of the premises of the vision of social democracy that the Rustins believe lies dormant in Kleinian psychoanalysis. The Rustins use her theory for inspiration as they advocate a sort of socialism in which individual needs are recognized as such and are not immediately subordinated to the demands of the group. With a more classically liberal approach, Roger Money-Kyrle, who also cites Melanie Klein, believes that a depressive morality based on love and a concern for others can be contrasted with totalitarianism and unbridled capitalism. The Rustins, for their part, present a model of democracy in which the state tends to social needs without hindering individual liberties in an effort to regulate an all-powerful liberalism. From that perspective, the authors draw the conclusion that Kleinian theory "provides one of the main theoretical bases for a better system of social provision, and also one of the main measures of their adequacy."[66]

Similarly, Fred C. Alford's *Melanie Klein and Critical Social Theory* attempts to develop a version of sociology that is capable of remedying the difficulties encountered when the Frankfurt School proposed a new concept of reason as part of its proponents' effort to understand human relations. Alford suggests that Marcuse, by basing his notion of Eros on sexual drives and the Oedipus complex, needlessly contrasted it with a society founded on repression, with the result that the sociology that stems from this notion runs the risk of descending into a "selfish instrumentalism."[67] A sociology derived from Kleinianism, on the other hand, could establish a social bond that is amenable to reparation and reconciliation.[68] Although Alford recognizes that his perspective "revises" Klein's clinical practice, he does not hesitate to deem Klein a "social theorist": by emphasizing the "passions" that are always linked to the other and adorned with a sense of direction and coherence more than are the "drives" that are more or less fragmenting and fragmented, Melanie Klein allows us to theorize a "reparative reason" and a "reparative individualism." The concern for the other would be the defining feature of such a paradigm, as would the creation of a social bond that is not coercive and that is defined as a "supple and flexible social structure." Such moral maturation directed toward reparation and reconciliation is possible with individuals and with small groups, whereas large groups, in contrast, defend themselves from anxiety through paranoid-schizoid mechanisms and thus impede the logical processes of a reparative individualism. The "instrumental reason" imposed by ultraliberalism, the speculations on the part of the financial markets, the unchecked exploitation of nature, and the wholesale mastery of society are rooted in a paranoid-schizoid position characterized by a tendency toward possession and domination. Reparative reason, on the other hand, reconciles and organizes a society that is founded more on the concern and respect for other people than on repression and instrumentalism. Melanie Klein's work promotes such a vision of human nature, a vision founded on a primal morality. To a sociologist's eyes, Klein appears less pessimistic than Freud, even though she was hardly unaware that destructive forces exist. The human being is not an isolated self but an eminently social self adorned with a "Eudaemonian ethic." Put another way, the Kleinian ego believes it has a "need to make reparation and that doing so will make [it] happier."[69] In summary, Alford reads Klein in a way that privileges the reparative thrust of her clinical approach at the cost of focusing on the more negative elements—the very ones that other people have been all too happy to emphasize.[70] Reparation aside, however, Alford is not unfamiliar with the tragic dimension of Klein's thought, for avarice, envy, and hatred make the world a hostile and empty one, and in Klein's view, the self encounters neither redemption nor complete salvation.[71]

Without renouncing the reparative fairy, it is important to note that Klein the wizard offers perspectives that are more disquieting that Alford's and that, as a result, provide more fertile ground for exploring human and social darkness. I will thus briefly discuss here another social reading inspired by Klein's clinical work.

It turns out that, long before the uprisings in May 1968 and the anarchist fugue attendant to Deleuze and Guattari's *Anti-Oedipus*, and right before the emergence of Lacan's passion for female paranoia,[72] Melanie envisioned the individual as an economy that is transformed by the death drive, is intrinsically paranoid-schizoid, and has little inclination to adapt to reality. The Anna Freudians criticized her for not paying attention to the real family and mother (not to mention the father) or to the burgeoning external reality, and for limiting herself instead to a world of sadistic fantasies, or at best essentially negative ones. This view is not really accurate, for the child's psychic dynamic depends, as Klein believed, on the mother's inner world—which the child deems to be an external object! It is true, however, that Klein did not believe in adaptation, and that she even thought it was not a psychoanalytic idea. As a result she rebuked Anna Freud for conducting herself like a schoolteacher in focusing exclusively on the ego's defenses as they relate to the aims of adequate education.

Klein proclaimed that we are all paranoid-schizophrenics, which was enough to raise the eyebrows of antiauthoritarian types in Great Britain. Even worse, she believed that all forms of authority, and parental authority in particular, generate inhibition and anxiety: we recall Fritz's atheist mother and believing father, who eventually let go of their hold on their son, per the analyst's advice, and allowed him to think for himself.

Underneath the authority (an authority that others will deem "symbolic") of the father, which she declines to discuss, Melanie diagnosed the power of the mother, which she believed provides the real support behind any law. Klein never defined femininity in terms of passivity, as Freud did. Rather, femininity in Klein unfolds into a form of receptiveness (the successor to the oral stage in both the girl and the boy, both of whom desire to incorporate the penis as well as the breast that contains it) and into a form of primordial terrifying maternal power, which is the backbone behind all tyrannical authority as well as the prototype (along with the father coupled with her) of the superego. For Klein, the law draws on this power of the "mother with a penis," which she attempts to distinguish from Freud's "mother phallic" because, in the Kleinian phantasy, the male organ is not a visible appendage but an internal supplement to the mother, more threatening than grotesque.

Although Klein revealed the base of phallic authority that consists of the mother-with-a-penis's fantasy-like power, she did not endorse a rival power, even more well founded, that she believed in—in the same way that other people believe in the father. On the contrary, she attempted to figure out how to get rid of this final henchman of power, this infantile pivot for tyranny. The mother as an internal object is the "double" of the real mother, and this doubling, which engulfs the baby, enables the world to avoid both judgment and verification through sensory perception.[73] The real mother is but a "colored" screen that is produced by our fantasies and/or by projective identification. To learn to judge reality in a way that is not based on terror, we can certainly depend on the satisfying care given by our mothers, who, as luck would have it, are capable of doing so, but we are also invited to depend on analysis so we might have a chance to work through our fantasies of omnipotence, which in the end is a maternal omnipotence.

The reason Melanie shifted maternal power from reality alone to the ego's fantasy was not to downplay either the real mother or the role of perception in children's experience, as the Anna Freudians accused her of doing during the Controversial Discussions. On the contrary, Klein's objective was to demystify the imaginary henchman of authority, whom we mistakenly believe to be real, and to moor analysis in the fantasy-like unconscious of the self he causes to suffer. Maternal power and paternal authority are thus remnants of a phyto- and ontogenetic memory made up of biology and representation, remnants that lurk inside us, as the subjects of psychoanalysis, and that we have the chance to deconstruct through the help of some mothers who are gratifying enough and distant enough—through the help, in the end, of analytic transference and interpretation.

To contend that what is truly taking place here is a never-ending attempt to settle scores with Libussa is less interesting, in the final analysis, than to understand how Melanie robs male authority, as well as its archaic maternal basis, of its power to encroach abusively upon our psychic lives. Bion and Winnicott would later develop this theme and would expand it into "the mother's capacity for reverie"[74] (the positive, productive version of psychic life) and into "encroaching mothers" (the noxious version that dismantles the structure of the psyche). More than anarchism, what emerges from Melanie's early writings, which deconstruct the imaginary power of the primitive mother, is a wholly genuine and sympathetic vision of the human experience. And her work continues to attract the attention of contemporary critics, particularly because, since the 1930s when Melanie first offered her hypotheses on tyrannical power, the world has only seen the worst in paranoid schizophrenia, abuse, and the collapse of authority.[75]

At the same time, this pivotal collapse—at the core of the human being as well as of the social bond—is, in Klein's view, of a destructive violence that proves to be no less saving. First, the masochistic anxiety-provoking drive, which breaks me up into bits until it disables or destroys my ability to think, possesses the unexpected virtue of being able to guide us toward the outside world and to take an object as its target. That object reverts back to me right away and takes refuge as an internal object so it can either gnaw at me from the inside (if it is a "bad" object) or become a stable focal point for my ego (it if is "good). For Klein, such reversions of the negative do in fact take into account reality (the parents, their care, their authority), but, in the end, they do so to a lesser degree than one might imagine. All that Melanie demands from the powers originating from the outside is that they exist as little as possible, that they do not encroach too much upon the adjustments made by internal objects bouncing between envy and gratitude.

As a result of this vision—one that I am just beginning to touch upon here—the Authority and the Real, the Law and the World can be kept as far apart as possible. The point is not to abolish them or ignore them, for Melanie is not a libertarian, nor is she a devotee of the Enlightenment who would deem the "social contract" a radical evil that must be destroyed, or at least ameliorated. Her tyrannical and retributive vision of Law and Authority sees the reality of the world as being essentially coercive. Even worse, this authority and this reality insinuate themselves in us from our birth, and even before, through the force of biological destiny; and they affect us from the inside in the form of a draconian superego that stems from the persecuting object, unless it is innate. The point, then, is not to deny authority, nor is it to adapt to reality in order to know it better: that authority and that reality are always already inside us, and we are what transports them. The only things that we can ever truly know are the violence of our death drive, the capacity for love that compensates for it, and the logic underlying our fantasies. This knowledge of the inner world makes it possible for us to approach reality, though in the form of a sporadic learning process. Bion's and Winnicott's subsequent developments regarding "learning by experience" and "transitional reality" are rooted in the negotiation of the death drive, as Klein would see it, as she reduced the fantasy as well as the coercive authority of the object in order to transform them gradually, after a great deal of work, into a reality susceptible to thought.

For Klein, there is no "real mother," or she counts for very little, because the only mother who interests her is the mother who can be thought. And a mother can be thought only if my awareness of the deadly fantasy that consumes me can imprint the real object with a portion of an object I can think about: an object I can play with—symbol, in the end. The external mother can gratify me (or not), which amounts to saying that she displays (or fails to display) her ability to the internal world of my fantasies. Accordingly, she helps me adapt the inner world to a "reality" that, in this context, emerges only at the end of a learning process that is creative, and, ultimately, infinite.

The model of this perpetually renewed knowledge of reality is nothing less than the transference relationship. By respecting the fantasy and interpreting it, the analyst does not establish the reality to be known or the law to be followed, but gives the ego a chance to constantly create a reality that, while increasingly objective, is the only one that is thinkable for me, livable for me, and desirable for me.

A version of freedom can be inferred from Klein's thought here, one that has proved to be particularly attractive to the British sociologists: a freedom based on a creativity that respects the self, one that is neither a normative adaptation nor a jubilant transgression of utopia in the antioedipal sense. Indeed, the balancing agent in this system of Kleinian self-regulation is nothing less than the experience of loss and its attendant depression, which arise when neurological maturation and the regulation of the two universes (the child's fantasy and the mother's fantasy and reality) allow for separation, which occurs in the realm of guilt and grief. Grief and guilt are the internal—and thus intrinsically psychosomatic—manifestations, like body-and-soul, of the severity of the law that shapes me in the form of a superego. At the end of this process, an optimal negotiation between internal violence and external authority successfully informs me that an Other exists and that this Other is both external (I learn to know my mother as a whole object, and all other forms of external reality thus become accessible to me) and internal (I am capable of symbols; "I think" after "I fantasize").

This vision of freedom, one that remained empirical for Klein, was developed most exhaustively through the Protestant ethic of Winnicott.[76] Winnicott offered a notion of play that in some ways recalls that of Anna Freud in the sense that his is a conception in which sexuality is still latent: once the child is able to extricate himself from fantasy-like meaning, he plays in order to play (this train is a train, and not daddy's penis, as Melanie would have it). It is through this absence of sexual meaning, as Klein understood it, that the child at play rediscovers the neutrality of the meanings he is supposed to re-create. Play comes to an end, on the other hand, with the first signs of sexual stimulation.[77] But isn't it also true that this encounter with sexuality, its gradual fading and *différance* through the indifferent speech of a third party who nevertheless takes it into account and who begins to restore its traumatic underpinnings, that is the object, more so than the oversimplifications of her school of thought to which she is often reduced, of Klein's own interpretation-in-the-context-of-play? In Miss Freud's view, education must precede such relief. For Lacan, the paternal function will do. Every analyst should learn how to play, to play a game of playing with each analysand, as Winnicott suggests. More soberly and directly, Melanie allowed the distanced truth of interpretive speech to function alongside the patient's projective identification, but alongside the analyst's as well: If I were you, we would play together, and I would acknowledge as much. We engage in a back-and-forth process of sexual identifications, projections, and attempts to distance ourselves . . .

We would search Klein's writings in vain to discover a focal point for these metamorphoses of the negative, although she does trace the creative and productive transformations of the underlying personal autonomy that so fascinates the English theoreticians. Lacan, for his part, had to fill in these gaps by situating the already-there of the Kleinian Oedipus complex and superego in the preexistence of the symbolic in human beings, as reflected by the Name-of-the-Father and the fecundity of the Phallus, whose paternal function is the conduit of the imaginary.

Klein, on the other hand, as if counterbalancing Lacan's intellectualizing or Thomistic Christianity, appears at first to be merciful as well as sensitive to an unfathomable destructiveness.[78] In the latter half of her work, however, she introduced notions that reflect positive psychic processes: the capacity for reparation and love with gratitude, as opposed to sadism, the tyranny of the superego, and envy. As they are also part of the constitution of the drives, those sublimating positive forces that are either innate or enhanced through optimal care from the parents, have the advantage of freeing up the perpetually enigmatic interfaces between psychoanalysis and biology. But they leave us bereft of thought in the face of the psychosomatic basis of the Kleinian version of Eros that does not blossom into pleasure but is manifested from the beginning as something propelled by a tenderness toward the other and by an overwhelming nostalgia that arises out of the depressive position.

Is this a way of inhibiting the aim of the drive? Other female analysts have said as much about the early sublimation of the libido into tenderness.[79] But these analysts do not specify what makes it possible: is it once again an innate capacity, this time for inhibiting the aim of the drive? Or is it a shift to a symbolic third party, to the father or to a father figure, that diminishes the sadomasochism of the mother-child dyad and who helps the *infans* down the road to sublimation?

Melanie left so much unsaid!

She did not reflect upon conversion hysteria or hysterical madness, for example. But isn't the phobic anxiety that internal objects project inside us a form of psychic conversion?

She also underestimated the mother's desire as well as her hatred, something that her successors, such as Kate Freidlander or D. W. Winnicott, addressed. But did she really underestimate it? Or was she simply engaging in a sort of rhetorical exaggeration that engages in distortion or hyperbole for persuasive effect alone? Perhaps she did so by putting herself in the place of the fragile ego (the baby, the child) rather than external reality (the mother, reality), so she could slowly construct this external reality, as well as the patient's symbolic creativity, herself.

Klein avoided perversion by reproaching the unfaithful Don Juan for merely wishing to prove to himself that he does not love his mother (whose death he dreads because he loves her with a possessive and destructive feeling) without recognizing in the excess of perverse libido either the force of desire or the defiance of the father, and by seeing in it only a defense against painful dependence.[80] But isn't the apparent denigration of desire really a thoughtful and serious reflection on what makes it a fatal wound? For Melanie, desire always bespeaks anxiety with much intensity: only in quieter times does it become a source of pleasure, in which case it is still prepared to seek delight through love and gratitude.

THE INNER MOTHER AND THE DEPTH OF THOUGHT

Klein never broached the subject of her impasse regarding the symbolic value of fatherhood. For proof of this, we need only reexamine the following reflection on the role of the father, which Klein likens to the role of a good mother:

> The gratification which a man derives from giving a baby to his wife [makes] up for his sadistic wishes towards his mother and making restoration to her. . . . An additional source of pleasure is the gratification of his feminine wishes by his sharing the maternal pleasure of his wife.[81]

Although it is true that Klein acknowledges here the femininity of man, which others have chosen to ignore, it is also true that

Melanie generally has little to say about men other than mentioning their dependence on the mother![82] In clinical practice, on
the other hand, the impact of interpretation does in fact inscribe
the paternal function. Through the relevance of what she says,
Melanie endorses the role of the familial Other that is assumed by
the father, and that the analyst describes through the understated
truth of her words. By implicitly safeguarding the function of the
father, Melanie thus holds herself out as an analyst and not as a
provider of social or maternal assistance. At the same time, this
implicit acknowledgment is accompanied by an unprecedented
inquiry into the maternal function. The feminists have congratu-
lated themselves on this alternative to Freudian male chauvinism
and Lacanian phallocentrism. Other women, on the other hand,
have expressed regret about what they consider to be Klein's "nor-
mativism," that is, her endorsement of the father-mother couple
and of heterosexuality as preconditions for a creative development of the psyche.

From that perspective, such feminists as Nancy Chodorow,[83]
Jessica Benjamin,[84] and Dorothy Dinnerstein[85] rely on Klein's theory of the object relation to show that the Oedipus complex is not
the subject's only ordeal of autonomy, as was believed by Freud
and Lacan, who are said to have used the primacy of Oedipus to
suggest that woman exhibit inferior moral and libidinal development. But aren't these theoreticians trying to replace the unconscious with the object relation and thus replace psychoanalysis
with a preventative measure of mental well-being? A special issue
of *Women: A Cultural Review*[86] responds to the excess of dogmatic
Freudianism and Lacanianism by advocating a "turn to Klein."
The most important contribution made by this rereading of Klein
is its exploration of the early relationship between mother and
baby—a relationship that is preoedipal in Freud's sense and part of
an early Oedipus complex in Klein's sense. The authors seek to
clarify the role played by the father in the primary logic of the fantasy, one in which the drive is nevertheless articulated in the context of a primary oral identification with a father desired by the
mother.[87]

By focusing her inquiry on the mother (first on the mother's hold on her child and then on the way the mother is put to death for the sake of symbolism), Melanie Klein the Oresteian situated herself, as I have said, at the heart of the crisis in modern values. Klein essentially contended that making reparation to the father and making restoration to our knowledge of reality are secondary goals of little concern because they have the potential for tyranny and cannot be actualized without the creation of a psychic life. No one has rejected more strongly than Melanie what Jean Gilbert has termed "the lowly desertion of the leader." Lacking a leader, as the mother is not a leader but an object of fantasy-like power that is the keeper of anxiety, the Kleinian universe is, it turns out, a decentralized universe—the only caveat being that the self, as it loses the object of anxiety and works through that loss, is able to access the life of the mind that Winnicott called "transitionality."

In order for there to be transitionality, the bond with the mother—not with a phallic mother but with a mother consumed with the desire for the father in the form of the penis—is essential. For Klein, this bond is a terrifying one, one that the inevitably phobic child learns to retreat from (Freud's Little Hans is the prototype of this) with the help of symbolization. To accomplish this, the sadistic-phobic baby relies on both his own capacity to experience pleasure and delight and his mother's response to his anxieties, as long as she remains sufficiently benevolent and distant.

Klein does not underplay desire; she demystifies it in parallel to her demystification of the death drive by showing that it can be thought—and is even a source of thought. The theoretical difficulties that the psychoanalyst encouraged along this path are metaphysical aporias that cannot be avoided by anyone familiar with the human being and its therapies. Such aporias enjoy the awesome privilege of placing us in the most withdrawn space we can imagine—a space that, when the promise of paternal protection that accompanies transcendental protection is taken away, the "thinking reed" that we are presumed to be must face the dramatic alternative that consists of the contemporary version of tragedy. This reduces us to wavering between a dissipation of the self and a contraction of identities, between schizophrenia and paranoia. And we can expect to be accompanied by a slew of paranoid, cruel, and fragile mothers. The analyst who presumes to lead us to the symbol is thus obliged to *belong to it*, to share this cruel and fragile paranoia in order to leave it behind more easily and, in this state of possession/dispossession, to constantly relive—and to make us relive—depression as a precondition for creativity: the analyst's own creativity, and his or her patients' creativity as well.

After joining Freud and Lacan in making eroticism our God and making the phallus the guarantor of identity, we are invited to join Klein as we return to the ambitions for freedom that lie within the coarsest and most archaic realms of our psyche, those in which the *one* (the identity) never manages *to be*. It is at this point that we realize that Melanie, despite her image as a matronly woman content to settle down in London to run her school, is our contemporary.

Consider the objects of the modern imaginary, the exhibitions or other events that are woven from the fabric of postcoital despair: is it not a bazaar of "internal objects" made up of breasts, milk, feces, and urine, objects underneath words and images of fantasies that are quite cruel and quite defensive, paranoid-schizoid-manic fantasies when they are not simply depressive? This reverses the symbolization process, not to mention the video games whose violence terrifies the associations of parents of school-age children—because such children "project" (and they do project!) themselves onto the video screen until they can longer distinguish between the image and reality—in a modern world that appears to be engulfed by the phantasy in Klein's retributive and realist sense of the word. What's different about Melanie's conception, though, is that in Kleinian practice the analyst accompanies this fantasy, articulates it, and interprets it so it is open to thought—and only then does the analyst get beyond it: not to forbid it, and not to repress it. The consciousless killers from the American high schools, on the other hand, had only a television screen for a baby-sitter and, deprived of access to any speech that could have freed them from the grips of the imaginary, were the castaways of an incomplete depressive position, the classic victims of paranoid-schizoid regression. By predicting the emergence of such children before the Second World War, Melanie was neither snickering nor reveling, for she welcomed them with the compassion of an accomplice who makes us believe that it is not really so bad to play if playing is part of an effort to put the desire for death into words. She posited, however, that we can do so together, in an entirely different way.

Therein lies the true "politics" of Kleinianism, which still leaves unanswered a fundamental question of psychoanalysis: if it is so obvious that the implicit ideology in Klein's observations provides a chapter of contemporary social philosophy, how does that inform the workings of her clinical practice? Has post-Kleinianism[88] not already done all that it can do? Current psychoanalytic research is characterized by an ecumenism that draws from various schools of thought (Freudian, Kleinian, Bionian, Winnicottian, Lacanian, and so forth) and refines the precise way of listening appropriate for each patient by remaining concerned about offering interpretations that are sensitive to the new maladies of the soul, and without trying to construct novel systems for untold battles to come. This retreat from militancy is not necessarily a lull, nor does it indicate that psychoanalysis has run its course.

Quite the contrary, in fact, psychoanalysis is being revived in two respects. First, it is exposing itself to other realms of human activity (society, art, literature, and philosophy) that it elucidates with an innovative mind-set, and it is thus expanding and unfolding the meaning of its own concepts outside the confines of clinical practice. Second, by honing in on specific symptoms, psychoanalysis is being stimulated and diversified, which improves its ability to understand and to care for each patient's unique qualities while avoiding structural generalities—and which is pressing psychoanalytic intervention to the frontiers of signification and biology. As with many other domains, the era of "geniuses" and overarching systems has been replaced today with personal ventures and exchanges that form a network of ideas. Because of—and despite—Klein's taste for power, which was encouraged by her era and her personal circumstances, at her core she was a forerunner of these two contemporary trends.

Klein believed that the *inside* of the mother (which is invisible but which is thought to be filled with threatening objects, beginning with the father's penis) imposed upon both sexes the most archaic anxiety situations: castration anxiety is only *a part*, admittedly an important one, of the more generalized anxiety that arises from the inside of the body itself. Klein also suggested that "good" objects counterbalance "bad" ones. Finally, Klein contended that thought is what allows *psychic interiority* to take shape, a depth that is at first grieving, then relieving and joyful, and that it is only thing that can help us conquer our fear of this maternal interior.

From one interior to the next, and from anxiety to thought: the Kleinian topography is a sublimation of the cavity, a metamorphosis of the womb, and a variation on female receptivity. Klein transformed her closeness with an unnameable depth into a form of self-knowledge—before she persuaded us that this imaginary knowledge is viable for everyone, women as well as men. Through psychoanalytic interpretation, the incarnate fantasy of the maternal interior becomes a way of knowing the self: psychoanalysis, and no longer faith, provides the optimal path toward self-knowledge.

With Melanie Klein, the fantasy connected to the mother lies at the heart of human destiny. In our Judeo-Christian culture, this important revaluing of the mother should not be underestimated. The fertility of the Jewish mother was blessed by Jahwe but removed from the sacred space that harbors the meaning of speech. The Virgin Mother then became the empty core of the Holy Trinity. Two thousand years ago the Man of Sorrow, Christ, founded a new religion that lays claim to the father, without wishing to know what he shared in common with his mother. The Kleinian child, phobic and sadistic, is the inner double of this visible and crucified man, his painful inside that is consumed by the paranoid fantasy of an omnipotent mother. That fantasy is one of a killing mother who must be killed, of an incarnate representation of female paranoia in which we discovered the projected paranoid-schizophrenia of our primitive and feeble ego. The subject is nevertheless able to free himself from this mortifying depth, provided, that is, that he can work through it indefinitely until it becomes the only value we still have: the depth of thought. ·

Like the analyst, but unknowingly so, the mother accompanies her child in this working through that causes him to lose her— and then to use words and thoughts to make reparation to her. The maternal function takes refuge in the alchemy that relies on the loss of self and the Other to attain and to develop the *meaning* of mortifying desire, but only through the love and gratitude that actualizes the subject. The bond of love with the lost object that is the mother—the mother from whom "I" distance myself— replaces matricide and takes on the aura of thought. It is hardly the least striking example of Melanie Klein's genius that she used the negative to link the fate of the female with the preservation of the mind and the spirit.

NOTES

INTRODUCTION: THE PSYCHOANALYTIC CENTURY

1. Meisel and Kendrik, *Bloomsbury/Freud*, p. 279.
2. Klein, *Envy and Gratitude*, p. 183. All future references to *Envy and Gratitude* will be indicated by *EG.*
3. Ibid., p. 202.
4. Freud used the word "psycho-analysis" for the first time in his "Heredity and the Aetiology of the Neuroses" (1896), in Freud, *Standard Edition*, 3:141–56. But it is Freud's *The Interpretation of Dreams*, which was published in 1900 on the heels of his and Joseph Breuer's *Studies on Hysteria* (1888), that has come to be viewed as the first psychoanalytic work.

I. JEWISH FAMILIES, EUROPEAN STORIES: A DEPRESSION AND ITS AFTERMATH

1. Grosskurth, *Melanie Klein.* All future references to Grosskurth's biography will be indicated by *MK.*
2. Ibid., p. 7.

3. Ibid., p. 15.
4. Ibid., pp. 10, 9.
5. Ibid., pp. 15, 16.
6. Ibid., p. 14.
7. Ibid., p. 20.
8. Ibid., p. 38.
9. Ibid., pp. 40–41.
10. Ibid., p. 41.
11. Ibid.
12. Ibid., p. 49.
13. Ibid., pp. 53, 51.
14. Ibid., pp. 84–85.
15. Ibid., pp. 83–84; emphasis added.
16. Ibid., p. 65.
17. Ibid., p. 66.
18. Cited in ibid., p. 69.
19. Ibid., p. 5.
20. Ibid., p. 113.
21. Meisel and Kendrik, *Bloomsbury/Freud*, pp. 192, 193.
22. Ibid., p. 294.
23. Ibid., p. 180.
24. *MK*, p. 148.
25. Ibid., p. 150
26. Ibid., p. 200.
27. Ibid., p. 392.
28. Freud, *Standard Edition*, 5:629–86.
29. *MK*, p. 70.
30. Ibid.
31. Freud, *Standard Edition*, 10:1–147.
32. Eugenia Sokolnicka published the case study of a little boy named Minsk in *Internationale Zeitschrift für Psychoanalyse* in 1920, around the same time that Klein presented her own study in July 1920 to the Budapest Psychoanalytic Society.
33. Cited in *MK*, p. 75.
34. Cited in ibid., p. 74.
35. "The Psycho-Analytic Play Technique: Its History and Significance," in Klein, *Envy and Gratitude*, pp. 122–40.
36. Abraham, *Dreams and Myths*; *On Character and Libido Development*.
37. *MK*, p. 98.
38. Ibid., p. 100.

39. See "A Short Study of the Development of the Libido, Viewed in the Light of Mental Disorders," an essay in which Abraham describes the similarities between obsessional neurosis and manic-depressive psychosis, which he believes is a reproduction of the "loss of the object," ibid. at 69, during the anal stage (feces) and of its equivalent in the unconscious, that is, the "expulsion of the object," ibid. at 75.

40. *MK*, p. 109.

41. "An Obsessional Neurosis in a Six-Year-Old Girl," in Klein, *The Psychoanalysis of Children*, pp. 35–57. All future references to *The Psychoanalysis of Children* will be indicated by *PC*.

42. Cited in *MK*, p. 131.

43. Meisel and Kendrik, *Bloomsbury/Freud*, p. 279

44. Cited in *MK*, p. 138.

45. Ibid., p. 155

46. Cited in ibid., p. 162.

47. Ibid., p. 215.

48. Michael Clyne, who was analyzed by Marion Milner and who became a brilliant scientist, named his daughter Melanie. Melanie Clyne was Melanie Klein's great-granddaughter.

49. Wollheim, "Melanie Klein," p. 469, cited in Sayers, *Mothering Psychoanalysis*, p. 256

50. *MK*, p. 366.

2. ANALYZING HER CHILDREN: FROM SCANDAL TO PLAY TECHNIQUE

1. See Stone, *The Family, Sex, and Marriage in England, 1500–1800*.

2. See Allestree, *The Whole Duty of Man*, p. 296 ("The Devil will be diligent enough to instill into [newborns] all wickedness and vice, even from their cradles, and there being also in all our natures so much the greater aptness to evil, than to good").

3. Mitchell, *Psychoanalysis and Feminism*, pp. 228–29.

4. On the place and the representation of the child, see Cullen, *Children in Society*; Cunningham, *Children and Childhood in Western Society Since 1500*; Hendrick, *Children, Childhood, and English Society, 1880–1990*; Hill, *Children and Society*; Becchi and Julia, *Histoire de l'enfance en Occident*; Barret-Ducrocq, *Love in the Time of Victoria* and *Pauvreté, charité et morale à Londres au XIXème siècle*. I am grateful to François Barret-Ducrocq for his guidance on this subject.

5. Sayers, *Mothering Psychoanalysis*, p. 224.
6. That was the term used by Karen Horney's daughter, who was Klein's analysand beginning in childhood and who later became Dr. Marianne Horney Eckhardt. *MK*, p. 105.
7. "Analysis of a Phobia in a Five-Year-Old Boy," in Freud, *Standard Edition*, 10:5–147.
8. See Bégoin-Guignard, "L'Évolution de la technique en analyse d'enfants," in *Melanie Klein aujourd'hui*, p. 55.
9. Klein, *Love, Guilt, and Reparation*, pp. 1–53. All future references to *Love, Guilt, and Reparation* will be indicated by *LGR*.
10. Ibid., p. 2.
11. The first part of this initial study is entitled "The Influence of the Sexual Enlightenment and Relaxation of Authority on the Intellectual Development of Children"; the second part, "The Child's Resistance to Enlightenment," was presented to the Berlin Psychoanalytic Society in 1921.
12. *LGR*, p. 4.
13. Ibid., p. 22.
14. Ibid., pp. 27, 21.
15. Ibid., p. 48.
16. Ibid., pp. 30–32.
17. Ibid., pp. 33–34.
18. See Miller, "Kleinian Analysis: Dialogue with Hanna Segal," p. 254.
19. *LGR*, pp. 22, 48; emphasis added.
20. Ibid., pp. 49–50.
21. Ibid., p. 3.
22. Ibid., p. 27.
23. Ibid.
24. The expression comes from Pontalis, *Frontiers in Psychoanalysis*, pp. 95 ff, 103.
25. See Winnicott, "Transitional Objects and Transitional Phenomena."
26. Klein acknowledged that she was not "a natural-born mother," whereas she believed that Winnicott had "a strong maternal identification, even though he had no children of his own." *MK*, p. 233.
27. *LGR*, pp. 106–27.
28. Ibid., pp. 108, 109.
29. Ibid.; emphasis added.

30. Ibid., pp. 45–46; see also *MK*, pp. 95–96.
31. *LGR*, p. 45, n.1.
32. Ibid., p. 45.
33. Ibid., p. 46.
34. Ibid; see also *MK*, pp. 95–96.
35. *LGR*, p. 66.
36. Ibid., p. 72.
37. See pp. 203–207.
38. *MK*, p. 101.
39. *PC*, pp. 32–33.
40. *EG*, p. 126.
41. *PC*, p. 21.
42. Ibid., p. 33.
43. Ibid., p. 17.
44. Ibid., p. 22.
45. Ibid., p. 20.
46. Ibid., p. 27.
47. Freud, *Standard Edition*, 19:235–39.
48. British analysts appear to be particularly drawn to Klein's innovation here, although Sylvia Payne has pointed out that some English analysts had engaged in transference interpretations before Melanie arrived in London. *See MK*, p. 340.
49. Montaigne, *Essays I*, p. 79.
50. *PC*, pp. 31–32.
51. Ibid., p. 34.
52. *EG*, p. 314.
53. Ibid.
54. *EG*, p. 124.
55. *PC*, p 32 n. 1, citing Freud, "Fragment of an Analysis of a Case of Hysteria" (1905), in Freud, *Standard Edition*, 7:48 ("J'appelle un chat un chat").
56. *PC*, p. 32, n. 2.
57. *LGR*, p. 33.
58. Ibid., p. 41.
59. Ibid., p. 42.
60. Ibid., p. 43.
61. *EG*, p. 124.
62. Etchegoyen, "Melanie Klein and the Theory of Interpretation," pp. 402–16.

63. See *PC*, "Preface," p. xi.

3. THE PRIORITY AND INTERIORITY OF THE OTHER AND
THE BOND: THE BABY IS BORN WITH HIS OBJECTS

1. *EG*, pp. 52–53; emphasis added.
2. We would be well served to put Klein's notion of the object always-already-there in the context of Hannah Arendt's emphasis, in the context of the debate that she engaged in concerning Heidegger's Platonic solipsism, on the being-in-the-world as an *in-between*, as an *appearance-to-other-people* within the bonds of the *polis*, in Aristotle's sense.
3. Freud, *Standard Edition*, 14:67–102.
4. Ibid., p. 76.
5. "Leonardo Da Vinci and a Memory of his Childhood," in Freud, *Standard Edition*, 11:57–137
6. "Psycho-Analytic Notes on an Autobiographical Account of a Case of Paranoia (Dementia Paranoides)," in Freud, *Standard Edition*, 12:1–79.
7. "From the History of an Infantile Neurosis," in Freud, *Standard Edition*, 17:1–122.
8. Freud, *Standard Edition*, 14:237–58.
9. Ibid., 18:1–64.
10. Ibid., p. 44. *Translator's note*: Following current psychoanalytic practice, I generally use "drive" rather than "instinct" when conveying the German *Triebe*.
11. Freud, *Standard Edition*, 19:1–59.
12. See Segal and Bell, "Theory of Narcissism in Freud and Klein."
13. *Translator's note*: Following current psychoanalytic practice, I generally refer to "cathexis" as "investment."
14. See, in particular, Laplanche and Pontalis, *The Language of Psycho-Analysis*, pp. 256–57.
15. Ibid., p. 257.
16. "Ego narcissism would therefore be, as Freud pointed out, a secondary narcissism that is shielded from objects. . . . Ego narcissism suggests the splitting of the subject, and it replaces auto-eroticism as a state of self-sufficiency. In this context, primary narcissism is the Desire for the One and an aspiration toward a self-sufficient and immortal totality whose self-generation is at once a condition, death, and the negation of death." See Green, *Narcissisme de vie, narcissisme de mort*, p. 132.

17. Petot, *Melanie Klein*, 2:116.

18. Wallon, *Les Origines du caractère chez l'enfant*; see also Petot, *Melanie Klein*, 2:277.

19. See Petot, *Melanie Klein*, 2:248, citing Carpenter, "Mother's Face and the Newborn."

20. See pp. 41, 71–72, 94, 106, 238.

21. See Balint, *Primary Love and Psycho-Analytic Technique*.

22. Petot, *Melanie Klein*.

23. Klein, Heimann, Isaacs, and Riviere, *Developments in Psycho-Analysis*. All future references to *Developments in Psycho-Analysis* will be indicated by *DP*.

24. Ibid., p. 293; emphasis added.

25. Ibid.; emphasis added.

26. Ibid., p. 199

27. This follows the terminology of W. R. Bion, who distinguishes between a *contained* (what is projected) and a *container* (the containing object), a dynamic that is concomitant with the formation of an "apparatus for thinking about thoughts." See generally Bion, *Learning from Experience*. Bion developed the notion of the analyst's mind as a "container" in his *Attention and Interpretation: A Scientific Approach to Insight in Psycho-Analysis and Groups*.

28. *EG*, p. 180.

29. On the heterogeneity between meaning and the drive, see part 3 ("Heterogeneity") of Kristeva, *Revolution in Poetic Language*; see also Green, "A Few Thoughts on Modern Linguistics."

30. I shall return to this point. See pp. 98–113.

31. See pp. 137–157.

32. *PC*, pp. 6–7; emphasis added.

33. Fairbairn, *Psycho-Analytic Studies of the Personality*.

34. Petot, *Melanie Klein*, 2:106.

35. *EG*, p. 6.

36. Ibid.

37. *DP*, p. 302.

38. Ibid., p. 318.

39. Cited in ibid., p. 317.

40. Ibid., p. 319.

41. Ibid.

42. Ibid., p. 320.

43. See generally "The Effects of Early Anxiety-Situations on the Sexual Development of the Boy," *PC*, pp. 240–78.

44. Ibid., p. 259

45. Ibid.
46. Segal, *Introduction to the Work of Melanie Klein*, p. 105.
47. Ibid., p. 106.
48. Ibid., p. 119.
49. Ibid., p. 120.
50. See Guignard, "L'Identification projective dans la psychose et dans l'interprétation."
51. Ibid., p. 93.
52. See Kristeva, *Powers of Horror*, pp. 1 ff.; and Kristeva, *Tales of Love*, pp. 46–48.
53. "A Contribution to the Psychogenesis of Manic-Depressive States," in *LGR*, pp. 262–89; "On the Theory of Anxiety and Guilt," in *DP*, pp. 271–91; "Some Theoretical Conclusions Regarding the Emotional Life of the Infant," in *DP*, pp. 198–236.
54. *MK*, p. 215.
55. *LGR*, p. 264.
56. See *A Psycho-Analytic Dialogue: The Letters of Sigmund Freud and Karl Abraham*, pp. 338–40.
57. *LGR*, p. 266.
58. Segal, *Introduction to the Work of Melanie Klein*, p. 57.
59. Proust, *In Search of Lost Time*, 6:268.
60. *LGR*, p. 268.
61. Ibid.
62. Ibid., p. 269.
63. Ibid., pp. 277–79.
64. Segal, *Introduction to the Work of Melanie Klein*, p. 60.
65. Ibid., pp. 81–82.
66. *LGR*, p. 270.
67. Ibid.
68. Freud, *Standard Edition*, 14:237–58.
69. Segal, *Introduction to the Work of Melanie Klein*, p. 62.
70. *LGR*, p. 289.
71. Ibid., p. 369.
72. See pp. 114–136.

4. ANXIETY OR DESIRE: IN THE BEGINNING WAS THE DEATH DRIVE

1. See Green, "Trop c'est trop," in Gammill, *Melanie Klein aujour-d'hui*, pp. 93–102.

2. Lacan, "The Subversion of the Subject and Dialectic of Desire," in *Écrits*, pp. 308 and 320.
3. Petot, *Melanie Klein*, 1:67
4. Cited in *DP*, p. 275.
5. Ibid., p. 276.
6. Ibid.; emphasis added.
7. Ibid., p. 275.
8. Ibid.
9. Ibid., p. 276.
10. See pp. 169–177.
11. See Kristeva, *Female Genius: Hannah Arendt*, pp. 3–8, 16–17, 31–38, 47–48, 213–215.
12. See pp. 158–191.
13. Freud, *Standard Edition*, 14:177. Specifically, Freud believed that the affect is never unconscious and that only its *representation* manages to succumb to repression. In addition, unconscious representation persists as a real formation in the unconscious following repression, "whereas all that corresponds in that system to unconscious affects is a potential beginning which is prevented from developing. Strictly speaking, then, and although no fault can be found with the linguistic usage, there are no unconscious affects as there are unconscious ideas" (ibid.). "The whole difference arises from the fact that ideas are cathexes—basically of memory-traces—whilst affects and emotions correspond to processes of discharge, the final manifestations of which are perceived as feelings" (ibid., p. 178).
    Freud returns to this debate in "The Ego and the Id" (1923) and refers to affect with a term that is curiously imprecise ("something") while emphasizing the *direct* path by which the motion of affect becomes conscious: "Let us call what becomes conscious as pleasure and unpleasure a quantitative and qualitative 'something' in the course of mental events; the question then is whether this 'something' can become conscious in the place where it is, or whether it must first be transmitted to the system *Pcpt*. . . . In other words: the distinction between *Cs* and *Pcs.* has no meaning where feelings are concerned; the *Pcs.* here drops out—and feelings are either conscious or unconscious. *Even when they are attached to word-presentations, their becoming conscious is not due to that circumstance, but they become so directly.*"Freud, *Standard Edition*, 19:22–23.
14. See pp. 38–45.
15. For a modern conception of affects, see Green, *The Fabric of Affect*

in the Psychoanalytic Discourse, pp. 73 ff. Although Green notes that Klein did not develop a theory of the affect, he shows how she has influenced all of those who have contributed since Freud to such a development, and he emphasizes that the affect is a "drive derivative" (ibid., p. 75); that it has a "direct" presentation (although it still is not associated with a representation) (ibid.); that it corresponds to antagonistic internal perceptions; and that affective motion involves a "psychization" (ibid., p. 237) that is inexpressible so long as the representation of things and the representation of words do not form along with it an intelligible amalgam. Yet unlike the Kleinians who, when faced with the difficulties of the affect problematic, highlighted the investment of an *object*, Green unfolds the cognitive and energetic traces of affect and explores its heterogeneity (its strength *and* its meaning) (ibid. pp. 303 and 313 ff.).

16. Petot, *Melanie Klein*, 1:155.
17. *EG*, p. 134.
18. Ibid.
19. Ibid.
20. See "Criminal Tendencies in Normal Children," in *LGR*, pp. 170–85.
21. Ibid., p. 181.
22. Green, "Trop c'est trop," p. 95.
23. *DP*, pp. 302, 297, 199.
24. Petot, *Melanie Klein*, 2:237.
25. *EG*, p. 181
26. Ibid., pp. 187–88.
27. "Poor soul . . . Than, soul, live thou upon thy servant loss . . . / So shalt thou feed on Death, that feeds on men, / And, Death once dead, ther's no more dying then."
28. Gammill, *Melanie Klein aujourd'hui*, p. 57.
29. Ibid., p. 63.
30. *EG*, p. 198.
31. Ibid., p. 199.
32. Ibid., p. 185.
33. Ibid., p. 180, n. 1.
34. Ibid., pp. 205–06.
35. Freud, *Standard Edition*, 20:129, cited in ibid., p. 190, n. 1.
36. Ibid., pp. 190–91.
37. Ibid., pp. 203–04.
38. *EG*, pp. 195–96.

39. Cited in *MK*, p. 435.
40. Anzieu, "Jeunesse de Melanie Klein," in Gammill, *Melanie Klein aujourd'hui*, p. 35.

5. A MOST EARLY AND TYRANNICAL SUPEREGO

1. *PC*, pp. 123–48.
2. *LGR*, pp. 370–419.
3. "This notion of a realm situated inside the mother's body that provides a space for the child to project himself has remained fundamental and has laid the foundation for the notion of a psychic realm." See Jean Bégoin, "Le Surmoi dans la théorie kleinienne et postkleinienne," p. 40.
4. *PC*, p. 123.
5. Ibid., pp. 136, 137, 139, citing Freud, "Totem and Taboo," in Freud, *Standard Edition*, 13:1–161.
6. *PC*, pp. 140–41.
7. Ibid., p. 130
8. "The Ego and the Id (1923), in Freud, *Standard Edition*, 13:1–161.
9. See "The Oedipus Complex in the Light of Early Anxieties" in *LGR*, pp. 370–419.
10. Ibid., pp. 416–17.
11. The "fact of being castrated" (in the girl) and the "threat of castration" (in the boy) mandate, in Freud's view, two different fates of the Oedipus complex. In the boy, the castration complex "destroy[s]" the Oedipus complex and, by inciting the abandonment of libidinal investments, ushers in a firm *masculine superego*, which is the true inheritor of the Oedipus complex. The girl, on the other hand, who does not have to be "threatened" by castration (because hers is a "fact") is introduced to the Oedipus complex by the very castration that she discovers when she assumes the feminine position of an object of love for the man, and she can abandon the Oedipus complex only very gradually, and perhaps not at all. As a result, "[women's] super-ego is never so inexorable, so impersonal, so independent of its emotional origins as we require it to be in men." See Freud, "Some Psychical Consequences of the Anatomical Distinction Between the Sexes," in Freud, *Standard Edition*, 19:241–58.
12. See "The Oedipus Complex in the Light of Early Anxieties" in *LGR*, pp. 416 ff.

13. See *EG*, pp. 198 ff.
14. Ibid., p. 193.
15. Ibid.
16. Ibid.
17. Jean Bégoin notes that the idealized object is "always two-sided." See Bégoin, "Le Surmoi dans la théorie kleinienne et postkleinienne," p. 65.
18. *EG*, p. 192.
19. Ibid.
20. Ibid.
21. Meltzer, "The Genesis of the Super-Ego Ideal."
22. "The being is thus enclosed in the very mechanism that he put in place to protect himself," as we are told by Athanassiou-Popesco in "L'Apport de Melanie Klein et des auteurs post-kleiniens à la compréhension du fonctionnement psychique," pp. 88 and 90 ff.
23. See pp. 190–191.
24. See Klein, *Narrative of a Child Analysis*. All future references to *Narrative of a Child Analysis* will be indicated by *NCA*.
25. See pp. 132–136.
26. See Kristeva, *Female Genius: Hannah Arendt*.
27. *NCA*, p. 225.
28. Ibid. p. 232.
29. Ibid. p. 235, n. 2.
30. *EG*, p. 249.
31. *NCA*, p. 231.
32. Ibid., p. 220.
33. Meltzer, *The Kleinian Development*. Part 2. "Richard Week-by-Week: A Critique of the 'Narrative of a Child Analysis' and a Review of Melanie Klein's Work," p. 70.
34. *NCA*, p. 461, n. 3.
35. See Gammill, *A partir de Melanie Klein*, p. 29.
36. "On the Sense of Loneliness" was published posthumously in *EG*, pp. 300–313. Klein's essay appears to respond to Winnicott's 1957 paper, "The Capacity to Be Alone," which was published in *The Maturlational Processes and the Facilitating Environment*, pp. 29–36. Winnicott distinguishes between the capacity to be alone on the part of a mature, postoedipal ego and a primitive capacity to be alone that is the domain of the baby granted "ego-support from the mother (ibid., p. 32). The youngest ego thus achieves "ego-relatedness" (ibid., p. 30), which is not "narcissism" but an

edification of an "internal world" (ibid., p. 33) that is more primitive than Klein's "introject[ed] . . . mother" (ibid.). We have here a good example of the back-and-forth exchange between Klein and Winnicott, an example that displays the originality of both analysts as well as their debt to each other. While Winnicott situates the capacity to be alone in a world of ecstasy, we will see that Melanie never distanced herself from a tone of desolation that strikes at the very heart of the serenity she had gained.

37. "On the Sense of Loneliness," p. 313.
38. Ibid., p. 301.
39. Ibid., p. 302.
41. Ibid. p. 313.
42. Ibid., p. 312

6. THE CULT OF THE MOTHER OR AN ODE TO MATRICIDE?
THE PARENTS

1. See pp. 202–207.
2. *EG*, p. 197.
3. *LGR*, p. 192, cited in Petot, *Melanie Klein*, 1:166.
4. *EG*, p. 197
5. See *PC*, chapter 8; *DP*, chapter 6.
6. *EG*, pp. 197–98; emphasis added.
7. Ibid., p. 198.
8. See p. 126.
9. *EG*, p. 200.
10. Ibid.
11. Ibid., p. 200; emphasis added.
12. Ibid.
13. Ibid., p. 201.
14. See Arnoux, *Melanie Klein*, p. 62.
15. Segal, *Introduction to the Work of Melanie Klein*, p. 97.
16. *PC*, pp. 240, 241, 249–51; emphasis added.
17. Guignard, *Epître à l'objet*, pp. 149–54.
18. Ibid., p. 152.
19. Ibid.
20. Ibid., p. 144.
21. See "The Effects of Early Anxiety-Situations on the Sexual Development of the Girl," in *PC*, pp. 194–239.
22. Ibid., p. 228.

23. Ibid., pp. 196, 212.

24. Ibid., p. 214.

25. "Last but not least, let me very heartily thank my daughter, Dr Melitta Schmideberg, for the devoted and valuable help which she has given me in the preparation of this book" (ibid., p. xii ["Preface to the First Edition"]).

26. Ibid., pp. 220, 229, 232.

27. Freud, *Standard Edition*, 20:77–175.

28. *PC*, p. 123.

29. Ibid., p. 196.

30. Ibid., p. 198.

31. Ibid., p. 202.

32. Ibid., p. 206.

33. Ibid., p. 210.

34. S. Cottet, "Melanie Klein et la guerre du fantasme," p. 110.

35. *PC*, p. 212

36. Ibid., p. 227.

37. Ibid., p. 228.

38. Ibid., p. 229.

39. Ibid., p. 236.

40. See Freud, "Civilization and Its Discontents," in Freud, *Standard Edition*, 21:223–43.

41. Ibid., pp. 238–39.

42. Winnicott endorsed this idea, but, by acting as an intermediary between Klein and Freud, he conceived of a relationship between mother and child that at first lacked drives (along the lines of "being") and that later became drive-based (along the lines of "doing"). See Winnicott, *Home Is Where We Start From*. We should also recall Bion's "a-toxic" or detoxifying mother, a mother who guards against excitation. See Bion, *Learning from Experience*; Bion, *Elements of Psycho-Analysis*.

43. Freud, *Standard Edition*, 23:70.

44. *PC*, p. 238.

45. Ibid., p. 239.

46. For a critical review of the history of psychoanalytic thought on female sexuality, see "On the Extraneousness of the Phallus; or, The Feminine Between Illusion and Disillusion," in Kristeva, *The Sense and Non-Sense of Revolt*, pp. 94–106.

47. Freud, *Standard Edition*, 16:250.

48. For the past few years, these notions have been developed assidu-

ously and creatively by French psychoanalysts, particularly by Monique Cournut-Janin and Jean Cournut in "La Castration et le féminin dans les deux sexes."

49. *PC*, pp. 243–44.
50. Ibid., p. 260.
51. Ibid.
52. Ibid.
53. Ibid., p. 263.
54. Ibid., p. 257.
55. Ibid., pp. 244, 249.
56. See pp. 171–175 and pp. 178–180.
57. *Translator's note*: See Freud, "Medusa's Head," in Freud, *Standard Edition*, 18:273–74.
58. See Kristeva, *Visions capitales*, the catalogue for the exhibition under the same name that was presented at the Hall Napoléon at the Louvre between April 27, 1998, and July 27, 1998.
59. See pp. 232–233.
60. Klein's essay on *The Oresteia* was published posthumously in *EG*, pp. 275–99.
61. See pp. 158–169.
62. *EG*, p. 299.
63. Ibid., p. 280.
64. Kristeva, *The Sense and Non-Sense of Revolt*, pp. 149–50, 161.
65. *LGR*, p. 7.

7. THE PHANTASY AS A METAPHOR INCARNATE

1. Susan Isaacs, "The Nature and Function of Phantasy," in *DP*, pp. 67–121.
2. See pp. 213–248.
3. *DP*, p. 83.
4. Freud, *Standard Edition*, 4:536.
5. Ibid., 5:543.
6. Ibid., 5:546.
7. Ibid., 14:269.
8. See Lacan, "The Topic of the Imaginary," in Lacan, *Freud's Papers on Technique (1953–1954)*, pp. 73–88.
9. See pp. 158–169.
10. Lacan, *Freud's Papers on Technique (1953–1954)*, p. 85.
11. We should keep in mind the words of Alain Gibeault, who said

that, for Freud, the "common language" of psychosis, as manifested by President Schreber, sets forth symbolic relationships that are remnants of archaic identities, and who noted that Freud enjoyed returning to theories on the origin of language that posited an "identity" between sexual words and the words used when one works. "Things that are symbolically connected to-day were probably united in prehistoric times by conceptual and linguistic identity." See Freud, *Standard Edition*, 5:352.

12. *DP*, p. 92.

13. Petot, *Melanie Klein*, 1:58.

14. *DP*, p. 89; emphasis added.

15. Freud, *Standard Edition*, 19:227–32.

16. The adjective *diplomatic* is drawn from Petot, *Melanie Klein*, 2:190.

17. See Bion's use of the elements *alpha* and *beta* in his *Attention and Interpretation*; and Piera Aulagnier and his pictograms in Aulagnier, *La Violence de l'interprétation*. See also my distinction between the semiotic and symbolic in Kristeva, *Revolution in Poetic Language*.

18. According to Freud's "Repression" (1915), the affect is a subjective translation of a quantity of instinctual energy, and it is often tantamount to the analogous expression of "quota of affect." Freud, *Standard Edition*, 14:152. Affect appears to be so bound up with self-consciousness that Freud wonders if it would be appropriate to speak of unconscious affect. Whereas unconscious representations remain repressed in the unconscious, the unconscious affect (the feeling of unconscious guilt, for example), corresponds only to a "rudiment." Melanie Klein, on the other hand, appears to extend her notion of the fantasy until it includes that rudiment. On the modern evolution of a theory of affects in a work that takes careful note of Klein's theories, see also Green, *The Fabric of Affect in the Psychoanalytic Discourse*.

19. Segal, *Introduction to the Work of Melanie Klein*, p. 2.

20. See pp. 158–169.

21. See Stern, "L'Enveloppe prénarrative." See also Nelson and Gruendel, "Generalized Event Representations: Basic Building Blocks of Cognitive Development"; Mandler, "Representation"; and Cellérier, "Le Constructivisme génetique aujourd'hui."

22. See pp. 213–225.

23. See p. 240.

24. Bion, *Learning from Experience*, p. 43.

25. See Nenunca Amigorena-Rosenberg, Leopoldo Bleger, and Eduardo Vera Ocampo, "Melanie Klein ou la métaphore incarnée," in *Psychanalyse: Cent ans de divan*. Paris: Arléa-Corlet, 1995, p. 101.

26. See my "Psychanalyser au féminin: De quelques contributions féminines à la théorie psychanalytique." Paper delivered at the Colloque d'histoire de la psychanalyse in July 1997.

27. Freud, *Standard Edition*, 21:227–28.

28. Kristeva, "On the Extraneousness of the Phallus; or, The Feminine Between Illusion and Disillusion," in *The Sense and Non-Sense of Revolt*; Kristeva, "La Fille au sanglot," pp. 41–42.

8. THE IMMANENCE OF SYMBOLISM AND ITS DEGREES

1. *LGR*, p. 221.

2. Ibid., p. 230.

3. See pp. 38–40.

4. *LGR*, p. 225.

5. Ibid., p. 231.

6. Ibid., p. 230.

7. Ibid., p. 220; emphasis added.

8. See pp. 176–177.

9. *LGR*, p. 221

10. Ibid.

11. Ibid.

12. Klein's hypothesis of a primary symbolism could be compared to what Freud described as the "organ-speech" of schizophrenics, which implicates the logic of *sameness* versus that of *resemblance*: "What has dictated the substitution is not the resemblance between the things denoted but the sameness of the words used to express them." Freud, *Standard Edition*, 14: 201; see also p. 263, n. 7.

13. *Translator's note*: See Segal, "Notes on Symbol Formation."

14. *LGR*, p. 225.

15. Translator's note: See Lacan, *Freud's Papers on Technique, 1953–1954*, p. 85.

16. *LGR*, p. 225

17. Ibid., p. 226.

18. Ibid., p. 224.

19. See also pp. 48–50.

20. *LGR*, pp. 226–27.

21. Ibid., p. 225.
22. Ibid., p. 227.
23. Ibid.
24. Ibid.
25. See pp. 139–140, 172–175.
26. See Gibeault, "Variation sur un thème ancien: construction et/ou reconstruction du psychisme de l'enfant."
27. The expression comes from Green, *The Work of the Negative.*
28. As Hanna Segal has pointed out, some of Freud's writings suggest that man is a "symbol user" (particularly when Freud suggests that the dream uses an array of collective symbolic creations that operate independently from the dreamer, that are made for good, and that are always available). Melanie Klein, on the other hand, "discovered man as the symbol maker." See Segal, "Psychoanalytic Dialogue: Kleinian Thought Today," p. 365.
29. See generally King and Steiner, *The Freud Klein Controversies,* pp. 567 ff.
30. See *DP*, pp. 73, n. 1, 124, n. 1; King and Steiner, *The Freud Klein Controversies,* pp. 531–35.
31. See Segal, "Notes on Symbol Formation."
32. Susan Isaacs taught logic and psychology and became the head of the Child Development Department at the Institute of Education at the University of London in 1933. See her "The Nature and Function of Phantasy," in *DP*, pp. 67–121.
33. Freud, *Standard Edition,* 18:14.
34. *DP*, pp. 72–74.
35. Freud, *Standard Edition,* 19:233–39.
36. *DP*, pp. 103–04; King and Steiner, *The Freud-Klein Controversies,* pp. 544 ff.
37. *DP*, p. 104.
38. Ibid., pp. 104–05.
39. Ibid., p. 105.
40. Ibid.
41. Ibid.
42. Heimann completed her psychoanalytic training in Berlin, where she was analyzed by Theodor Reik. After emigrating to England in 1933 to escape the Nazis, she was at first a loyal follower of Klein, but later expressed her discontent and joined the "Independents."
43. *DP*, p. 326.
44. Ibid., p. 146.

45. Ibid., p. 124.
46. Ibid.
47. Freud, *Standard Edition*, 19:235.
48. See pp. 169–171.
49. See Lacan, *The Seminar of Jacques Lacan, Book I*, pp. 73–88; and "A Spoken Commentary on Freud's *Verneinung* by Jean Hyppolite," in ibid., appendix, pp. 289–97.
50. From an entirely different perspective, Hannah Arendt also explored the deep logical processes in which "taste" encounters "judgment." See Kristeva, *Female Genius: Hannah Arendt*, pp. 220–230
51. See "A Spoken Commentary on Freud's *Verneinung* by Jean Hyppolite," in *The Seminar of Jacques Lacan, Book I*, appendix, pp. 289–97. The "new psychoanalysis" developed by Klein was also recognized in the March 1952 issue of the *International Journal of Psychoanalysis*, which was devoted to Klein's seventieth birthday and which was reprinted in *New Directions in Psychoanalysis*. See pp. 227–228.
52. See "A Spoken Commentary on Freud's *Verneinung* by Jean Hyppolite," in *The Seminar of Jacques Lacan, Book I*, appendix, p. 292.
53. Ibid.
54. Ibid., p. 293.
55. Ibid.
56. Ibid., pp. 292, 290–91.
57. Ibid., p. 292.
58. Ibid., p. 295.
59. Ibid., p. 297.
60. Ibid. See Rose, "Negativity in the Work of Melanie Klein," in Stonebridge and Phillips, *Reading Melanie Klein*. These remarks come to mind as we read Hanna Segal and her commentary on the shift from "equations" to the "symbol proper." See Segal, "Notes on Symbol Formation"; see also pp. 176–177. The *equivalent* (as Hyppolite understands the term) of *Verneinung* is accompanied or supported by a *suspension* of destructiveness: "equivalent" and "suspension" indicate thought and allow it to free itself from the realm of "equations" that characterizes archaic fantasies.
61. Lacan, *Écrits*, p. 388.
62. Ibid, p. 396. Jacqueline Rose has carefully tracked these various intersections and divergences in her "Negativity in the Work of Melanie Klein," in Stonebridge and Phillips, *Reading Melanie Klein*, pp. 137–38.
63. Lacan, *Écrits*, pp. 390–92.

64. *MK*, p. 488.
65. King and Steiner, *The Freud-Klein Controversies*, p. 569.
66. Ibid.
67. See Heimann, "On Countertransference"; and Heimann, "Further observations on the analyst's cognitive process."
68. In light of Winnicott's February 5, 1947, paper delivered to the British Psycho-Analytical Society entitled "Hate in the Counter-Transference," which observes that during certain stages in the analysis, the analyst's hate is sought by the patient, and that the analyst must acknowledge the errors arising out of his hate in order for the analysis to continue effectively, and in light of similar notions presented by Margaret Little, Paula Heimann insisted to the Zurich Congress in 1949 that the analyst functions like "the patient's mirror reflection." See *MK*, p. 379.
69. See Kristeva, *New Maladies of the Soul*, pp. 79–86.
70. Segal, "Notes on Symbol Formation," p. 393.
71. See, for example, Kristeva, *Tales of Love*, pp. 26–53. On the castration ordeal, see Kristeva, *The Sense and Non-Sense of Revolt*, pp. 94–106.
72. Bion, *Learning from Experience*, p. 31.
73. Ibid., p. 6.
74. Ibid., p. 26.
75. Ibid., p. 6.
76. Ibid., p. 26.
77. Ibid., p. 35.
78. Ibid., p. 83.
79. Ibid., p. 33.
80. Ibid., pp. 36–37.
81. See Fain and Braunschweig, *La Nuit, le jour*, pp. 147–50, 175–76.
82. Bion, *Learning from Experience*, p. 83.
83. Ibid., p. 43.
84. See Rosenfeld, *Psychotic States*, which distinguishes between a projective identification that evacuates the bad parts of the self and a projective identification that is destined to communicate with objects and to make the patient amenable to the analyst's understanding of him. From that perspective, we should recall Hanna Segal's work on the symbol that followed her 1957 article on symbol formation (see pp. 176–177): in that work she recognized that there is a mutually beneficial relationship between *container* and *contained* that facilitates the development of the

depressive position and the genesis of the symbol. See Segal, "On Symbolism."

85. See generally Meltzer et al., *Explorations in Autism.*

86. See Bick, "The Experience of the Skin in Early Object-Relations.

87. See, in particular, Mazet and Leibovici, *Autisme et psychoses de l'enfant*; Hochmann and Ferrari, *Imitation, identification chez l'enfant autisme*; Privat and Sacco, *Groupes d'enfants et cadre psychanalytique*; Athanassiou, *Bion et la naissance de l'espace psychique*; Golse, *Du corps à la pensée*; Haag, "De la sensoralité aux ébauches de pensée chez les enfants autistes"; Haag, "Autisme infantile précoce et phénomènes autistiques: Réflexions psychanalytique"; Anzieu, "Les Liens originaires du moi à l'objet concret"; Anzieu, "Concrétude de l'objet et construction du moi"; Houzel, "Aspects spécifiques du transfert dans la cure d'enfants autistes"; Houzel, "La Psychothérapie psychanalytique d'un enfant autiste" and "Ce que la psychanalyse peut apporter aux parents d'enfants autistes"; Houzel, "Les Formations archaïques."

88. See Tustin, *Autistic Barriers in Neurotic Patients.*

89. See Tustin, "Les états autistiques chez l'enfant," in *Rencontres avec Frances Tustin.*

90. See Rayner, *The Independent Mind in British Psychoanalysis.* Translator's note: The "Independents" were also known as the "Middle Group."

91. *MK*, p. 234.

92. Winnicott, *Human Nature*, pp. 106–07.

93. Ibid., pp. 114–15.

94. Winnicott, *The Maturational Processes and the Facilitating Environment*, p. 65.

95. See pp. 111–113.

96. See Winnicott, "Birth Memory, Birth Trauma, and Anxiety" (1949), in *Collected Papers: Through Paediatrics to Psycho-Analysis.*

97. *LGR*, p. 214.

98. Ibid., p. 211.

99. Ibid., p. 214.

100. Ibid., p. 215.

101. Ibid., p. 216.

102. Ibid., p. 217.

103. Ibid., p. 218.

104. See "On Identification," in *EG*, pp. 141–75.

105. Ibid., pp. 164, 169.

106. Ibid., p. 159.
107. Ibid., p. 175.

9. FROM THE FOREIGN LANGUAGE TO THE FILIGREE OF THE LOYAL AND DISLOYAL

1. Meisel and Kendrik, *Bloomsbury/Freud*, p. 188.
2. *MK*, p. 380.
3. *DP*, p. 198, n. 1.
4. I was made privy to these facts and observations by Phyllis Grosskurth, whom I thank very much.
5. *MK*, p. 7.
6. Ibid.
7. Ibid., p. 6.
8. Through other means but in like manner, Hannah Arendt was obliged to carry out her work in a foreign language, English, a predicament that no doubt affected her thought, particularly her disputatious didacticism and her clarity, which kept her away from the presumed or feared madness of the mother tongue. See Kristeva, *Female Genius: Hannah Arendt*, pp. 185–187, 238–239.
9. "Language is the house of Being. In its home man dwells." Heidegger, "Letter on Humanism," p. 193
10. See pp. 188–190.
11. See pp. 94–97.
12. *MK*, p. 284.
13. King and Steiner, *The Freud-Klein Controversies*, p. 535.
14. Ibid., pp. 538–39.
15. Ibid., p. 535.
16. Ibid., p. 558.
17. Rose, "Negativity in the Work of Melanie Klein," in Stonebridge and Phillips, *Reading Melanie Klein*, p. 143.
18. *DP*, p. 32.
19. See Joan Riviere's remarks in *DP*, p. 36.
20. Ibid.
21. Ibid., p. 20.
22. Ibid., p. 35.
23. *MK*, p. 452.
24. Ibid.
25. *MK*, pp. 46, 53.
26. See pp. 46–48. This rumor has not been confirmed definitively, however.

27. *MK*, p. 183.
28. See p. 122.
29. Cited in *MK*, p. 199.
30. Ibid., p. 214.
31. Ibid., pp. 297–98.
32. Ibid., p. 297.
33. Ibid., p. 291.
34. Ibid., p. 293.
35. Ibid., p. 316.
36. Ibid., p. 242.
37. Ibid., p. 461.
38. Ibid., p. 462.
39. Ibid., p. 354.
40. Ibid.
41. See p. 74.
42. *MK*, p. 215.
43. Ibid., p. 231.
44. Ibid., p. 424.
45. Ibid., p. 216.
46. See generally Paula Heimann's writings, particularly those included in *DP*; see also Heimann's innovative theory of countertransference, discussed pp. 171–172.
47. *MK*, p. 381.
48. Ibid., p. 369.
49. Ibid., pp. 419 ff.
50. Ibid., p. 420.
51. See pp. 170–171.
52. See Isaacs, "The Nature and Function of Phantasy," in *DP*, pp. 67–121.
53. *MK*, p. 398.
54. Ibid., p. 208.
55. See Riviere, "A Contribution to the Analysis of the Negative Therapeutic Reaction."
56. *MK*, p. 382.
57. Ibid., p. 419.
58. With respect to the possibility of analyzing other cultures, Klein asserted, "I've never tried it. I would have liked it." *MK*, p. 443.
59. Ibid., p. 438.
60. Ibid., p. 448.
61. In her biography of Klein, Phyllis Grosskurth speaks of "a strong element of homosexuality" in Melanie, and describes her as "the

androgynous female whose true children were her concepts." *MK*, pp. 362 and 385.

62. See Ramnoux, *La Nuit et les enfants de la nuit de la tradition grecque*, which structures this preontological universe into binary pairs (high/low, void and black, earth and depth, Night herself bearing two children, one black and one white: Thanatos and Hypnos, and so forth), whose reversibility teaches us to look death in the face.

63. While any human relation is ambivalent, since it contains traces of hostile sentiments, "the relation of a mother to her son" is the solitary exception: "based on narcissism, [it] is not disturbed by subsequent rivalry, and is reinforced by a rudimentary attempt at sexual object-choice." Freud, *Standard Edition*, 18:101, n. 2.

10. THE POLITICS OF KLEINIANISM

1. *MK*, p. 162.
2. *Translator's note*: See King and Steiner, *The Freud-Klein Controversies*, p. 627.
3. Anna Freud, *Einführung in die Technik der Kinderanalyse* (Vienna: Verlag, 1927). A translation of this work appeared in the United States in 1929, "On the Theory of the Analysis of Children," in *International Journal of Psychoanalysis* 10 (1929), but the first British edition (Anna Freud, *The Psycho-Analytic Treatment of Children* [London: Imago, 1946]) did not appear until 1946.
4. Cited in *MK*, p. 164.
5. Cited in ibid., p. 168.
6. See King and Steiner, *The Freud-Klein Controversies*. Although the editors of this work did not have access to all relevant documents, particularly to Anna Freud's personal archives, this work makes an exemplary contribution to the history of ideas in psychoanalysis.
7. King and Steiner, *The Freud-Klein Controversies*, p. 24.
8. *MK*, p. 241.
9. King and Steiner, *The Freud-Klein Controversies*, p. 238.
10. See *MK*, p. 257.
11. Cited in ibid.
12. André Green refers to it as such in his preface to the French edition of *The Freud-Klein Controversies*.
13. Cited in King and Steiner, *The Freud-Klein Controversies*, p. 235.
14. Reprinted in Jones, *Papers in Psycho-Analysis*, pp. 452–84.

15. Cited in King and Steiner, *The Freud-Klein Controversies*, p. 229.
16. First at the Jackson Nursery in Vienna, then at the Hampstead War Nursery in London, and, since 1952, at the Hampstead Child Therapy Clinic, Anna Freud endeavored to directly observe children alongside her faithful colleague Dorothy Burlingham. With the assistance of Joseph Sandler, she created a developmental profile that enabled her to relate pathological divergences to the course of normal development and thus to determine whether therapeutic intervention or analytic intervention would be indicated. With its focus on the direct observation of children rather than on analytic reconstruction, the work of the Hampstead nurseries appears to have adopted a deductive approach that employed a high degree of systematization to foster the child's socialization.
17. John Bowlby and Esther Bick went to the Tavistock Clinic in 1948 to offer training in child psychotherapy; Bick took over later on. Their treatment was based on observation and in particular on the analysis of projective identification in the analyst's countertransference. Yet some critics objected to the religious character of some of the work being done at the Tavistock, which they felt was dominated by "matriarchal elements" as opposed to "the Freudian emphasis on the father." See Eli Zaretsky, "Melanie Klein and the Emergence of Modern Personal Life," p. 36.
18. King and Steiner, *The Freud-Klein Controversies*, p. 227
19. Jones did so during the June 10, 1942, meeting, for example. Ibid., p. 195.
20. See Klein's "The Emotional Life and Ego-Development of the Infant with Special Reference to the Depressive Position," in King and Steiner, *The Freud-Klein Controversies*, pp. 752–97 and the account of the discussion of May 3, 1944, at ibid., pp. 823 ff.
21. Ibid., pp. 758 ff.
22. *MK*, p. 299.
23. King and Steiner, *The Freud-Klein Controversies*, pp. 231–32.
24. Cited in *MK*, p. 289.
25. Particularly Freud's early case study of "Little Hans," which she cites at length, and his essay entitled "Negation." See King and Steiner, *The Freud-Klein Controversies*, pp. 792, n. 19, 843, n.4.
26. Ibid., p. 842.
27. Ibid., p. 839.
28. Ibid., p. 778.
29. Ibid., p. 834.

30. Ibid., p. 779.
31. Ibid., p. 916.
32. *Translator's note*: See *MK*, p. 403 ff. regarding Anna Freud's reaction to Bowlby's paper "Grief and Mourning in Infancy."
33. Ibid., pp. 928–29.
34. *MK*, p. 428.
35. Bion, *Experiences in Groups.*
36. Ibid., p. 187.
37. See pp. 202–212.
38. See Rayner, *The Independent Mind in British Psychoanalysis.*
39. See Winnicott, *The Maturational Processes and the Facilitating Environment*, pp. 29–36.
40. *EG*, pp. 300–313.
41. See pp. 111–113.
42. See Lacan, "Aggressivity in Psychoanalysis," in Lacan, *Écrits: A Selection*, pp. 8–29; Roudinesco, *Jacques Lacan*, p. 194; *MK*, p. 376.
43. Lacan, *Écrits*, p. 70.
44. Ibid., p. 15.
45. Ibid., p. 20.
46. Lacan, *Écrits*, pp. 136–37.
47. Lacan, *Écrits: A Selection*, pp. 1–7
48. See pp. 138–140, 169–177.
49. Lacan, *Écrits: A Selection*, p. 21.
50. Letter from Melanie Klein to Clifford Scott, January 28, 1948, cited in *MK*, p. 377.
51. Ibid, pp. 376–77.
52. See Roudinesco, *Jacques Lacan*, p. 197.
53. See the March 1952 issue of the journal. A revised version, buttressed with two essays by Melanie herself and a preface by Ernest Jones, was published under the title *New Directions in Psychoanalysis: The Significance of Infant Conflict in the Pattern of Adult Behavior.*
54. See pp. 169–177.
55. "They practically ignored the papers and books of Freud's late period. . . . Also they rarely used Freud's very important, short paper 'On Negation' (Freud, S. 1925a), a real small masterpiece, on which the Kleinians based many of their claims that Freud could support their views." King and Steiner, *The Freud-Klein Controversies*, p. 255.
56. See pp. 138–140.

57. Lacan, *Écrits*, p. 345.
58. Ibid., p. 667.
59. Ibid., pp. 728–29.
60. I thank Catherine Millot for bringing this point to my attention.
61. Lacan, *Écrits*, pp. 750–51.
62. Ibid.
63. See Klein's "On the Sense of Loneliness," in *EG*, pp. 300–13.
64. See, for example, Rustin, "A Socialist Consideration of Kleinian Psychoanalysis"; Rustin and Rustin, "Relational Preconditions of Socialism"; Rustin and Rustin, *The Good Society and the Inner World*; Alford, *Melanie Klein and Critical Social Theory*.
65. See Stonebridge and Phillips, *Reading Melanie Klein*.
66. Rustin and Rustin, "Relational Preconditions of Socialism," p. 218.
67. Alford, *Melanie Klein and Critical Social Theory*, p. 170.
68. "In caring for others from within ourselves, we seek not to overcome their separateness but to assert our individuality through an act of *caritas*, an act that reaches outward from my boundaries to another's without denying either" (ibid., p. 184).
69. Ibid., p. 49.
70. See pp. 169–177.
71. "A Kleinian perspective holds out little hope for such a transformation [of humanity]. Nevertheless, it finds in human nature as it is currently constituted cause for hope—a hope, to be sure, that remains tragically unfulfilled, especially in the large group." Alford, *Melanie Klein and Critical Social Theory*, p. 136.
72. See Lacan, "Le Cas 'Aimée' ou la paranoïa d'auto-punition" (1932) and "Motifs du crime paranoïaque: le crime des soeurs Papin" (1933), in *De la psychose paranoïaque dans ses rapports avec la personnalité*, pp. 153–343 and 389–98.
73. See *LGR*, pp. 345–46.
74. Bion, *Learning from Experience*, pp. 36–37.
75. See John Phillips, "The Fissure of Authority: Violence and the Acquisition of Knowledge," in Stonebridge and Phillips, *Reading Melanie Klein*, pp. 160–78.
76. See p. 38.
77. See Hochmann, "Winnicott et Bion dans l'après coup des Controverses," pp. 141–42.
78. The very destructiveness that theologians, particularly Protestant and Orthodox ones, call kenosis, from *ekenosen* ("emptied," "useless," "gratuitous," in the realm of "nonbeing," "futility," and

"nothingness"). Kenosis evokes incarnation as a limit experience because the culmination of the human form that Christ endured is structured through annihilation and death.

79. See Parat, *L'Affect partagé*.

80. See *LGR*, p. 86.

81. Ibid., p. 81.

82. With the exception, perhaps, of the phallic stage, particularly in the boy, see p. 127, but also in the girl, see p. 123.

83. Chodorow, *The Reproduction of Mothering*. Chodorow emphasizes the way the desire for motherhood is shifted inside the object relation between the mother and her daughter.

84. Benjamin, *The Bonds of Love*. In the light of the bond between mother and baby, Benjamin focuses on the intersubjective tension in the erotic bond between two people more than on the tension inside the individual.

85. Dinnerstein, *The Mermaid and the Minotaur*. Dinnerstein analyzes the "androgyny" of the woman as a result of the "couple" relationship formed between the young girl and her mother during the preoedipal phase.

86. *Women: A Cultural Review* 1, no. 2 (Spring 1990). The special issue includes articles by Ann Scott, Janet Sayers, Elaine Showalter, Margot Waddell, Mary Jacobus, Noreen O'Connor, and Juliett Newbigin, as well as an interview of Hanna Segal by Jacqueline Rose.

87. See Mary Jacobus, ibid.; see also Sayer, *Mothering Psychoanalysis*; and Brennan, "The Foundational Fantasy."

88. I discuss some of these contributions on pp. 177–185.

BIBLIOGRAPHY

WORKS BY MELANIE KLEIN

The Writings of Melanie Klein. 4 vols. New York: Delacorte/Seymour Lawrence, 1975.

———. Vol. I, *Love, Guilt, and Reparation, and Other Works, 1921–1945.*

———. Vol. II, *The Psychoanalysis of Children.* Trans. Alix Strachey.

———. Vol. III, *Envy and Gratitude, and Other Works, 1946–1963.*

———. Vol. IV, *Narrative of a Child Analysis: The Conduct of Psycho-Analysis of Children as Seen in the Treatment of a Ten-Year-Old Boy.*

———. (With Paula Heimann and Roger Money-Kyrle) *New Directions in Psychoanalysis: The Significance of Infant Conflict in the Pattern of Adult Behavior.* London: Tavistock, 1955.

———. (With Paula Heimann, Susan Isaacs, and Joan Riviere) *Developments in Psycho-Analysis.* Ed. Joan Riviere. London: The Hogarth Press and the Institute of Psycho-Analysis, 1952.

———. *The Selected Melanie Klein.* Ed. Juliet Mitchell. New York: Penguin, 1986.

WORKS ABOUT MELANIE KLEIN

Alford, F. *Melanie Klein and Critical Social Theory: An Account of Politics, Art, and Reason Based on Her Psychoanalytic Theory*. New Haven, Conn.: Yale University Press, 1989.

Amigorena-Rosenberg, N., L. Bleger, and E. Vera Ocampo, "Melanie Klein ou la métaphore incarnée." In *Psychanalyse: Cent ans de divan*. Paris: Arléa-Corlet, 1995.

Arnoux, D. *Melanie Klein*. Paris: PUF, 1997.

Athanassiou-Popesco, C. "L'Apport de Melanie Klein et des auteurs postkleiniens à la compréhension du fonctionnement psychique." In *Psychoses I: Théories et histoire des idées*. Ed. J. Chambrier. Paris: PUF, 1999.

Bégoin, J. "Le Surmoi dans la théorie kleinienne et postkleinienne." In N. Amar, G. Le Gouès, and G. Pragier, *Surmoi II: Les développements post-freudiens*. Paris: PUF, 1995.

Cottet, S. "Melanie Klein et la guerre du fantasme." In Nicholas Wright, ed., *Madame Klein*. Paris: Seuil, 1991.

Etchegoyen, R. H. "Melanie Klein and the Theory of Interpretation." In *The Fundamentals of Psychoanalytic Technique*. London: Karnac Books, 1991, pp. 402–16.

Gammill, J. *A partir de Melanie Klein*. Paris: Césura, 1998.

———. *Melanie Klein aujourd'hui: Hommage à l'occasion du centenaire de sa naissance*. Paris: Césura, 1985.

Grosskurth, Phyllis. *Melanie Klein: Her World and Her Work*. New York: Aronson, 1986.

King, P., and R. Steiner. *The Freud-Klein Controversies*. London and New York: Tavistock/Routledge, 1991.

Miller, J. "Kleinian Analysis: Dialogue with Hanna Segal." In *States of Mind*. New York: Pantheon Books, 1983.

Meltzer, D. *The Kleinian Development*. London: Karnac Books, 1999.

Petot, J-M. *Melanie Klein*. 2 vols. Trans. Christine Trollope. Madison, Conn.: International Universities Press, 1991.

———. Vol. I, *First Discoveries and First System, 1919–1932*.

———. Vol. II, *The Ego and the Good Object, 1932–1960*.

Rustin, M. "A Socialist Consideration of Kleinian Psychoanalysis." *New Left Review* 131 (1982): 71–96.

Segal, H. *Introduction to the Work of Melanie Klein*. New York: Basic Books, 1990.

———. "Psychoanalytic Dialogue: Kleinian Thought Today." *Journal of the American Psychoanalytic Association* 25, no. 2 (1977): 363–70.

Stonebridge, L., and J. Phillips. *Reading Melanie Klein.* New York: Routledge, 1998.

Wollheim, R. "Melanie Klein." *Spectator* (September 30, 1960).

OTHER WORKS

Abraham, K. "A Short Study of the Development of the Libido, Viewed in the Light of Mental Disorders" (1924). In *On Character and Libido Development,* pp. 67–150. New York: Basic Books, 1966.

Allestree, R. *The Whole Duty of Man.* 1663. Reprint, London: James Goodwin, 1747.

Anzieu, A. "Concrétude de l'objet et construction du moi." In *Journée d'étude: L'Objet et l'enfant,* pp. 39–52. Arles: Hôp J. Imbert, 1990.

———. "Les Liens originaires du moi à l'objet concret." *Journal de la psychanalyse de l'enfant* 14 (1993): 338–64.

Athanassiou, C. *Bion et la naissance de l'espace psychique.* Paris: Popesco, 1997.

Aulagnier, P. *La Violence de l'interprétation.* Paris: PUF, 1975.

Balint, M. *Primary Love and Psycho-Analytic Technique.* New York: Liveright, 1965.

Barret-Ducrocq, F. *Love in the Time of Victoria: Sexuality, Class, and Gender in Nineteenth-Century London.* Trans. John Howe. London: Verso, 1991.

———. *Pauvreté, charité et morale à Londres au XIXème siècle: Une sainte violence.* Paris: PUF, 1991.

Becchi, E., and D. Julia. *Histoire de l'enfance en Occident.* 2 vols. Paris: Seuil, 1998.

Benjamin, J. *The Bonds of Love: Psychoanalysis, Feminism, and the Problem of Domination.* New York: Pantheon Books, 1988.

Bick, E. "The Experience of the Skin in Early Object-Relations." *International Journal of Psychoanalysis* 49 (1968): 484–88.

Bion, W. R. *Attention and Interpretation: A Scientific Approach to Insight in Psycho-Analysis and Groups.* New York: Basic Books, 1970.

———. *Elements of Psycho-Analysis.* New York: Basic Books, 1963.

———. *Experiences in Groups, and Other Papers.* New York: Basic Books, 1961.

———. *Learning from Experience.* London: Karnac, 1984.

Brennan, T. "The Foundational Fantasy." In *History after Lacan.* London: Routledge, 1993, pp. 79–117.

Carpenter, C. G. "Mother's Face and the Newborn." In R. Lewin, ed., *Child Alive*. London: Temple Smith, 1975.

Cellérier, G. "Le Constructivisme génetique aujourd'hui." In B. Inhelder and G. Cellérier, eds., *Le Cheminement des découvertes de l'enfant*. Lausanne: Delachaux and Niestlé, 1992.

Chodorow, N. *The Reproduction of Mothering: Psychoanalysis and Sociology of Gender*. Berkeley and Los Angeles: University of California Press, 1992.

Cournut-Janin, M., and J. Cournut. "La Castration et le féminin dans les deux sexes." *Revue française de psychanalyse* 57 (1993): 1353–1558.

Cullen, S. *Children in Society: A Libertarian Critique*. London: Freedom Press, 1991.

Cunningham, H. *Children and Childhood in Western Society Since 1500*. London: Longman, 1995.

Deleuze, D. and F. Guattari. *Anti-Oedipus: Capitalism and Schizophrenia*. Trans. Robert Hurley, Mark Seem, Helen R. Lane. New York: Viking Press, 1977.

Dinnerstein, D. *The Mermaid and the Minotaur: Sexual Arrangements and Human Malaise*. New York: Harper and Row, 1976.

Etchegoyen, R. H. *The Fundamentals of Psychoanalytic Technique*. London: Karnac Books, 1991.

Fain, M., and D. Braunschweig. *La Nuit, le jour: Essai psychanalytique sur le fonctionnement mental*. Paris: PUF, 1975.

Fairbairn, W. *Psycho-Analytic Studies of the Personality*. London: Routledge and Kegan, 1952.

Freud, A. *The Ego and the Mechanisms of Defense*. Trans. Cecil Baines. London: Hogarth Press, 1937.

Freud, S. *The Standard Edition of the Complete Psychological Works of Sigmund Freud*. Ed. James Strachey. 24 vols. London: Hogarth Press, 1953–1974.

Gibeault, A. "Variation sur un thème ancien: Construction et/ou reconstruction du psychisme de l'enfant." In *Les Textes du Centre Alfred Binet* 15 (December 1989): 1–21.

Golse, B. *Du corps à la pensée*. Paris: PUF, 1999.

Green, A. *Narcissisme de vie, narcissisme de mort*. Paris: Editions de Minuit, 1983.

———. *The Fabric of Affect in the Psychoanalytic Discourse*. Trans. Alan Sheridan. New York: Routledge, 1999.

———. *The Work of the Negative*. Trans. Andrew Weller. London and New York: Free Association Books, 1999.

Guignard, F. *Epître à l'objet*. Paris: PUF, 1997.

Haag, G. "Autisme infantile précoce et phénomènes autistiques: Réflexions psychanalytique." *Psychiatrie de l'enfant* 27, no. 22 (1984): 293–354.

———. "De la sensoralité aux ébauches de pensée chez les enfants autistes." *Revue internationale de psychopathologie* 3 (1991): 51–63.

Heidegger, M. "Letter on Humanism." In David Farrell Krell, ed., *Basic Writings*. New York: Harper and Row, 1977.

Heimann, P. "Further Observations on the Analyst's Cognitive Process." *Journal of the American Psychoanalytic Association* 25 (1977): 313–33.

———. "On Countertransference." *International Journal of Psychoanalysis* 31, no. 2 (1950): 81–84.

Hendrick, H. *Children, Childhood, and English Society, 1880–1990*. Cambridge: Cambridge University Press, 1997.

Hill, M. *Children and Society*. London: Longman, 1997.

Hochmann, J. "Winnicott et Bion dans l'après coup des Controverses." *Bulletin de la Société psychanalytique de Paris* 50 (July/August 1998).

Hochmann, J. and P. Ferrari. *Imitation, identification chez l'enfant autisme*. Lyon: Inserm, 1989.

Houzel, D. "Aspects spécifiques du transfert dans la cure d'enfants autistes." In *Hommage à Frances Tustin*, pp. 77–128. Paris: Audit, 1993.

———. "La Psychothérapie psychanalytique d'un enfant autiste" and "Ce que la psychanalyse peut apporter aux parents d'enfants autistes." *Parents et professionels devant l'autisme* 220 (1997): 179–89 and 167–77.

———. "Les Formations archaïques." In D. Widlöcher, ed., *Traité de psychopathologie*. Paris: PUF, 1994, pp. 393–419.

Jones, E. "The Phallic Phase." In *Papers in Psycho-Analysis* (1948), 5th ed., pp. 452–84. Reprint, London: Karnac Books, 2000.

Kristeva, J. "La Fille au sanglot: Du temps hystérique." *L'Infini* 54 (Spring 1996).

———. *Female Genius: Hannah Arendt*. Trans. Ross Guberman. New York: Columbia University Press, 2001.

———. *New Maladies of the Soul*. Trans. Ross Guberman. New York: Columbia University Press, 1995.

———. *Powers of Horror: An Essay on Abjection*. Trans. Leon S. Roudiez. New York: Columbia University Press, 1982.

———. *Revolution in Poetic Language*. Trans. Margaret Waller. New York: Columbia University Press, 1984.

———. *The Sense and Non-Sense of Revolt: The Powers and Limits of Psychoanalysis*. Trans. Jeanine Herman. New York: Columbia University Press, 2000.

———. *Tales of Love.* Trans. Leon S. Roudiez. New York: Columbia University Press, 1987.

Lacan, J. *De la psychose paranoïaque dans ses rapports avec la personnalité.* Paris: Seuil, 1975.

———. *Écrits: A Selection.* Trans. Alan Sheridan. New York: Norton, 1977.

———. *Écrits.* Paris: Seuil, 1966.

———. *Freud's Papers on Technique (1953–1954)* (The Seminar of Jacques Lacan, Book I). Ed. Jacques-Alain Miller. Trans. Sylvana Tomaselli. New York: Norton, 1988.

Laplanche, J., and J.-B. Pontalis. *The Language of Psycho-Analysis.* Trans. Donald Nicholson-Smith. New York: Norton, 1973.

Mandler, J. "Representation." In P. Mussen, *Handbook of Child Psychology*, vol. 3. New York: Wiley, 1983.

Marsh, Bernard, and Hilda C. Abraham, eds. *A Psycho-Analytic Dialogue: The Letters of Sigmund Freud and Karl Abraham, 1907–1926.* New York: Basic Books, 1965.

Mazet, P., and S. Leibovici. *Autisme et psychoses de l'enfant: Les points de vue actuels.* Paris: PUF, 1990.

Meisel, P., and W. Kendrik. *Bloomsbury/Freud: The Letters of James and Alix Strachey, 1924–1925.* New York: Basic Books, 1985.

Meltzer, D. "The Genesis of the Super-ego-Ideal." In D. Meltzer, *Sexual States of Mind*, pp. 74–80. Perthshire, Scotland: Clunie Press for the Roland Harris Trust, 1990.

Meltzer, D., et al. *Explorations in Autism: A Psycho-analytical Study.* Strath Tay, Scotland: Clunie Press, 1975.

Middlemore, M. *The Nursing Couple.* London: Hamish Hamilton, 1941.

Nelson, K., and J. Gruendel. "Generalized Event Representations: Basic Building Blocks of Cognitive Development." In M. Lamb, *Advances in Developmental Psychology*, vol. 1. New York: Lawrence Erlbaum Assoc., 1981.

Parat, C. *L'Affect partagé.* Paris: PUF, 1995.

Pontalis, J.-B. *Entre le rêve et la douleur.* Paris: Gallimard, 1977.

———. *Frontiers in Psychoanalysis: Between the Dream and Psychic Pain.* Trans. Catherine Cullen and Philip Cullen. London: The Hogarth Press and the Institute of Psycho-Analysis, 1981.

Privat, P., and F. Sacco. *Groupes d'enfants et cadre psychanalytique.* Toulouse: Erès, 1995.

Proust, M. *In Search of Lost Time.* Trans. Andreas Mayor and Terence

Kilmartin. Revised D. J. Enright. London: Chatto and Windus, 1992.

Ramnoux, C. *La Nuit et les enfants de la nuit de la tradition grecque*. Paris: Flammarion, 1959.

Rayner, E. *The Independent Mind in British Psychoanalysis*. London: Free Association Books, 1990.

Riviere, J. "A Contribution to the Analysis of the Negative Therapeutic Reaction." *International Journal of Psychoanalysis* 17 (1936): 304–20.

Rosenfeld, H. *Psychotic States: A Psycho-analytical Approach*. New York: International Universities Press, 1965.

Roudinesco, E. *Jacques Lacan*. Trans. Barbara Bray. New York: Columbia University Press, 1997.

Rustin, M., and M. Rustin. "Relational Preconditions of Socialism." In B. Richards, ed., *Capitalism and Infancy*. London: Free Association Books, 1984.

———. *The Good Society and the Inner World: Psychoanalysis, Politics, and Culture*. London: Verso, 1991.

Sayer, J. *Mothering Psychoanalysis: Helene Deutsch, Karen Horney, Anna Freud, and Melanie Klein*. London: Hamish Hamilton, 1991.

Segal, H. "Notes on Symbol Formation." *International Journal of Psycho-Analysis* 38 (1957): 391–97.

———. "On Symbolism." *International Journal of Psychoanalysis* 59 (1978): 315–19.

Segal, H., and D. Bell. "Theory of Narcissism in Freud and Klein." In J. Sandler, S. Persone, and P. Fonagy, *Freud's "On Narcissism": An Introduction*. New Haven, Conn.: Yale University Press, 1991, pp. 149–74.

Stern, D. "L'Enveloppe prénarrative: Vers une unité fondamentale d'expérience permettant d'explorer la réalité psychique du bébé." *Journal de la psychanalyse de l'enfant* 14 (1993): 13–65.

Stone, Lawrence. *The Family, Sex, and Marriage in England, 1500–1800*. London: Weidenfeld and Nicolson, 1977.

Tustin, F. *Autistic Barriers in Neurotic Patients*. New Haven, Conn.: Yale University Press, 1986.

———. *Rencontres avec Frances Tustin*. Toulouse: CREAI, 1981.

Wallon, H. *Les Origines du caractère chez l'enfant: Les préludes du sentiment de personnalité*. Paris: PUF, 1993.

Winnicott, D. W. *Collected Papers: Through Paediatrics to Psycho-Analysis*. London: Tavistock Publications, 1958.

———. *Home Is Where We Start From: Essays by a Psychoanalyst*. Ed.

Clare Winnicott, Ray Shepherd, and Madeleine Davis. New York: Norton, 1986.

―――. *Human Nature.* London: Free Association Books, 1988.

―――. *The Maturational Processes and the Facilitating Environment: Studies in the Theory of Emotional Development.* New York: International Universities Press, 1965.

―――. "Transitional Objects and Transitional Phenomena." *Journal of Psycho-Analysis* 34 (1953).

EUROPEAN PERSPECTIVES

A Series in Social Thought and Cultural Criticism

LAWRENCE D. KRITZMAN, Editor

ELISABETH ROUDINESCO	*Jacques Lacan: His Life and Work*
ROSS GUBERMAN	*Julia Kristeva Interviews*
KELLY OLIVER	*The Portable Kristeva*
PIERRA NORA	*Realms of Memory: The Construction of the French Past*
	vol. 1: *Conflicts and Divisions*
	vol. 2: *Traditions*
	vol. 3: *Symbols*
CLAUDINE FABRE-VASSAS	*The Singular Beast: Jews, Christians, and the Pig*
PAUL RICOEUR	*Critique and Conviction: Conversations with François Azouvi and Marc de Launay*
THEODOR W. ADORNO	*Critical Models: Interventions and Catchwords*
ALAIN CORBIN	*Village Bells: Sound and Meaning in the Nineteenth-Century French Countryside*
ZYGMUNT BAUMAN	*Globalization: The Human Consequences*
EMMANUEL LEVINAS	*Entre Nous*
JEAN-LOUIS FLANDRIN and MASSIMO MONTANARI	*Food: A Culinary History*
ALAIN FINKIELKRAUT	*In the Name of Humanity: Reflections on the Twentieth Century*
JULIA KRISTEVA	*The Sense and Non-Sense of Revolt: The Powers and Limits of Psychoanalysis*
RÉGIS DEBRAY	*Transmitting Culture*
SYLVIANE AGACINSKI	*The Politics of the Sexes*
ALAIN CORBIN	*The Life of an Unknown: The Rediscovered World of a Clog Maker in Nineteenth-Century France*
MICHEL PASTOUREAU	*The Devil's Cloth: A History of Stripes and Striped Fabric*
JULIA KRISTEVA	*Hannah Arendt*
CARLO GINZBURG	*Wooden Eyes: Nine Reflections on Distance*
ELISABETH ROUDINESCO	*Why Psychoanalysis?*
ALAIN CABANTOUS	*Blasphemy: Impious Speech in the West from the Seventeenth to the Nineteenth Century*

A child or young person
enters the classroom. That child
becomes the point around which plans
becomes less interpretive, ideological, discursive
current less interpretive over her transparency her weight
streams which pour over her substance and weight
into an figure whose substance and classification position
whose measurements and classification position
will influence her treatment. And the figure
who greets who is meant to teach this child
will direct a focus and and apply a series of
interventions based on the various interpretive
streams in which the student emerges
The teacher herself will remain primarily
a site from which various actions will
emanate, a self-reflexive loop in
which self + reflection consist of
the measured attainment of
pre-set goals.